Wilson Horace Hayman

Works

Wilson Horace Hayman

Works

ISBN/EAN: 9783741165641

Manufactured in Europe, USA, Canada, Australia, Japa

Cover: Foto ©Andreas Hilbeck / pixelio.de

Manufactured and distributed by brebook publishing software (www.brebook.com)

Wilson Horace Hayman

Works

WORKS

BY

THE LATE

HORACE HAYMAN WILSON,
M.A., F.R.S.,

MEMBER OF THE ROYAL ASIATIC SOCIETY, OF THE ASIATIC SOCIETIES OF
CALCUTTA AND PARIS, AND OF THE ORIENTAL SOCIETY OF GERMANY;
FOREIGN MEMBER OF THE NATIONAL INSTITUTE OF FRANCE;
MEMBER OF THE IMPERIAL ACADEMIES OF ST. PETERSBURGH AND VIENNA,
AND OF THE ROYAL ACADEMIES OF MUNICH AND BERLIN;
PH. D. BRESLAU; M. D. MARBURG, ETC.;
AND BODEN PROFESSOR OF SANSKRIT IN THE UNIVERSITY OF OXFORD.

VOL. II.

LONDON:
TRÜBNER & CO., 60, PATERNOSTER ROW.
1862.

ESSAYS AND LECTURES

CHIEFLY ON THE

RELIGION OF THE HINDUS.

BY THE LATE

H. H. WILSON, M.A., F.R.S.,

BODEN PROFESSOR OF SANSKRIT IN THE UNIVERSITY OF OXFORD,
ETC., ETC.

COLLECTED AND EDITED BY

DR. REINHOLD ROST.

IN TWO VOLUMES.

VOL. II.

MISCELLANEOUS ESSAYS AND LECTURES.

LONDON:
TRÜBNER & CO., 60, PATERNOSTER ROW.
1862.

TABLE OF CONTENTS.

	Page
I. Notice of Three Tracts received from Nepal	1 – 39
II. Two Lectures on the Religious Practices and Opinions of the Hindus	40 – 120
III. Summary Account of the Civil and Religious Institutions of the Sikhs	121 – 150
IV. The Religious Festivals of the Hindus	151 – 246
V. On Human Sacrifices in the ancient Religion of India	247 – 269
VI. On the supposed Vaidik Authority for the Burning of Hindu Widows, and on the Funeral Ceremonies of the Hindus	270 – 292
VII. Remarks by Rájá Rádhákánta Deva on the preceding article; with observations	293 – 309
VIII. On Buddha and Buddhism	310 – 378
IX. Account of the Religious Innovations attempted by Akbar	379 – 400
Index	401 – 416

I.

NOTICE

OF

THREE TRACTS RECEIVED FROM NEPAL.

From the Asiatic Researches, Vol. XVI, Calc. 1828, p. 450–78.

THE accounts hitherto published of the Religious System of the Nepalese are far from being comprehensive or satisfactory. They only establish the general conclusion that there are two predominant forms of belief, as well as two principal divisions of the people, the *Párvatíya*, or Mountain Hindus, who follow the faith of the Brahmans, and the *Newárs*, or original inhabitants, who adhere to the worship of *Buddha*.

The indistinctness and inaccuracy that pervade the descriptions of KIRKPATRICK and BUCHANAN are not however, in all probability, the fault of the describers. Much is, no doubt, attributable to their want of access to original authorities, on which alone dependence can be placed for a correct view of any mode of faith in India. The Spirit of Polytheism, always an accommodating one, is particularly so in this country, and the legends and localities of one sect are so readily appropriated by another, that it speedily becomes difficult to assign them to their genuine source. In like manner formulæ and ceremonies very soon become common property, and whatever may be the ruling principles, the popular practice easily adopts a variety of rites that are peculiar to different creeds. This is every where the case throughout Hindustan, and the sectaries of Vishṅu often assimilate to those of Śiva, whilst the worshippers of the female Principle are constantly identifiable with both. Nepal, evidently, constitutes no exception, and the worship of Śiva, and *Tantra* rites, are so widely blended with the practices and notions of the *Bauddhists*, that an accurate appreciation of the latter is no longer derivable from any but original and authentic sources, or the ancient works of the *Bhotiyas* in which the pure and primitive doctrines are enshrined.

Of the number and character of those works which are the authorities of the *Bauddhas* of Nepal, the only description on which any reliance can be placed is contained in the preceding communication*, from Mr. Hodgson, to whose active and intelligent zeal the Society is so largely indebted. It yet remains, however, to estimate** the contents of the volumes he

---

* [Notices of the Languages, Literature, and Religion of the Bauddhas of Nepal and Bhot. As. Res. XVI, 409 49. Reprinted in the "Illustrations of the Literature and Religion of the Buddhists". By B. H. Hodgson, Esq. Serampore: 1841, p. 1 49.]

** [On the results of the estimate since made compare Mr. Hodgson's "Quotations from original Sanskrit authorities", in

has enumerated, and which for the far greater part, it is believed, are written in the language of *Tibet*, and not in Sanskrit, as he seems to suppose. We must wait therefore for the acquirement of this language by European scholars, before we can pronounce with confidence upon the character and contents of the *Bauddha* Scriptures, and how far they may be originals or translations. If the latter, which, except to a limited extent, is very unlikely, we may safely assert, that the *Sanskrit* originals are no longer procurable in Hindustan.

The paper already referred to furnishes us also with the only outline of the BAUDDHA philosophy and mythology that can be consulted with advantage, for, although some of the particulars are to be found in GEORGI's ponderous volume, they are so obscured by his parade of learning, and spirit of theory, that they are to be selected only with great trouble and uncertainty. The account given by PALLAS, as quoted by BUCHANAN, seems also to be derived from oral information only, and to be confined to superficial and popular details. To what extent the Doctrines or Divinities of *Bhot Buddhism* are of local origin or modification, can only be determined when the condition in which this form of faith exists in other countries is

---

Journ. As. Soc. Bengal, Vol. V, p. 28 ff., 71 ff. (reprinted in his "Illustrations" p. 94–136), and Burnouf's "Introduction à l'histoire du Bouddhisme indien". Paris: 1844, p. 1 ff. J. B. Saint-Hilaire, "Bouddha et sa religion". Paris: 1860, p. IX ff. A. Weber, "Ind. Studien", III, 135 ff.)

more authentically explained; but as far as we may infer from what has yet appeared in the Asiatic Researches, or elsewhere, on the *Buddhism* of *Ceylon* and *Ava*, many and important varieties occur between the heavenly hierarchy of those countries and of *Bhot*. Of the scale of *Buddhas* which prevails in the latter, we have no trace whatever in the communications of BUCHANAN, MAHONY and JOINVILLE. Their enumeration of the human *Buddhas*, the only *Buddhas* of whom they speak, differs also from that of Mr. HODGSON. Amidst the perplexity that this disagreement is calculated to occasion, any further illustration that is available will be, no doubt, welcome to the Society, and I have therefore thought that the following notice of the only works sent down by Mr. HODGSON, which I have been able to distinguish as connected with the religion of *Nepal* in any language known to me, might not be unacceptable. The works are short, and are evidently of a popular, not a scriptural character. As authorities, therefore, they are of no great value, although they may be taken as guides to common and corrupt practice and belief. They evidently, however, spring from the mythological system sketched by Mr. HODGSON, and so far corroborate his statements, as well as derive confirmation from his remarks, whilst they serve also to show how far the *Buddha* creed has been modified by *Tántrika* admixture.

The works in question are three tracts, comprised in one volume, and severally entitled—*Ashtamí vrata Vidhána*, Ritual for the religious observance of the

Eighth (day of the lunar fortnight), *Naipálya Devatá Kalyáña Panchaviṅsatiká*, Twenty-five Stanzas invocatory of the favor of the Deities of *Nepal*—and *Sapta Buddha Stotra*, Praise of the seven *Buddhas*. The text of these tracts is *Sanskrit*, interspersed with a gloss in *Newári*, copiously infused with pure *Sanskrit* terms. The two latter are so short that they may be translated entire. A specimen of the first will be sufficient.

TRANSLATION.
SAPTA BUDDHA STOTRA.

"I adore JINENDRA, the consuming fire of sorrow, the treasure of holy knowledge, whom all revere, who bore the name VIPAŚYÍ, who was born in the race of mighty monarchs, in the city *Bandumati*, who was for eighty thousand years the preceptor of gods and men, and by whom, endowed with the ten kinds of power, the degree of *Jinendra* was obtained at the foot of a *Pátalá* tree.

"I adore ŚIKHÍ, the mine of heavenly wisdom, the supreme sage who crossed the boundaries of the world, who was born of a royal race in the great city *Aruńa*, whose life, adorned with every excellence, extended to the term of 70,000 years, by whom, out of affection for mankind, holy wisdom was obtained at the foot of a *Puṅdaríka*.

"I adore VIŚWABHÚ, the friend of the universe, the king of virtue, who was born in *Anupamá*, of a race of illustrious monarchs, whose life lasted 60,000 years, and who, having triumphed over earthly afflictions, obtained immortality at the foot of a *Sāl* tree.

"I adore KRAKUCHCHANDA, the Lord of Munis, the unequalled *Sugata*, the source of perfection, who was born in *Kshemavati*, of a family of Brahmans, revered by kings; the life of that treasure of excellence was 40,000 years, and he obtained, at the foot of a *Sirīsha* tree, the state of *Jinendra*, with the weapons of knowledge that annihilate the three worlds.

"I adore KANAKA *Muni*, the sage and legislator, exempt from the blindness of worldly delusion, who was born in the city *Sobhanavati*, of a race of Brahmans honoured by kings. His resplendent person existed thirty thousand years. The degree of *Buddha* was obtained by him, munificent as the mountain of gems, at the foot of an *Udumbara* tree.

"I adore KÁSYAPA, the Lord of the world, the most excellent and eminent sage, who was born at *Benares*, in the family of Brahmans venerated by princes; the life of his illustrious frame endured 20,000 years, and the waters of the three worlds were dried up by the lamp of divine wisdom, which he acquired at the foot of a *Nyagrodha* tree.

"I adore SÁKYA SINHA, the *Buddha*, the kinsman of the Sun, worshipped by men and gods, who was born at the splendid city of *Kapilapur*, of the family of the chief of the *Sákya* kings, the life of which best friend to all the world lasted 100 years. Having speedily subdued desire, unbounded wisdom was acquired by him at the foot of the *Aswattha* tree.

"I adore the Lord MAITREYA, the chief of Sages, residing at *Tushitapur*, who will assume a mortal birth at *Ketumati*, in the family of a Brahman honoured by the king, and who, endowed with immeasurable excellence, will obtain the degree of *Buddha*, at the foot of a *Nága* tree; his existence will endure 8000 years.

"Having praised the seven *Buddhas*, supreme over all, and resplendent as so many Suns, as well as the future eighth *Buddha*, MAITREYA, dwelling at *Tushitapur*, may the merit of such praises be quickly productive of fruit, so that having divided all corporal bonds I may speedily obtain the final liberation of the holy Sages."

REMARKS.

The enumeration given in these verses is, therefore, very different from that of Dr. BUCHANAN and Capt. MAHONY, and instead of five or six we have eight deified *Buddha* teachers or human *Buddhas*: the former writer has only specified two names, GAUTAMA and SÁKYA, of which the first does not occur in the Nepal list, whilst in another place he observes that SÁKYA is considered by the Burmese *Buddhists* as an impostor: the latter has mentioned the names of the *Buddhas*, and they are evidently the same as the last five of the Nepal *Stotra*.

KAKOOSONDEH,	or KRAKUCHHANDA,
KONAGAMMEH,	„ KANAKA,
KASERJEPPEH,	„ KÁSYAPA,

GOTTAMA, or SÁKYA,
MAITREE, MAITREYA,
possibly the other three are regarded as *Bauddhas* of a different Kalpa, or period, and therefore only were omitted in the list furnished to Capt. MAHONY (Asiatic Research. VII, 32): the Nepal enumeration, however, is not a mere provincial peculiarity, nor of very modern date, and the same must have prevailed in Hindustan, when there were *Bauddhas* in the country. *Hemachandra*, who wrote his vocabulary, probably in *Guzerat*, in the 12th century, specifies the same *Buddhas* as the *Sapta Buddha Stotra*, or *Vipaśyí, Śikhí, Viśwabhú, Krakuchhanda, Kánchana, Káśyapa,* and *Śákya Sinha**.

How many of these *Buddhas* are real personages, is very questionable. KÁSYAPA is a character known to the orthodox system, and perhaps had once existence: he seems to have been the chief instrument in extending civilisation along the *Himalaya* and *Caucasian* mountains, as far as we may judge from the traditions of Nepal and Kashmir, and the many traces of his name to be met with along those ranges. SÁKYA, as identifiable with GAUTAMA, was possibly the founder of the *Bauddha* system as it now exists, in the sixth or seventh century before Christianity. The names of the cities in which these *Buddhas* are said to have been born, or to have appeared in a human form, are not verifiable, with the exception

---

* [ii. 236.]

of Benares*. They contribute therefore to throw doubt on the reality of the persons. The extravagant periods assigned to their lives is another suspicious circumstance. But these periods are, no doubt, connected with some legendary classification of the *Kalpas*, or ages of the world, in which mankind enjoyed a length of life far exceeding any thing in these degenerate days. So GEORGI states that, in the second age of the world and the first of men, the limit of life was 80,000 years; in the third age it was 40,000; in the fourth it was 20,000, and in the fifth one hundred. The *Buddhas* therefore only partake of the longevity of the periods to which they belong.

The omission of the name of GAUTAMA proves that he is not acknowledged as a distinct *Buddha* by the Nepalese, and he can be identified with no other in the list than ŚÁKYA SINHA. The *Newári* comment adds, that the latter was born in the family of ŚUDDHODANA RÁJÁ, and ŚUDDHODANA is always regarded as the father of GAUTAMA. Other names in the text, which are translated as epithets, *Ádityabandhu*, the friend of the sun, and *Lokaikabandhu*, the sole or superior friend of the world, occur as synonymes of GAUTAMA as well as ŚÁKYA SINHA, as in the vocabularies of *Amara* and *Hemachandra*; "*Śákya Muni, Śákya Sinha, Sarvárttha Siddha, Sauddhodani* (the

---

* [Compare, however, St. Julien, "Voyages des pèlerins Bouddhistes", I, 315 f. R. Spence Hardy, "Manual of Buddhism", 96 f. Burnouf, "Introduction", 116 & 388.]

son of *Śuddhodana*), *Gautama*, *Arkabandhu* (the kinsman of the sun), *Máyádeví Suta*." *Amara Kosha**. "The seventh *Buddha* is named *Śákya Sinha—Arkabándhava*, the parent of *Ráhula* (*Ráhulasú*), *Sarvárttha Siddha*, *Gotamánwaya* (of the family of *Gotama*), *Máyá Suta* (the son of *Máyá*), *Suddhodana Suta* (the son of *Śuddhodana*), *Devadattágraja* (the elder brother of *Devadatta*)." *Hemachandra***. On what authority BUCHANAN asserts that the Priests of Ava consider GAUTAMA and ŚÁKYA as distinct, and the latter as a heretic, he has not mentioned; but, as I have had occasion to remark elsewhere, no such distinction is made in the Pali version of the *Amara Kosha*, which is used by the Priests of Ava and Ceylon. GAUTAMA, and ŚÁKYA SINHA, and ÁDITYABANDHU, are there given as synonymes of the son of SUDDHODANA. "*Suddhodani cha Gotamo Sakyasího tathá Sakyamuni ch' Ádichchabandhu cha*" ***.

It may seem scarcely worth while to notice the mention made in these verses of the acquisition of the state of a *Buddha*, or of a condition exempt from the infirmities of humanity, under particular trees: the meaning is, according to the Translation, that the sages chose such spots for the performance of their *Tapas*, or course of religious austerities. The specification, however, may be turned probably to some account. It is often exceedingly difficult to discriminate between *Bauddha* and *Jain* sculptures, and to

---

* [1, 1, 1, 10.]   ** [236. 237.]   *** [sl. 4. 5.]

decide to which sect images and architectural remains belong—any characteristic peculiarity will therefore be very acceptable to Indian antiquarians and travellers, and a figure, in other respects possessing the usual features, the spiral locks, thick lips, and large ears of a *Jina*, or a *Buddha*, engaged in devotion, under the shade of a tree, may generally, perhaps, be ascribed with safety to the latter. It is more common to find the Jain Pontiffs shaded by the expanded hoods of the many-headed snake.

The next work takes a wider range than the preceding in its enumeration of the objects of veneration in Nepal, and comprehends so many local peculiarities, that a correct translation of it is impracticable any where out of Nepal, except by a person familiar with the country and the system. The translation originally made was, therefore, referred to Mr. Hodgson, to whose revision and explanatory remarks it is indebted for any pretension to accuracy. The notes appended to the translation are almost wholly derived from communication with him on the subject of the text.

TRANSLATION.

NAIPÁLÍYA DEVATÁ KALYÁŇA PANCHA-VIŃŚATIKÁ.

May the first-born, the Holy SWAYAMBHÚ, AMITA-RUCHI, AMOGHA, AKSHOBHYA, the splendid VAIRO-

CHANA, MANIDHAVA, the King of sages and the Pure VAJRASATTWA[1], preserve you in your sojourn in the world; may ŚRÍ PRAJNÁ, VAJRADHÁTWÍ, the all-bountiful holy TÁRÁ, and the rest[2], be propitious to you — I adore them.

2. May the goddesses SAMPAT PRADÁ, GAŃAPATI-HRIDAYÁ, VAJRAVIDRÁVIŃÍ, USHŃÍSHÁRPAŃÁ, KITIVARA-VADANÁ, GRAHAMÁTHIKÁ, KOTILAKSHÁKSHI, with her

---

[1] These, as will have been seen by the preceding dissertation of Mr. HODGSON, are the personages of the *Aiśwarika*, or Theistical pantheon — the *Ádi Buddha*, or self-existent original Creator — the five *Dhyáni Buddhas*, under other appellations, corresponding severally to AMITÁBHA, AMOGHASIDDHA, AKSHOBHYA, VAIROCHANA, and RATNASAMBHAVA (as in As. Res. XVI, p. 441), and a sixth *Buddha*, VAJRASATTWA, emanating from *Ádi Buddha* — the secondary agent in the creation of immaterial substances — the other five being charged with the creation of material bodies. [Burnouf, "Introduction", 525. W. Wassiljew, "Der Buddhismus", St. Petersburg: 1860, I, p. 205 f.]

[2] These female divinities are, in the vulgar *Aiśwarika* system, the wives of *Ádi Buddha* and the *Dhyáni Buddhas*. The powers of inert matter are typified by a Goddess in the *Swábhávika* system; but neither in that nor the primitive *Aiśwarika* doctrine are the intellectual Essences of the divine *Buddhas* linked to female forms — either literally or figuratively, as their *Śaktis*, or active energies. The complete list of these Goddesses, and their appropriation, are specified by Mr. HODGSON, as follows:—

ÁDI BUDDHA,	his Wife	PRAJNÁ.
VAIROCHANA,	„	VAJRADHÁTWÍ
AKSHOBHYA,	„	LOCHANÁ.
RATNASAMBHAVA,	„	MÁMUKHÍ.
AMITÁBHA,	„	PÁŃDARÁ.
AMOGHA-SIDDHA,	„	TÁRÁ.
VAJRASATTWA,	„	VAJRASATTWÁTMIKÁ.

train, and the protecting¹ PANCHARAKSHÁ, be propitious to you—I adore them.

3. May RATNAGARBHA, DÍPANKARA, the *Jina* MANIKUSUMA, VIPAŚYÍ, ŚIKHÍ, VIŚWABHÚ, KAKUTSA*, KANAKA, the *Muni* of *Munis* KÁŚYAPA, and ŚÁKYA SINHA², the *Buddhas* past, present, and future, the ocean of whose excellence is not to be passed by the ten faculties, be propitious to you—I adore them.

4. May the chief of sages and saints, the excellent son of *Jina*, AVALOKITEŚWARA, may MAITREYA, ANANTAGANJA, VAJRAPÁNI, and the great chief MANJUNÁTH, SARVANIVARANA, and the illustrious pair KSHITIGARBHA and KHAGARBHA³, be propitious to you—I adore them.

---

¹ These Goddesses are considered by Mr. HODGSON as belonging to the genuine Bauddha system and the *Swábhávika* school—being spontaneous manifestations of matter, like other existent beings, man included. Some of them are known by other names, as SAMPATPRADÁ, the giver of wealth, is also VASUNDHARÁ, the earth—KITIVARAVADANÁ, the hog-faced, is also MARICHI, perhaps intending Radiance; KOTILAKSHÁKSHÍ, the innumerably-eyed, is named PRATINGIRÁ. The *Pancharakshdh*, the five *Rakshas*, or protecting powers, are styled PRATISARÁ, MAHÁSAHASRAPRAMARDINI, MAHÁMAYÚRI, MAHÁSETAVATÍ, and MAHÁMANTRÁNUSÁRINÍ. Without possessing the legends attached, no doubt, to each it would be unsafe to analyse these terms.

* [i. e. KRAKUCHCHHANDA.]

² We have here *Ten* mortal *Buddhas*. The last seven have been already the object of remark. The three first are assigned by some, not the best authorities, to the *Satya yuga*.

³ These nine are *Bodhisattwas*, supposed to bear to the *Dhyání*, or celestial *Buddhas*, the relation of Sons: thus—

5. May that collective aggregate of the five *Buddhas* preserve you, who, for the preservation of mankind, created, from his own abode, the one light[1] in the supreme Lotus, named *Nágavása*, which sprang from the root planted by VIPAŚVÍ, which being one portion became five-fold, and which plays eternally—I adore it.

6. May that mysterious portion of PRAJNÁ as GUHYESWARI[2], born of the Lotus with three leaves,

AVALOKITEŚWARA,	is the Son of	AMITÁBHA.
MAITREYA,	„	VAIROCHANA.
ANANTAGANJA,	„	AKSHOBHYA.
SAMANTABHADRA,	„	VAIROCHANA.
VAJRAPÁŃI,	„	AKSHOBHYA.
MANJUNÁTH,	„	Ditto.
SARVANIVARAŃA VISHKAMBHI,	„	AMOGHA.
KSHITIGARBHA,	„	RATNASAMBHAVA.
KHAGARBHA,	„	AMITÁBHA.

Of these the first, who is the same with PADMAPÁŃI, the fourth and the fifth, are included in original systems amongst the *Dhyánibodhisattwas*, but the others are of mortal origin, and, therefore, very inconsistently derived from celestial progenitors.

[1] The object of Invocation is the *Ádi Buddha*, in the form of Light, manifested on the *Sambhundáh* mountain; the flame is said to burn eternally in the centre of the hemisphere of *Sambhu Chaitya*.

[2] The *Sakti* of *Ádi Buddha* is here addressed as manifested in the element of water, the following legend is cited by Mr. HODGSON from the *Sambhu Purdna*—"When MANJUNÁTH had let off the waters, the luminous form of *Buddha* appeared. MANJU-NÁTH resolved to erect a temple over it, but water bubbled up so fast that he could find no foundation. On his having recourse to prayer, the Goddess GUHYEŚWARI appeared, and the water subsided—GUHYEŚWARI, the Goddess of the hidden form, is very

by the will of MANJUDEVA, void of being, the personification of desire, favourable to many, and praised by BRAHMÁ, VISHNU, and SIVA, who in DURGÁ, the giver of boons, was manifested on the ninth day of the dark half of the month *Márgaśírsha*, be propitious to you—I adore her.

7. May SWAYAMBHÚ, in a visible form as *Ratna Lingeswara*, of the *Śrívatsa* shape, the chief of the eight *Vitarágas*[1], the raft by which the ocean of life

---

like an adoption from *Saiva* mysticism." This, and the preceding verse, are both very obscure.

[1] This, and the following seven verses, refer to the eight *Vitarágas* of the nine *Bodhisattwas* addressed in verse four, all but the first manifested portions of themselves under some visible but inanimate shape, thus

MAITREYA,	was visible as a flame called	*Srívatsa*.
ANASTAGANJA,	as a	*Lotus*.
SAMANTABHADRA	as a	*Flag*.
VAJRAPÁNI	as a	*Water-Jar*.
MANJUNÁTH,	as a	*Chauri*.
VISHKAMBHI,	as a	*Fish*.
KSHITIGARBHA,	as a	*Umbrella*.
KHAGARBHA,	as a	*Conch Shell*.

These are called *Vitarágas*, the exempt from Passion, or rather perhaps the liberators from Passion—as the compound admits of either sense. They are also called the eight *Mangalas*, or auspicious objects. They are found sculptured on *Bauddha* monuments, and especially on the stone or marble *Feet*, which are frequently placed in the temples of the sect. They appear to have been merely the symbols of the *Bodhisattwas*; but they have been connected evidently in popular belief with notions derived from the Hindu religion and local legends, and bear the character of so many *Lingas* erected by different individuals, some of whom are specified. [Burnouf, "Lotus", 647.]

may be crossed, who was produced from a portion of MAITREYA uniting with the light of RATNACHÚDA[1] in the forest rock, be propitious to you—I adore it.

8. May GOKARṆEŚWAHA, the son[2] of KHAGANJA, in the form of a Lotus, assumed on the bank of the *Vágmatí*, by desire of LOKANÁTH, to preserve the wicked GOKARṆA[3] engaged in austere devotion, and who, for the benefit of mankind and their progenitors, is still at the confluence of the rivers[4], be propitious to you—I adore him.

---

[1] RATNACHÚDA or MAṆICHÚDA, he of the Jewel-crest: he is said to have been a King of *Saketa Nagar*, on whose head grew a gem of inestimable value, which he offered to the Gods, and which was united with the portion of MAITREYA to form the *Jewel*-Linga. The *Srivatsa* is, properly, the Jewel worn by KRISHṆA, but is here understood to imply a waving flame. Amongst the ancient *Bauddha* sculptures at *Amaravati*, on the *Krishṇá*, and removed by Colonel MACKENZIE, was one of a Lingam, surmounted by a flame of this description.

[2] The *Uttardga* is styled *Khaganja Tanaya*, meaning, however, emanation or derivation, not literally son.

[3] GOKARṆA is said to have been a prince of *Panchála*. The name of the *Uttardga*, in conjunction with his appellation, is a clear indication of a *Linga* being intended, these symbols, throughout all India, being commonly named from some circumstance connected with their first erection; with *Íswara*, the name of Śiva, affixed. *Gokarṇeswara* is, therefore, the Linga set up by GOKARṆA. It is probable, however, that GOKARṆA is a fabulous person, and that the real origin of the name is the existence of a similar *Lingam* on the Malabar Coast, which has been very celebrated for some centuries.

[4] Of the *Vágmatí* and *Amogharatí*, where oblations to ancestors are offered.

9. May *Maheśa*, named *Kíla*[1], the *Vítaràga*, emanating from Samantabhadra, in the form of a flag, on the holy mountain[2], for the benefit of mankind, frightening, as with a stake, the fierce serpent Kulika[3], the King of the *Nágas*,—

10. May that *Sarveśwara*, the son of the great *Jina*, holding a trident and a bell, a portion of Vajrapáṇi, in the form of a water-jar, assumed at the command of Lokeśwara, to cherish Sarvapáda[4], and left on earth for the benefit of mankind[5], be propitious to you—I adore him.

11. May *Garttesa*[6], the all-bestowing form assumed by Manju Deva, for a portion of himself, in order to awake the ignorant, and idle, and sensual *Manjugartta*[7], and convert him (it) to a profound and learned sage (or region), be propitious to you—I adore him.

---

[1] Or *Kílekcara*.

[2] The text has *Srigiri*, which the comment calls *Chárugiri*.

[3] Kulika is one of the eight chiefs of the *Nágas*, or serpents of *Pátála*.

[4] A sage also named Vajrácháryá, but the term is also used in a generic sense.

[5] The *Linga* is called *Ghaleśwara*.

[6] The emblem of Manju Deva is a Chaurí; but *Gartta* is a cavern, a hole, or hollow. The text in this instance, therefore, does not preserve its symbolic consistency as in the preceding stanzas.

[7] The comment seems to understand by *Manju-gartta*, *Nepal*, the hollow or valley of Manjudeva, who, according to Mr. Hodgson, appears to be a historical personage. [Burnouf, "Lotus de la bonne loi", 500 f.]

12. May that pious SARVANIVARAŃA VISHKAMBHÍ, desirous of the form of a fish, and decorated with the lord of snakes, who gave all to the sage UDIYA, and throwing off a portion of himself became the passionless *Vítarága, Phańíndreśwara*[1], be propitious to you—I adore him.

13. As UDIYÁNA[2], shaded by his umbrella, was engaged in devotion on the bank of the *Vágmatí*, PRITHWIGARBHA suddenly appeared and established that portion of himself, the *Vítarága Gandheśa*[3], the friend of all, standing in the presence of LOKANÁTH, may he be propitious to you—I adore him.

14. As UDIYÁNA, having obtained super-human faculties from his austerities, was delighted, remem-

---

[1] A fish is the symbol of VISHKAMBHÍ; but it is clear that in this, as in other stanzas, the primitive symbol is lost sight of in the new *Lingaïte* personification, which is more especially referred to in every instance, and which is not always alluded to under the same type. In this case it is the *Íswara*, or *Linga*, of the Lord of Hooded Snakes.

[2] The person mentioned in this, and alluded to, although not named (in the original) in the next verse, is no further specified than as an *Áchárya*, or holy man. LOKANÁTH, LOKEŚWARA, and the son of AMITA, are considered by Mr. HODGSON to imply PADMAPÁŃI, who is held to be the especial Lord of the eight *Vítarágas*.

[3] The authors of this nomenclature seem to have been rather at a loss for an appropriate name, and have apparently taken *Gandheśa*, the Lord of Odour, from smell being the property of the element of earth, from which the *Bodhisattwa*, named PRITHWÍ and KSHITI-GARBHA, derives the first member of his name.

bering the son of AMITA, and blowing the shell KHA-
GARBHA, his heart devoted to the will of LOKESWARA,
was manifest; may he who, having established a portion of himself as *Vikrameśa*[1], resurned to his own
abode, be propitious to you—I adore him.

15. May the holy *Tirtha*[2] *Puñya*, where the *Nága*

---

[1] The same remark applies still more especially to this form
—*Vikrama*, valour, prowess, being used to signify the austerities
practised by the Sage.

[2] From this verse to the 18th, the twelve great *Tirthas*, or
places of pilgrimage in Nepal, are addressed. They are all at
the confluence of rivers, the greater number of which are mere
mountain torrents. The circumstances from which they derive
their sanctity, are briefly alluded to in the text; the legends are
related in the *Sambhu Purána*, and are too prolix to be cited,
the places themselves, which are still numerously frequented,
are all identified by Mr. HODGSON as follows:

Puñya T. at *Gokarna*, where the *Vágmati* and *Amoghaphala-
ddyini* rivers unite.

Sánta T. at *Guhyeśwari Ghát*, where the *Mandirik'á* flows
into the *Vágmati*.

Śankara T. Immediately below *Patan*, at the confluence of
the *Vágmati* and *Manimati*.

Rája T. at *Dhantila*, where the *Ráj-manjari* runs into the
Vágmati.

Káma T. called in Newari *Phusiakhel*, at the junction of the
Keśavati and *Vimalavati*; the former is now known as the *Vishnuvati*.

Nirmala T. at the junction of the *Keśavati* and *Bhadravati* at
a place called *Bijiśoko*.

Akara T. at the junction of the *Keśavati* and *Suraṁnavati*.

Jñána T. at the confluence of the *Keśavati* and *Pápanásini*.

Chintámaṇi T. at *Pachilivairi*, where the *Keśavati* and *Vágmati*
unite, just below the present capital—this is the chief *Sangam*,
or conflux of rivers in Nepal.

obtained rest from TARKSUTA; may the holy *Tirtha Sánta*, where PÁRVATÍ performed penance to allay dissension; may the holy *Tirtha Sankara*, where RUDRA, with his mind fixed on obtaining PÁRVATÍ, practised severe austerities, be propitious to you— I adore them.

16. May the holy *Rájatirtha*, where VIRÚPA obtained the sovereignty of the earth; may the holy *Kámatirtha*, where the hunter and deer went to *Indra's* heaven; may the holy *Tirtha Nirmalákhya*, where the Sage VAJRÁCHÁRYA performed his ablutions, be propitious to you—I adore them.

17. May the holy *Tirtha Ákara*, where treasure is obtained by the despairing poor; may the holy *Jnána Tirtha*, where the only wisdom is obtained by the ignorant paying reverence to the stream; may the holy *Tirtha Chintámani*, where every desire is obtained by those duly performing ablutions there, be propitious to you—I adore them.

18. May *Pramoda Tirtha*, where ablution secures pleasure; may *Satlakshaña Tirtha*, where waters engender auspicious attributes; may *Srí Jaya Tirtha*, where BALÁSURA bathed when he undertook to subdue the three worlds, be propitious to you—I adore them.

Pramoda T. at a place called *Danaga*, where the *Vágmatí* and *Ratnavatí* unite.

Satlakshaña T. at the junction of the *Vágmatí* and *Chárumatí* rivers.

Jaya T. at the junction of the *Vágmatí* and *Prabháratí*.

19. May the goddesses VIDYÁDHARI, ÁKÁŚAYOGINÍ, VAJRAYOGINÍ, and HÁRITÍ[1]; may HANUMÁN, GAŃEŚA, MAHÁKÁLA[2], and CHÚḌÁ *Bhikshińí*[3]; may BRÁHMAŃÍ

[1] These four goddesses belong to the *Swábhávika* system. According to one comment, *Vidyádhari* and *Ákáśayogini* are produced from the Lotos in the Solar sphere—above *Sumeru*, which is above the earth; below the earth is the region of water—below that, of fire, and below that, of air. *Vajrayogini* is a goddess of a superior, *Háriti* of an inferior rank. [St. Julien, Mém. sur les Contr. occident., I, 120, Note.] These goddesses resemble the *Yoginís* and *Yakshińís* of the *Tántrika* system in their terrific forms, malignant disposition, and magical powers, and in having each her *Vija Mantra*, a mystical syllable, appropriated to prayers addressed to her. *Háriti* has a temple in the precincts of *Sambhunáth*, and is worshipped as *Sítalá* by the Brahmanical Hindus. [Burnouf, "Introduction", 550 f.]

[2] These three divinities, adopted from the orthodox Pantheon, are great favorites with the *Bauddhas* of Nepal, the legends justifying their adoption being ingenious and popular. The prevailing notion of these and similar importations from the Brahmanical theocracy is, that they are the servants of the Buddhas, and are only to be reverenced in that capacity. It is related of HANUMÁN, in the *Lankávatár*, that when RÁVAŃ found himself overmatched by the monkey, he took refuge in a temple of ŚÁKYA. HANUMÁN, unable to violate the sanctuary, applied to RÁMA, who recommended him to go and serve the *Buddha*. In ŚÁKYA's temple are found images of RÁVAŃ, HANUMÁN, MAHÁKÁLA and HÁRITÍ. MAHÁKÁLA is considered by the *Swábhávikas* as self-born, and is invoked by them as *Vajravíra*. The *Aiśwarikas* regard him as the son of PÁRVATÍ and ŚIVA. [See also St. Julien, l. l. I, 43, Note.]

[3] CHÚḌÁ BHIKSHIŃÍ is a female mendicant. *Bauddha Ascetics* are classed in four orders, the *Arhan*, or perfect saint, *Srávaka*, studious sage, *Chailaka*, naked *ascetic*, and *Bhikshu*, mendicant. [See Hodgson's "Illustrations", 75, and Burnouf, "Lotus", 392.]

and the rest¹, with Sinhiní, Vyághriní², and Skanda⁴, be propitious to you—I adore them.

20. May the lesser *Tírthas*, the source and term of the *Vágmati*, and the rest¹; the *Keśa Chaitya*, on the *Sankochha*⁵ hill, the *Lalita Chaitya*, on the *Jalochha* hill⁶, the *Devi* of the *Phullochha* hill⁷, and the *Bhagavati*, of the *Dhyánaprochha* hill⁸, be propitious to us—I adore them.

---

¹ *Brahmaní* and the rest are the *Mátrikás*, the divine mothers, or personified energies of the Hindu gods.

² *Sinhiní* and *Vyághriní*, or the Lion and Tiger-goddesses, are inferior spirits attached to the *Mátris*.

³ *Skanda* is the Hindu deity, according to the *Aiśwarikas*; according to the *Swábháviḱas*, self-engendered.

⁴ These are four pools at *Vágheúra*, named *Tárá T., Agastya T., Apsara T.,* and *Ananta T.*—Mr. Hodgson classes the source and term of the chief river *Vágmati*, amongst the greater *Tírthas*, but the text cannot be so understood.

⁵ *Sankochha* hill is called, by the Gorkhas, *Śivapura*; by the Newárs, *Shipphucho*: the Legend of *Keśa Chaitya* states, that Khakcchchhanda *Buddha* here cut off the forelocks of 700 *Brahmans* and *Kshatriyas*, or, in other words, made them *Bauddhas*; half the hair (*keśa*) rose to heaven, and gave rise to the *Keśavati* river, the other half fell on the ground, and sprung up in numberless *Chaityas* of the form of Lingas. [See also Hodgson, "Illustrations", 168.]

⁶ *Lalita Chaitya* is said to have been founded by the disciples of *Virásvi*; the hill on which it stands is the *Arjun* of the Gorkhas, the *Jamachho* of the Newárs.

⁷ The goddess is *Vasundhará*, in the form of a *conical stone*: the hill is called, by the Gorkhas, *Phulchok*.

⁸ Another goddess, a portion of *Guhyeśwari*, in the shape of a *conical stone*. The hill is called, by the Gorkhas, *Chandragiri*.

21. May the *Chaitya* of Śrí Manju hill, erected by his disciples¹; may the five deities established in the cities founded by Śrí Śánta²; may the *Puchhágra* mountain, where Śákya expounded the unequalled *Puráña*³, be propitious to you—I adore them.

22. May the King of Serpents, the *Nága*, the destroyer of *Vighnarája*, residing with his train in the *Ádhára* lake⁴; may the five Lords of the three worlds⁵, Ánanda *Lokeśwara*, Harihariharivána *Lokeśwara*, Yakshamalla *Lokeśwara*, Amoghapáśa *Lokeśwara*, and Trilokavaśankara *Lokeśwara*, be propitious to you—I adore them.

---

¹ *Srímanju* hill is the western part of mount *Sambhu*; between which and *Srímanju* there is a hollow, but no separation.

² Śántaśrí, according to the *Sambhu Puráña*, was a Kshatriya King of Gaur, named Puschańda Deva, who, having come to Nepal, was made a *Bauddha* by Gunakar *Bhikshu*: the five divinities are Vasundhará Deví in *Vdaypur*, Agni Deva in *Agnipur*, Váyu Deva in *Vdyupur*, Nágadeva in *Nágpur*, and Guhyadeví in *Sántapur*. They are all on mount Sambhu round the great temple.

³ The *Puchhágra* mountain is the hollow of mount *Sambhu*; the *Puráña* intended is the *Sambhupuráña* [i. e. *Srayambhúpuráña*. See Burnouf, "Introduction", 581. Hodgson, "Illustrations", 25.]

⁴ The *Nága* here is Karkota, one of the eight *Nágas*, who in Nepal, as well as in Kashmir [Rája Tar. III, 530.], is reported to have resided in the waters which filled those valleys; when the country was drained, he repaired to a reservoir near Kathmandu. The *Ádhára* tank is called, by the Newárs, *Tadahung*.

⁵ The five *Lokeśwaras*, regents of the worlds, are *Bodhisattwas*: *Ananta* is called by the Newárs *Chobhá Dev*, and *Yakshamalla*, *Tújú Khwá*.

23. May the divinities HEVAJRA, SAMVARA, CHANDA-VÍRA, TRILOKAVÍRA and YOGÁMBARA, with their train; may the destroyer of YAMA and the rest of the ten Kings of wrath, with all hidden and revealed spirits; may APARIMITÁYU NÁMSANGÍTI, be propitious to you[1]—I adore them.

24. May MANJUNÁTH[2], who having come from *Sirsha*, with his disciples, divided the mountain with his scymitar, and on the dried-up lake erected a city, the pleasant residence of men, worshipping the deity sitting on the elemental Lotus, be propitious to you—I adore him.

25. May ANJAPÁNI, the chief of the companion train of HAYAGRÍVA, and JATÁDHARA[3], who came to the mountain *Potala* after having gone from *Saukhavati*[4]

---

[1] Most of these belong to the *Bauddha* system and the *Swábhávika* division. APARIMITÁYU and NÁM SANGÍTI are both *Buddhas*, to each of whom various associates are attached.

[2] Some observations on the historical purport of this and the next verse will be subjoined to the text.

[3] The construction of this passage might warrant the use of *Jaṭádhara* as the epithet of HAYAGRÍVA, the wearer of the *Jaṭá*, or matted hair, denoting a follower of *Śiva*, particularly as HAYAGRÍVA is said to be a *Bhairava*, one of *Śiva's* attendants: but the comment calls *Jaṭádhara* a *Lokeśvara*: according to Mr. HODGSON, also HAYAGRÍVA and JATÁDHARA are two of the menial attendants of ANJAPÁNI or PADMAPÁNI, one of the *Dhyáni Buddhas*; others are named *Sudhana, Kumára, Ajita, Apardjita, Marśainya, Varada, Akálamrityu, Jaya, Vijaya, Abhayaprada,* and *Dhanada*, most of which names are well known to the Hindus as those of the attendants on *Śiva* and *Párvati*.

[4] [Köppen, "Religion des Buddha", II, 28. Wassiljew, I. I. I, 222.]

to *Venga*, and being afterwards called by the King[1] to remove accumulated evils, entered *Lalitapur*, be propitious to you—I adore him[2].

REMARKS.

Besides the peculiar purport of the allusions contained in the preceding verses, they suggest a few general considerations which may be here briefly adverted to.

It is clear that the *Bauddha* religion, as cultivated in Nepal, is far from being so simple and philosophical a matter as has been sometimes imagined. The objects of worship are far from being limited to a few persons of mortal origin, elevated by superior sanctity to divine honours, but embrace a variety of modifications and degrees more numerous and complicated, than even the ample Pantheon of the Brahmans. A portion of the heavenly host is borrowed, it is true, from the Brahmanical legends, but a sufficient variety is traceable to original sources, both amongst the *Swábhávikas* and *Aiśwarikas*, and either spontaneously engendered, or created by some of the manifestations of the *Ádi Buddha*, or Supreme Being. Such are the *Bodhisattwas*, and the *Lokeśwaras*, and a

---

[1] The *Deva*; the Comment says *Narendra Deva*, a King of Nepal.

[2] [A translation of the same Tantra, by Mr. Hodgson, appeared in the Journal As. Soc. Bengal, XII, 400-409; but unfortunately it is disfigured by numerous misprints.]

number of inferior divinities, both male and female, that are not borrowed from either the Śaiva or Śákta sects.

It is a subject of important inquiry, in what degree these divinities are peculiar to Nepal, and whether they are acknowledged by the *Bauddhas* in other countries. There can be little doubt, that they are recognised by the *Bauddhas* of Tibet and Chinese Tartary, and some of them are traceable in China. It is very doubtful, however, if they form part of the theocracy of Ceylon, Ava, and Siam. In the first of these we find inferior divinities, some of them females, worshipped; but they do not, as far as any description enables us to judge, offer any analogy to the similar beings reverenced in Nepal. In Ava and Siam nothing of the kind apparently occurs, although in the existence of *Nats*, it is admitted, that other animated creatures than man and animals exist. It has already been observed, that nothing analogous to the Metaphysical, or *Dhyáni Buddhas* occurs in the *Buddhism* of Southern India.

There is, however, some evidence to shew, that the whole of the Nepal hierarchy of heaven, even of the *Swábhávika* class, is not confined to the nations of the North. In the vocabulary of HEMACHANDRA* we have the names of sixteen goddesses, at a little distance from the synonymes of the *Buddhas*, entitled the *Vidyádevís*, who are unknown to the Brahmanical system. One of these is *Prajnaptí*, who may be the

* [239. 240.]

same as the *Prajná* of our text. It is however, in the vocabulary, entitled the *Trikáṅḍa Śesha*, that the fullest confirmation occurs, that many of the inferior personages belonging to the Bauddhas were known in India, when that faith was current there. Besides the names of ŚÁKYA and those of general or individual *Buddhas*, as SWAYAMBHÚ, PADMAPÁṆI, LOKANÁTH, LOKEŚA, VÍTARÁGA, AVALOKITA, and MAÑJUŚRÍ, that work specifies a variety of goddesses, whose titles are found in the text as *Tárá, Vasundhará, Dhanadá* or *Sampatpradá, Márichi, Lochaná*, and others. The vocabulary is Sanskrit, and is apparently a compilation of the tenth or eleventh century[1].

The allusions in the twenty-fourth and other verses to MAÑJU NÁTH seem to point to him as the first teacher of the *Bauddha* religion in Nepal. Tradition assigns to him the same part that was performed by KÁŚYAPA in Kashmir[2], the recovery of the country from the waters by which it was submerged, by giving them an outlet through the mountains: this he performed, according to the text, by cutting a passage with his scymitar. He is described in the same stanza, as coming from *Śirshá*, which the *Newárí* comment says is the mountain of *Mahácháin*, and the *Sambhu Puráṅa* also states the same. The city founded by MAÑJU, called *Manju Pattan*[*], is no longer in exis-

---

[1] Introduction of Wilson's Dictionary p. xxvii.
[2] As. Res. Vol. XV. [Burnouf, "Lotus", 505.]
[*] [Lassen, Ind. Alt., III, 777 f. Burnouf, "Lotus", 504.]

tence, but tradition places it half-way between Mount
Sambhu, and the Pasupati Wood, where the remains
of buildings are often dug up. Both BUCHANAN and
KIRKPATRICK advert to the legend of MANJU's drying
up the valley of Nepal, and express themselves satisfied that it is founded on the fact of the valley having
once been an extensive lake. MANJU has a number
of synonymes in the Trikáṅḍa, as MANJUŚRÍ, MANJU
GHOSHA, MANJUDHADRA, KUMÁRA, the youth or prince;
NÍLA, the dark-complexioned; VÁDIRÁJ, the King of
controversy; KHADGÍ, wearing a sword; DAṄḌÍ carrying a staff; ŚIKHÁDHARA, having a lock of hair on
the crown of his head; SINHAKELÍ, who sports with a
Lion; and ŚÁRDÚLAVÁHANA, who rides on a Tiger:
some of these epithets are, of course, not to be understood literally, but their general tendency is to assign
to MANJU the character of a Military Legislator, one
whose most convincing argument was the edge of
his sword.

The religion introduced by MANJU and his disciples
was, possibly, that of pure Buddhism, either in the
Swábhávika or Aiswarya form; but whence were the
Brahmanical grafts derived? It is not extraordinary
that we should have ŚIVA, or VISHNU, or GANESA, or
perhaps even HANUMÁN, admitted to some degree of
reverence, for there is nothing in the Bauddha doctrines negative of the existence of such beings, and
the popularity of the legends relating to them with
the whole Hindu people recommended them to the
favour and adoption of their neighbours; but the Śákta

form of *Hinduism* is a comparatively obscure and unavowed innovation, and had not therefore the same claims to consideration. It is, nevertheless, the chief source of the notions and divinities foreign to *Buddhism* with those *Bauddhas*, amongst whom the *Panchaviṅśati* is an authority. It could only have been brought to their knowledge by contiguity, for the *Tantras*, and *Tántrika Puráṅas*, form a literature almost peculiar to the eastern provinces of Hindustan, the origin of which appears to be traceable to KÁMARÚP or western Asam. There is no doubt that the system has principally prevailed in Bengal, Rungpore, Cooch Behár, and Asam; and, following the same direction, has probably spread into Nepal. There seem to be some hints to this effect in the concluding stanza of the Tract that has been translated.

The literal purport of this verse is, that ABJAPÁṄI, whoever he might be, came to *Lalitapur*, after having gone from *Saukhavati* to *Banga*. *Saukhavati* is called a *Lokadhátu*, a peculiar *Bauddha* division of the universe, and probably not in this world; but *Banga desa* is never applied to any country, except the east or north of Bengal. ABJAPÁṄI, or PADMAPÁṄI, is a metaphysical *Bodhisattwa*, but in the present work all these nonentities are converted into substances, and he is therefore a mortal teacher of the *Bauddha* faith, or employed for the occasion in that capacity. He was invited, the tradition records, to reside in Nepal on the occasion of a famine, by NARENDRA DEVA, Rájá of *Bhatgong*, and BANDHUDATTA, a *Vajráchárya*, and came in consequence. He comes attended by *Bhairavas* and wearers of *Jatás*, and may therefore be suspected of having come in the garb of a *Saiva* priest, if not as his identical self, yet as an *Ansa*, or portion, which the orthodox *Bauddhas* leave out of view. They have, however, no objection to the *Siva Márgís* worshipping AIMAPÁNI under any name they please, and his annual festival is attended by all sects alike.

The invitation of a foreign teacher by NARENDRA DEVA is noticed by Colonel KIRKPATRICK; but the individual is called by him MATSYENDRA NÁTH[1], one of the first propagators, apparently, of the *Pásupata* form of the *Saiva* religion, which seems to be that prevailing in Nepal. There is also mention of some alteration of the national rites, by another Prince of the same denomination, by which it is recorded a fall

---

[1] An original legend sent me by Mr. HODGSON narrates, that the *Lokéswara* PADMAPÁNI descended by command of ÁDI BUDDHA as MATSYENDRA. He hid himself in the belly of a fish, in order to overhear ŚIVA teach PÁRVATÍ the doctrine of the *Yoga*, which he had learned from ÁDI BUDDHA, and which he communicated to his spouse on the sea-shore. Having reason to suspect a listener, ŚIVA commanded him to appear, and PADMAPÁNI came forth, clad in raiment stained with ochre, smeared with ashes, wearing ear-rings, and shaven, being the chief of the *Yogis*: He was called MATSYENDRA NÁTHA, from his appearance from a fish (*Matsya*), and his followers took the appellation *Náth*. We have in this story a decided proof of the current belief of a union between the *Yoga* sectaries, and the *Bauddhas*, effected, perhaps, by the *Yogi* MATSYENDRA, known in Hindustan as the pupil of GORAKHNÁTH, but converted by the *Bauddhas* into a manifestation of one of their deified Sages. [See Vol. I, 214.]

of snow was obtained. The first NARENDRADEO appears to have lived in the 7th, the second in the 12th century. The first would answer well enough for the introduction of the *Páśupata* creed, which might have been popular in India about that time, and the latter date is that about which the *Tántrika* ritual seems to have obtained currency. It is not unlikely that the expressions in the *Panchaviṃśati* refer to one or other of these events, although, as usual, in all such appropriations of legendary history, the circumstances are adapted to the peculiar notions of those by whom they are borrowed. According to local traditions, the invitation of *Padmapáni* occurred in the fifth century, or 1381 years ago*.

ASHTAMÍ VRATA VIDHÁNA.

This tract is of much greater extent, than either of the preceding, but is of less value for the illustration of ideas originally *Bauddha*. It belongs to that faith, but is still more copiously interspersed with notions from a foreign source than even the preceding, being, in fact, a ritual of the *Tántrika* practices of persons professing the religion of *Buddha*. A few observations and extracts will be sufficient to give an idea of its character, and of the observances it enjoins.

The eighth lunar day of every half month is a day

---

* [See Köppen, "Religion des Buddha", II, 21-32.]

peculiarly appropriated to religious ceremonies in the orthodox system. In the *Vaidik* creed it was customary to fast, and offer oblations to the gods in general on this day, and the *Pauraniks* made it sacred to different divinities, particularly to VISHNU. The *Tántrikas* have devoted the eighth day of certain months to the celebration of rites, which have no exclusive object, but are intended to secure the prosperity of the observer, and in this they have been apparently imitated by the *Bauddhas* of *Nepal*.

The opening of the work, announcing the intention of the worshipper, refers briefly to several of the leading topics of the verses of the *Panchavinsatiká*. Thus:

"In the period of the *Tathágata* ŚÁKYA SINHA, in the *Bhadrakalpa*, in the *Lokadhátu* named *Sahá*, in the *Vaiwaswata Manwantara*, in the first quarter of the Kali age, in the *Bharata* division of the earth, in Northern *Pancháia*, in the *Devasúka Kshetra*, in the *Upachhandoha Pitha*; in the holy land *Aryávartta*; in the abode of the King of Serpents, KARKOTA, in the lake called *Nágavása*, in the region of the *Chaitya* of SWAYAMBHU, in the realm over which GUHYEŚWARÍ PRAJNÁ presides, and which the fortune of MANJU ŚRÍ protects, in the kingdom of *Nepal*, of the form of that of *Śrí Samvara*, and invincible, encircled by the eight *Vitarágas*, *Mahilingeśwara, Gokarneśwara, Kileśwara* and *Kumbheśwara, Gartteśwara, Phanikeśwara, Gandheśa* and *Vikrameśwara*, watered by the four great rivers *Vágmati, Keśavati, Manimati*, and *Prabhávati*, sanctified by the twelve greater and six lesser Tírthas, and by the edifices on the four mountains, governed by the seven Sages, honoured by the *Yoginís*, the eight *Mátrikás*, the eight *Bhairavas*, *Sinhiní*, *Vyághriní*, *Ganesa*, *Kumára*, *Mahákála*, *Hárití*, *Hanumán*, the ten ministers of wrath. In such a place, at such a time, before such a divinity, I (naming himself and family) perform this rite, with my wife and household." The objects of the ceremony are then enunciated, generally, aversion of all evils, the preservation of health, and the attainment of fortune. Most of the allusions have been already explained, and others belong to Brahmanical Hinduism. The name of the *Lokadhátu*, or division of the universe, *Saha*, is applicable apparently to the *Himálaya* range, and includes *Kashmír*, as we know from the *Rája Taranginí*[1].

The ceremonial of the *Tantras* is distinguished by the repetition of mystical syllables, the employment of *Yantras*, or diagrams, a superabundance of gesticulations, the adoration of the spiritual teacher, or *Guru*, and the fancied identification of the worshipper with the divinity worshipped. In all these, as well as

---

[1] See As. Res. Vol. XV, p. 110, where *Kashmír* is termed, in the *Nágarí* text [1, 172.], *Sahalokadhátu*, rendered erroneously 'the essence of the world,' the admissible, although not the technical purport of *Lokadhátu*, in composition with *Saha*, no available information then suggesting the latter to be a proper name, and the former a division of the Universe in *Bauddha* Geography. [For the explanation of the term *Sahalokadhátu*, world of patience, see Burnouf, "Introduction", 594—7, and Köppen, "Religion des Buddha", I, 264.]

in the order and nature of the presentations, the *Ashtami Vidhána* is as applicable to Calcutta as to *Kathmandu*; the only difference being in the object or objects addressed: in the present case, the principal person propitiated is AMOGHAPÁSA, apparently the same with SWAYAMBHÚ NÁTHA; but prayers are made, and offerings are addressed to all the personages of the *Bauddha* Pantheon, and to a great number of the divinities of the *Hindus*, especially to the terrific forms of SIVA and SAKTI, and to all the *Bhútas*, or spirits of ill, and the *Yoginis* and *Dákinis*, the perpetrators of all mischief. A few passages will substantiate the accuracy of these assertions.

In the hall where the ceremony is held various *Mandalas*[1], or portions are marked off and appropriated to the different objects of the rite, and a complete course of worship is addressed to each. The following is that directed for the *Buddha Mandala*. The directions are, in general, in *Newári*, the texts and prayers to be repeated in *Sanskrit*.

Let the sacrificer touch the *Buddha Mandala* with his fore-finger, repeating: "The universal *Tathágata*, may all be propitious." He is then to address himself to the *Dúrvá*[2] (or holy grass which is placed in the

---

[1] The *Mandala* is sometimes an imaginary circle on the body of the worshipper; but it is defined here to be made with various substances, according to the means of the performer of the rite, as with gold dust, or pounded gems, or stone. [See also Wassiljew, l. l. I, 212.]

[2] [Dr. Ainslie, in his "Materia Indica", Vol. II, p. 27 f., gives a description of this beautiful grass and its properties.]

centre of the circle). "Om. I adore the *Vajra*[1] *Dúrvá*
—glory be to it." He is then to throw flowers, or
wave incense in the air, saying: "May all the *Buddhas*
residing in all quarters gather round me. I, such a
one so named, observing this rite, have become a
mendicant *(Bhikshu).* Let all the *Buddhas* approach,
who will grant me the permission of my desires. I
wave this *Vajra Pushpa,* in honor of the auspicious
teachers, the possessors of prosperity and the Lord;
I invite them to appear."

The worshipper is then to present water to wash
the feet, and to rinse the mouth (saying: "Receive
water for the feet of the Saint of ŚRI BUDDHA; *Swáhá,*
Receive the *Áchamana; Swáhá*").

The *Pushpa Nyása* (presentation of flowers) next
occurs; with these ejaculations: "Om! to the holy
VAIROCHANA: *Swáhá.* Om! to the holy AKSHODHYA:
Swáhá. Om! to the holy RATNASAMBHAVA: *Swáhá.*
Om! to the holy AMITÁBHA: *Swáhá.* Om! to the holy
AMOGHA SIDDHA: *Swáhá.* Om! to the holy LOCHANÁ:
Swáhá. Om! to the holy MÁMAKI: *Swáhá.* Om! to
the holy TÁRÁ: *Swáhá.*"

This is followed or accompanied by the presentation
of incense, lights, water, and whole rice.

Then ensues the *Stotra,* or praise: "I ever offer my
salutation with my head declined; To the holy bene-

---

[1] The term *Vajra*, which signifies 'the thunderbolt', or 'a diamond',
is employed in these compounds, evidently in the sense of auspicious,
holy, or sacred, [Burnouf, "Introduction", 527, or serving for
the removal or keeping off of difficulties. See Wassiljew, L I. I, 211.]

factor of the world VAIROCHANA. To the holy AKSHOBHYA. To the illustrious RATNODBHAVA, the best of Saints. To AMITÁBHA, the Lord of the *Munis*. To the holy AMOGHA SIDDHA, the remover of the ills of the *Kali* age. To LOCHANÁ, to MÁMAKÍ, and to TÁRÁ, named PÁNDURÁ. I adore SÁKYA SINHA, the ruler of all, propitious, the asylum of clemency, the all-wise, the lotus-eyed, the comprehensive *Buddha*."

The *Deśaná*, a sort of confession, is next performed. "Whatever sin may have been committed by me, child and fool that I am, whether originating in natural weakness, or done in conscious wickedness, I confess all, thus standing in the presence of the Lords of the world, joining my hands, afflicted with sorrow and fear, and prostrating myself repeatedly before them. May the holy Sages conceive the past as with the past, and the evil I have done shall never be repeated."

This is to be said by the disciple before the GURU, placing his right knee in the *Mandala* on the ground: He then continues: "I, such a one, having uttered my confession, take refuge with *Buddha* from this time forward, until the ferment of ignorance shall have subsided: for he is my protector, the Lord of exalted glory, of an imperishable and irresumable form, merciful, omniscient, all-seeing, and free from the dread of all terrors; I do this in the presence of men."

To this the *Guru* is to reply repeatedly: "Well done, well done, my son; perform the *Niryátana*."

The worshipper accordingly takes rice, flowers, and

water, and performs the rite, or sprinkles them on the *Mandala,* with this text: "This is the Lord ARHAT, the comprehensive *Buddha,* replete with divine knowledge, *Sugata,* knowing the universe, the supreme, the curber of the wild steeds of human faults, the ruler of the mortals and immortals: *Buddha.* To him, gem of *Buddhas,* I address the rites performed to this flower *Mandala.*"

The offering is then made with this formula: "Om! *Namah* to the gem of *Buddhas,* whose heart is laden with the burthen of compassion, the supreme spirit, the universal intellect, the triple essence, the endurer of ills for the benefit of existing beings; accept this offering, savoury and fragrant, and confirm me and all men in the supreme all-comprehending wisdom. *Om, Ám, Hrit, Hum, Phat, Swáhá.*"

The whole of the above is thrice repeated, with what are called the *Dharma, Sangha,* and *Múla Mandalas.* The names of the *Buddhas* being changed, and the prayers varied in length, though not in purport: these, however, form but a small part of the whole ceremony; although it is made up entirely of such prayers and observances.

After worship has been offered to the different *Buddhas, Bodhisattwas,* regents of the quarters, and other mythological beings, the ceremony concludes with the following address to the "spirits of heaven and goblins damned".

"Glory to VAJRASATTWA—Gods and demons, Serpents and Saints, Lord of the plumed race, and all

Gandharbas, Yakshas, Regents of the planetary orbs, and spirits that dwell upon the earth. Thus, kneeling on the ground, I invoke you. Let all, hearing my invocation, approach with their wives, and children, and associates. Hear Demi-Gods, who frequent the brow of *Meru,* the groves of *Indra,* the palaces of the Gods, and the orbit of the sun, spirits who sport in streams, in ponds, in lakes, in fountains, and the depths of the sea. Goblins, who dwell in villages, in towns, in the deserted temples of the Gods, in the stalls of Elephants, and the cells of Monks. Imps, that haunt the roads, the lanes, the markets, and where cross-ways meet. Ghosts, that lurk in wells and thickets, in the hollow of a solitary tree, in funeral paths, and in the cemeteries of the dead, and Demons of terrific form, who roam as bears and lions through the vast forest, or rest in the mountain's caverned sides. Hear and attend. Receive the lights, the incense, the fragrant wreaths and the offerings of food presented to you in sincerity of faith; accept, eat and drink, and render this act propitious. INDRA, the thunder-bearer, AGNI, YAMA, Lord of the earth, Lord of the main, God of the winds, Sovereign of riches, and King of spirits (ÍSÁNA), Sun, Moon, progenitors of mankind, accept this offering of incense, this offering of lights. Accept, eat and drink, and render the act propitious.

KRISHNÁ RUDRI, MAHÁ RUDRI, ŚIVÁ, UMÁ, of black and fearful aspect, attendants of DEVÍ, JAYÁ, VIJAYÁ, AJITÁ, APARÁJITÁ, BHADRAKÁLÍ, MAHÁKÁLÍ, STHALA-

KÁLÍ, YOGINÍ, INDRÍ, CHAŚDÍ, GHORÍ, VIDHÁTRÍ, DÚTÍ, JAMBUKÍ, TRIDAŚEŚWARÍ, KÁMBOJINÍ, DÍPANÍ, CHÚ- SHUSÍ, GHORARÚPÁ, MAHÁRÚPÁ, DRISHTARÚPÁ, KAPÁ- LINÍ, KAPÁLAMÁLÁ, MÁLINÍ, KHATWÁNGA, YAMAHÁRD- DIKÁ, KHADGAHASTÁ, PARAŚUHASTÁ, VAJRAHASTÁ, DHANUHASTÁ, PANCHADÁKINÍ, MAHÁTATTWÁ. The accomplisher of all acts, the delighter in the circle of the Jogís, the Lord of VAJREŚWARÍ, all hear and obey this the order of VAJRASATTWA, who was created by the *Yoya* of the unimpassioned form of *Tathágata*. *Om-Ka-ka-kardana-kardana! Khá-khá, khádana- khádana!* destroy, destroy, all obnoxious to me; *Gha gha, ghátaya, ghátaya!* cherish and preserve the life and health, the wishes and the prosperity of the sacrificer, the holder of the thunder-bolt, commands: *Hrum, Hrum, Hrum, Phat, Phat, Phat; Swáhá!*"

Such is the nonsensical extravagance with which this and the *Tántrika* ceremonies generally abound; and we might be disposed to laugh at such absurdities, if the temporary frenzy, which the words excite in the minds of those who hear and repeat them with agitated awe, did not offer a subject worthy of serious contemplation in the study of human nature.

II.
TWO LECTURES
ON THE
RELIGIOUS PRACTICES AND OPINIONS OF THE HINDUS.

Delivered before the University of Oxford on the 27th and 28th of February, 1840.

LECTURE I.

It has always been my wish and intention to offer to those members of the University who may take an interest in the subject, a general view of the institutions and social condition, the literature and the religion of the Hindus. The purpose, although unfulfilled, is not abandoned. Various impediments have retarded its accomplishment, and still delay its execution; but I hope, at no very distant period, to be able to carry it into effect. In the mean time, the invitation which has been addressed to the University by the Bishop of Calcutta, and which, I am happy to think, has been accepted, to contribute to the religious enlightenment of a benighted, but intelligent and interesting and amiable people, has suggested to me the propriety and the duty of giving some earnest of my desire to render to any who may apply their talents and learning to the proposed task—a task peculiarly appropriate to a society equally eminent for piety and erudition—whatever assistance the direction of my studies, my personal knowledge of the Hindus, and the extent of my ability may qualify me to afford them.

The task that has been proposed to the members of the University is twofold. They are invited to confute the falsities of Hinduism, and affirm to the conviction of a reasonable Hindu the truths of Christianity. For the second branch of this undertaking the qualifications are widely disseminated. Deep impressions of the importance of Christian truth, and of the obligation to extend it to the ends of the earth—knowledge of that truth, and skill to make it known—are not likely to be deficient in this University. For the effective performance, however, of the first branch of the undertaking, some preparation is requisite—some preliminary study is necessary—some information not yet sought for is to be obtained. It is obviously essential to know that which we engage to controvert. It is indispensable that we should be well acquainted with the practices and doctrines and belief, the erroneousness of which we would demonstrate; and in this respect whatever may be the zeal and the ability, the like extent of available fitness cannot at present be reasonably expected. Yet the plan submitted to the University requires this fitness, and judiciously requires it. Besides the general principles upon which the necessity of such competency is obvious, it is still more imperative in regard to the circumstances and character of those with whom we have to deal. The Hindus will not listen to one who comes amongst them strong only in his own faith and ignorant of theirs. "Read these translations," said a very worthy clergyman to a sect of religionists at Benares, who were already seceders from idolatrous worship, and were not indisposed for argument upon the comparative truth of different creeds. "We have no objection to read your books," was the reply, "but we will enter into no discussion of their contents with you until you have read ours." This was inconvenient or impracticable, and no further intercourse ensued. This is one instance out of many where precious opportunities have been lost, because the only means of communicating fully with the natives — conversancy not merely with their language but with their literature — has been wanting or incomplete; and with an acute and argumentative people like the Hindus you must satisfy them that they are in error before you can persuade them to accept the truth. To overturn their errors we must know what they are; and for the purpose of conveying to you some notion of their nature and extent, and of putting you in the way of acquiring more precise information on the subject, I have thought it possible that even some brief observation may be of use. With this hope I propose to give in this and a succeeding Lecture a general sketch of the principal religious practices and opinions of the Hindus.

The account which it is thus proposed to submit to

you must be unavoidably of a very general nature. The interval that has elapsed since the invitation was accepted has not permitted the preparation of a very comprehensive detail; nor is the subject, perhaps, in that stage of its consideration in which minuteness of detail would be of advantage. What is now wanted, and that as early as possible, is some determinate direction in which inquiry may be prosecuted — some definite point to which the thoughts may be made to converge. In a topic necessarily unfamiliar to the customary tenor of academic study, it is not possible that any exact ideas should have been yet formed as to the degree or kind of preparation that is requisite, and few are likely to be acquainted with the situation and sufficiency of those stores from which they must provide their outfit for an untried voyage. The scene is so new, the prospect so indistinct, that enterprise may lose heart, and zeal may languish in vain aspirations, unless something of a chart, however rude and imperfect, be laid before the adventurer whilst he yet hesitates to make his first advance. It is this help which it is my present purpose to supply, in the hope that some, who, although competent to do honour to themselves and the University, might shrink from encountering they know not what, may be induced, if the mist may be in some degree cleared away, to look a little nearer, advance a little farther into the now-seeming labyrinth, assured that every step they take the path will become less intricate, and the goal be more perceptibly in view; assured, too—unless my own experience deceive me—that there will not be wanting on their journey objects, if not of beauty, yet of exceeding curiosity and interest, to enliven their way, and beguile them of the consciousness of fatigue.

The history of the Hindu religion, although not traceable with chronological precision, exhibits unequivocal proof that it is by no means of that unalterable character which has been commonly ascribed to it. There are many indications which cannot be mistaken, that it has undergone at different periods important alterations in both form and spirit. These are little heeded, have been little investigated, and are little known by even the most learned of the Brahmans. Some have been pointed out by the late Hindu reformer Rájá Rammohan Roy, but even he was unaware of their full extent, and they are of themselves fatal to the pretensions of the Hindu faith, as it now mostly prevails, to an inspired origin and unfathomable antiquity.

The oldest monuments of the Hindu religion are the Vedas. It is much to be regretted that we have not a translation of these works in any of the languages of Europe; if we had, they would no doubt, in like manner as the Koran of the Mohammedans and the Zend-avesta of the fire-worshippers of Persia, supply us with irrefutable arguments against the credibility of the religion of which they were once the oracles. A summary of the contents of the Vedas— as satisfactory as a summary can be—was published by Mr. Colebrooke, the most eminent of all our Sanskrit scholars, in the eighth volume of the Researches of the Asiatic Society of Bengal[1]. The account, with a variety of instructive dissertations on the religion, philosophy, science, and literature of the Hindus, has been reprinted in a Collection of Miscellaneous Essays[2], published by Mr. Colebrooke, or rather for him, not long before his death. The text also, with a Latin translation of one book out of eight, of one of the Vedas, the Rig-Veda, has been printed by the Committee of the Oriental Translation Fund[3]. It was

---

[1] Asiatic Researches. Transactions of a Society instituted in Bengal, for inquiring into the History, &c., of India. 20 Vols. 4to. Calcutta.

[2] Miscellaneous Essays, by H. T. Colebrooke. 2 Vols. 8vo. London. Allen and Co. 1837. [2nd ed. London, 1858.]

[3] Rig-veda Sanhita. Liber Primus. 1 Vol. 4to. London. Oriental Translation Fund. Allen and Co. 1838.

[Since the above was written, the Sâmaveda has been edited and translated by Stevenson (1842) and Benfey (1848); the white Yajurveda edited by Weber (1849 ff.); the black Yajurveda is in the course of publication in the Bibliotheca Indica; the Atharvaveda has been edited by Roth and Whitney (1855 ff.), and an edition of the Rigveda with the commentary of Sâyana was commenced by M. Müller in 1849, which is still in progress. Prof. Wilson's translation of the Rigveda (1850-57, 3 Vols.) reaches to the end of the 4th Ashtaka. Dr. Aufrecht is editing the text of the Rigveda in Roman characters (Vol. I, 1861). On Vedic literature generally see Weber's Vorlesungen über indische Literaturgeschichte (1852), his Indische Studien (5 Vols. 1850-61), Müller's history of ancient Sanskrit literature (1859), and Goldstücker's article on the Vedas in the English Encyclopædia (Arts and Sciences, Vol. VIII. 1861).]

the work of Dr. Rosen, a distinguished oriental scholar, who died in the prime of life and in the spring of his fame. A portion of the same Veda has also been translated by the Rev. Mr. Stevenson, and published at Bombay.

From these authorities a tolerably correct notion may be formed of the character of the Vedas. They are four in number, Rich, Yajush, Sáman, and Atharvan, or, as usually compounded, Rig-veda, Yajur-veda, Sáma-veda, and Atharva-veda. The latter, however, differs, as far as it is known, materially in purport and even in style from the others; it is rarely met with, and is not uncommonly omitted from the specification of the Vedas even by early writers, who not unfrequently speak of the Vedas collectively as but *three*. It evidently enters in a less degree than the rest into the formation of the national religion as taught by the Vedas. Neither of the Vedas can be considered as a distinct work, composed upon a definite plan, having either a consistent method or a predominating subject. Each is an unarranged aggregate of promiscuous prayers, hymns, injunctions, and dogmas, put together in general, though not always, in similar succession, but not in any way connected one with the other. It is not at all unusual for even what is considered as the same hymn, to offer perfectly isolated and independent verses, so that they might be extruded without injury to the whole. In the belief of the Hindus, the Vedas were coeval with creation, and are uncreated, being simultaneous with the first breath of Brahmá—the creative power. This is sometimes questioned; but the opinion is universal that Brahmá was their author, and that they were amongst the first created things. There are, however, legends of their having been lost; and there is one account of their recovery, which states that they were then taught to a number of Brahmans by a son of Brahmá. This refers, probably, to the period of their composition by different Brahmans. They themselves furnish evidence of their composition by different hands, and at different periods. Each hymn is said to have its Rishi—the sage by whom it was first communicated; and these Rishis comprise a variety of secular as well as religious individuals, members of the Kshatriya or military, as well as the Brahmanical order, who are celebrated at different æras in Hindu tradition. It is also admitted that the Vedas existed in a scattered form until the parts of which they now consist were collected and arranged in their actual form by a person of very equivocal origin — the son of a Rishi, by the daughter of a fisherman, and therefore, properly speaking, of very impure caste — and who from his arranging the Vedas is known by the name of Vyása—the arranger. He is supposed by the Hindus to have lived about 5000 years ago. It seems not improbable that he, or the school of which he is the reputed founder, flourished about thirteen centuries before the Christian era. He was assisted in his labour, it is reported, by various sages, and it is here again evident that the composition of the

Vedas was the work of many hands—of a school or religious community which first reduced the straggling institutes and practices, and popular prayers and hymns of the people, into a compact and permanent authority. The proceedings of Vyása and his coadjutors, and the formation of various branches from the main stem, or of subordinate and subsequent from one primary and principal school, are described by Mr. Colebrooke, and will also be found detailed in the Vishńu Puráńa[1], of which a translation is about to appear from the press of the University.

In the state in which they are now found, the Vedas are each distinguishable into two portions— a practical and a speculative: the one still forms the chief basis of speculative opinion; the other is, except in a few particulars, obsolete.

The practical portion of the Vedas consists of little else than detached prayers addressed with a few exceptions to divinities no longer worshipped, some of whom are even unknown. There is one for instance named Ŕibhu, of whose history, office, or even name, a person might ask in vain, from one end of India to the other. The prayers have consequently gone out of fashion along with their objects, and when they are employed they are used as little else than unmeaning sounds, the language in which they are written differing much, both in words and construction, from the

---

[1] The Vishńu Puráńa. A System of Hindu Mythology and Tradition, translated from the original Sanskrit. 1 Vol. 4to. London. Murray. 1840.

Sanskrit of later writings. In many parts of India the Vedas are not studied at all; and when they are studied it is merely for the sake of repeating the words; the sense is regarded as a matter of no importance, and is not understood even by the Brahman who recites or chaunts the expressions. Now this is in itself a vital departure from the sacred institutes of the Hindus, by which the first portion of life, the first of the four orders or stages through which all males of the three first castes, the Brahman, Kshatriya, and Vaisya, were peremptorily commanded to pass, was that of the religious student; the term of whose studentship was to be spent with a Brahman teacher of the Vedas, and the sole object of whose studies was the understanding of the Vedas. For a Brahman to be wholly ignorant of the Vedas was a virtual degradation. "A Brahman," says Manu, "unlearned in holy writ, is extinguished in an instant like dry grass on fire*." "A twice born man (that is, a man of either of the three first castes) not having studied the Veda, soon falls, even while living, to the condition of a Śúdra, and his descendants after him**." It is also declared that a Brahman derives not that name from birth alone, but from his knowledge of the Vedas***. According therefore to the letter of the law, there are very few Brahmans now in India who have a right to the respect and privileges which the designation claims.

---

* [III, 168.]   ** [II, 168.]   *** [XI, 84.]

The religion of the Vedas, as far as we are acquainted with it, differs in many very material points from that of the present day. The worship they prescribe is, with a few exceptions, domestic, consisting of oblations to fire, and invocations of the deities of fire, of the firmament, of the winds, the seasons, the moon, the sun; who are invited by the sacrificer, if a Brahman, or by his family priest, if he is not a Brahman, to be present and accept the offering, either oiled butter, or the juice of the Soma, a species of asclepias, which are poured upon the sacrificial fire, in return for which they are supplicated to confer temporal blessings upon the worshipper, riches, life, posterity; the short-sighted vanities of human desire, which constituted the sum of heathen prayer in all heathen countries.

The following is the second hymn of the Rig-veda:

1. Approach, O Váyu (deity of the air); be visible: this Soma juice has been prepared for thee; approach, drink, hear our invocation.

2. Those who praise thee, Váyu, celebrate thee with sacred songs, provided with store of Soma juice, and knowing the season suitable for their oblations.

3. Váyu, thy assenting voice comes to the sacrificer, it comes to many through the offering of the libation.

4. Indra and Váyu, this juice has been prepared; come with benefits for us; verily the libation desires you.

5. Váyu and Indra, observe the libations, being present in the offerings; come quickly.

6. Váyu and Indra, mighty men, approach the priest of the sacrificer quickly, on account of his prayers.

7. I invoke Mitra (the sun), the source of purity; I invoke Varuña, able to destroy; both cherishing earth with water.

8. Mitra and Varuña, be pleased with this propitiatory offering; for to you, assuredly, do sacrifices owe their success, as the waters do their abundance.

9. Mitra and Varuña, all wise divinities, born for the benefit of multitudes, and multitudinously present, give efficacy to our acts.

The titles and functions of the deities commonly addressed in these invocations give to the religion of the Vedas the character of the worship of the elements, and it is not unlikely that it was so in its earliest and rudest condition. It is declared in some texts that the deities are only three; whose places are the earth, the middle region, between heaven and earth, and the heaven; namely, fire, air, the sun. Upon this, however, seems to have been grafted some loftier speculation, and the elements came to be regarded as types and emblems of divine power, as there can be no doubt that the fundamental doctrine of the Vedas is monotheism[*]. "There is in truth," say repeated texts, "but one deity, the Supreme Spirit." "He from whom the universal world proceeds, who is the Lord of the universe, and whose work is the universe, is the Supreme Being." In-

---

[*] [Colebr., Essays, p. 12 ff. M. Müller, History of ancient Sanskrit Literature, p. 558 – 71.]

junctions also repeatedly occur to worship Him, and Him only. "Adore God alone, know God alone, give up all other discourse;" and the Vedánt says, "It is found in the Vedas, that none but the Supreme Being is to be worshipped, nothing excepting him should be adored by a wise man."

It was upon these and similar passages that Rámmohan Roy grounded his attempts to reform the religion of his countrymen, to put down idolatry, and abolish all idolatrous rites and festivals, and substitute the worship of one God by means of prayer and thanksgiving. His efforts were not very successful, not so successful as they might have been, had he confined himself to their legitimate objects; but he involved himself in questions of Christian polemics and European politics, and intermitted his exertions for the subversion of Hindu idolatry. He did not, however, labour wholly in vain: and there is a society* in Calcutta, which although not numerous is highly respectable, both for station and talent, which professes faith in one only Supreme God, and assembles once a week, on a Sunday, to perform divine service, consisting of prayers, hymns, and a discourse in Bengali, or Sanskrit, on moral obligations, or the attributes and nature of the Deity. A leading preacher at those meetings, when I left India, was a learned Brahman, who was professor of Hindu law in the Sanskrit college of Calcutta: and another influential

---

* [the Tattvabodhini sabhá.]

member, a man also of Brahminical birth, of good
family, and of property, set on foot, and I believe
still continues, an English newspaper, called the Reformer, in which the opinions of the party, not only
on religion, but on the measures of the government
of India, are advocated, by natives solely, although in
our language, with remarkable boldness and ability.

To return however to the purpose of the Vedas.
It seems very doubtful, if at the time of their composition idolatry was practised in India: images of
the deified elements are even now unworshipped, and
except images of the sun, I am not aware that they
are ever made. The personification of the divine
attributes of creation, preservation, and regeneration,
Bráhmá, Vishńu, and Śiva, originate no doubt with
the Vedas, but they are rarely named, they are blended
with the elementary deities, they enjoy no preeminence, nor are they ever objects of special adoration.
There is no reason, from the invocations addressed
to them in common with the air, water, the seasons,
the planets, to suppose that they were ever worshipped under visible types. Ministration to idols in
temples is held by ancient authorities infamous; Manu
repeatedly classes the priest of a temple with persons
unfit to be admitted to private sacrifices, or to be
associated with on any occasion*; and even still, the
priests who attend upon the images in public are considered as of a scarcely reputable order by all Hindus

---

* [III, 152. 180.]

of learning and respectability. The worship of images is declared to be an act of inferior merit even by later authorities, those perhaps with which it originated, and it is defended only upon the same plea which has been urged in other times and other countries — that the vulgar cannot raise their conceptions to abstract deity, and require some perceptible object to which their senses may be addressed. "Corresponding to the natures of different powers and qualities," it is said, "numerous figures have been invented for the benefit of those who are not possessed of sufficient understanding." And again: "The vulgar look for their gods in water; men of more extended knowledge, in the celestial bodies; the ignorant, in wood, bricks, and stones." It is almost certain therefore, that the practice of worshipping idols in temples was not the religion of the Vedas.

The dwelling-house of the householder was his temple: if qualified, he was his own priest: but this practice even among the Brahmans probably soon fell into desuetude, as they more extensively engaged in secular avocations, and it became almost universally the practice to retain a family priest. This is still the custom. Instead of being however a Brahman of learning and character, he is very commonly illiterate, and not always respectable. The office has also undergone an important modification. The family priest was formerly also the Guru, or spiritual adviser of the family. The priest now rarely discharges that function, he merely conducts the domestic rites; and the Guru, to whom extravagant deference, such as is due to deity alone, is paid, is a very different individual, very usually not a Brahman at all, but a member of some of the mendicant orders that have sprung up in comparatively modern times, a vagrant equally destitute of knowledge, learning, and principle.

Again: although Brahmá, Vishńu, and Śiva are named in the Vedas, yet it is very doubtful if even the names of those incarnations and types, under which they are now exclusively worshipped, occur. Ráma the son of Dasaratha, Krishńa the son of Vasudeva, are, it is believed, unnoticed in authentic passages of the Sanhitá or collected prayers, and there is no mention of the latter as Govinda or Gopála the infant cowherd, or as the uncouth and anomalous Jagannáth. The only form in which Śiva is now worshipped, the Linga or Phallus, it is generally agreed, has no place whatever amongst the types and emblems of the mythos of the Vedas. It is clear therefore that the great body of the present religious practices of the Hindus are subsequent in time and foreign in tenor to those that were enjoined by the authorities which they profess to regard as the foundations of their system.

Some parts of the private and domestic ceremonial of the Vedas are however still in use, although mixed up with much extraneous matter. For these I may again refer to Mr. Colebrooke, who published originally in the fifth and seventh volumes of the Asiatic Researches three papers on the religious ceremonies of the Hindus and of the Brahmans especially. They are reprinted in his Essays*, and describe the constant and occasional offices of the Hindus, the rites to be performed daily, and those appropriated to seasons of joy or sorrow, those by which marriage is consecrated and death is solemnized.

Characteristic features in these observances—and they are common to all formal religions—are the prodigal demand which they make upon the time of the observer, and the minuteness of their interference in all the most trivial actions of his life. The Hindu rules compel a Brahman to get out of bed before daylight, and prescribe how many times he shall rince his mouth, and with what sort of a brush and in what attitude he shall clean his teeth. He is then to repair to a river, or piece of water, and bathe. This is not a simple ablution, but a complicated business, in which repeated dippings alternate with a variety of prayers, and a still greater variety of gesticulations. The whole is to precede the rising of the sun, whose appearance is to be waited for and welcomed with other gesticulations and other prayers**. The most celebrated of the latter is the Gáyatrí, held to be the holiest verse in the Vedas, and personified as a goddess, the wife of Brahmá. It is preceded by a mysterious monosyllable, the type of the three divinities, Brahmá, Vishńú, Śiva, and the essence of the Vedas —OM, and by three scarcely less sacred words, *Bhur*,

---
* [Ed. 1858, p. 76 – 142.]
** [See for details the Áchárádarśa. Banares: 1856, p. 1 – 64.]

Bhuvar, Swar, denoting earth, atmosphere, heaven. The prayer is merely, "Let us meditate on the sacred light of that divine sun, that it may illuminate our minds*." This is to be repeated mentally as often as the worshipper can do it whilst he closes his mouth and nostrils, effecting the latter by rule. It is the most orthodox of the gesticulations, and is performed by placing the two longest fingers of the right hand on the left nostril, inhaling through the right, closing the right with the thumb, and when the breathing can no longer be suspended raising the fingers and exhaling by the left nostril. There are other gesticulations**, all, to our seeming, very absurd, but they are not subjects of ridicule, because they are seriously and reverentially practised by men of even sense and learning. The excuse made for them is that they contribute to fix the attention, and prevent the thoughts from straying. It cannot be regarded as a very arduous attempt to shew how ill calculated must be the subject of an individual's meditations to occupy his mind, how little either his understanding or his feelings can be interested in his devotions, if he is obliged to have recourse to sleight of hand to prevent their being put to flight.

After his morning ablutions, a Brahman ought to devote part of his time to the perusal of the Vedas. This, as already intimated, is never done; but other works—the Puránas—may sometimes be substituted.

---

* [Rigveda M. III, 62. 10.]
** [See "The Sandhyá", by Mrs. Belnos, plates 6 and 9-12.]

Then follows domestic worship, now idol worship; for in most houses there is an image of the favourite deity of the householder, in a room or recess appropriated to its accommodation. And to this the family Brahman, in the presence of the master of the house, makes offerings, and addresses prayers, diversifying his recitation by blowing a conch-shell, ringing a bell, beating a drum, waving lights, or other unmeaning accompaniments. A considerable portion of the forenoon is thus unprofitably expended. There is no doubt that many Hindus of respectability feel these rites as grievous burdens, although the influence of prescription, example, and fear of scandal, prevent them from casting them off.

The marriage ceremonies of the Hindus vary much with caste and condition, but they are always, in relation to the circumstances of the parties, troublesome and expensive. It is very little the object of the rite to impress upon the married couple any reverence for the union so contracted. Some injunctions are directed to the bride; as, "Be gentle in thy aspect; be loyal to thy husband; be amiable in thy mind, be lovely in thy person*." But no reciprocity of duty is recommended to the bridegroom. The greater number of the prayers and invocations are mythological and unmeaning. It may be remarked of the rite, however, that it evidently contemplates responsible persons. The Vedas then did not sanction

---

* [Colebr., Essays, p. 133.]

the marriage of children. In fact, it was impossible
for a man to marry before maturity, as nine years
are specified as the shortest term of his studentship,
until the expiration of which he was not allowed to
marry. He did not enter his studentship till he was
seven or eight, and therefore, at the earliest, he could
not have been married before he was seventeen; an
early age enough, in our estimation, but absolute
manhood, as compared with the age of nine or ten,
at which Hindu boys are, according to the present
practice, husbands. There is no doubt that many
other innovations for the worse have been made in
the marriage ritual and usages of the Hindus. And
the whole system, the premature age at which the
parties are married, the practice of polygamy, and
the circumstances under which the alliance is commonly contracted, involving the utter degradation of
the female sex, is equally fatal to the development of
the moral virtues and intellectual energies of the man,
and is utterly destructive both of public advancement
and domestic felicity.

The funeral ceremonies originate also in part from
the Vedas. It may be necessary here to explain that
the use of forms and prayers, derived from the Vedas,
is not incompatible with the neglect of the study of
these works. The necessity of an acquaintance with
the text has been obviated by the compilation of ma-
nuals and breviaries, if they may be so termed, in
which the rules are laid down, and the formulæ
(whether from the Vedas or other authorities) are

inserted. These are always modern. The great authority for Bengal is a Pańdit, who lived less than a century ago, named Raghunandana. He composed eighteen works of this kind, denominated Tattwas. One treats of daily rites; one of weekly or monthly rites; one of marriage; one of obsequies, and the like. These are the sources, not always exempt from suspicion of unfaithfulness or interpolation, and always objectionable as confounding authorities, and attaching weight to works of various eras, and of very opposite tendency, by which the practices of the Hindus are regulated.

The Hindus, as is well known, burn their dead; a usage recommended by the peculiarities of climate, and the habits of the people, as much as by authority. The custom of carrying the dying to the banks of the Ganges, or some river considered sacred, has no warrant from antiquity, any more than it has from reason or humanity. The final commitment of the corpse to the funeral pile is decorously conducted. The tone of the ceremony, though not open to much exception, is cold and selfish. It offers no consolation from the future condition of the dead, although it rebukes the natural emotions of the living: it represses affliction by expatiating upon its inutility; it seeks not to soothe sorrow by inspiring hope.

The practice of the Satí*, the burning of the widow

---

* [L. v. Orlich, "Indien", 1861, II, 2, 234—40.]

on her husband's funeral pile, is now* prohibited in the territories subject to the British government. Its prohibition was prudently gradual, and was facilitated by the difference of opinion entertained by the Hindus themselves as to its obligation, as well as by those natural feelings of which not even superstition can wholly divest mankind. Although noticed by the historians of Alexander's invasion**, and therefore then prevailing, there is no authority, it is believed, for the practice in the Vedas***. There is certainly none even in the laws of Manu.

A peculiar feature in the funeral ceremonies of the Hindus is the performance of the Śráddha†: periodical offerings of cakes, of flesh, or other viands, and libations of water, to the manes. These are incumbent on every householder, and are presented on a variety of occasions. They are offered in the first instance to such of his own ancestors as are deceased, and then to the general body of the progenitors of mankind, to the collective Pitris, or Patres of the human race. When a person dies, the nearest of kin presents an obsequial oblation to his ghost daily, for ten days, and again at stated intervals for a twelvemonth.

---

* [since 1829. See Neumann, Geschichte des englischen Reiches in Asien. II, 168–73. J. W. Kaye, Administration of the E. I. Company, p. 538 f.]

** [See the quotations in Lassen's Ind. Alt., III, 347.]

*** [See No. V. of this volume.]

† [Full particulars of this are contained in the Śráddhaviveka. Benares: 1856.]

A ceremony is then performed by which the spirit of the defunct is supposed to be associated with the Pitṛis, and to take his place in their sphere or heaven. On every anniversary of his demise the rite is repeated. These Śrāddhas are imperative, but the Pitṛis should be worshipped once every fortnight at least; and offerings should be made to them on every occasion of private or public festivity, and whenever a householder is desirous of acknowledging or soliciting any temporal good. The character, offices and situation of the Pitṛis formed, no doubt, part of the ancient system, and various appellations and functions are ascribed to them in the laws of Manu[*], and in some of the Purāṇas. The subject is little considered or understood in the present day. The inefficacy of all such ceremonies has not escaped the satire of some of the Hindus themselves; and it would not be difficult to shew that their object is incompatible with the condition of the soul after death, as it is more commonly represented by their own authorities.

These are some of the practices of the domestic worship of the Hindus, which, although very materially modified, are no doubt referable to their original institutes. The public worship of the Hindus has, unquestionably, undergone still greater change.

The system of the universe and the theory of creation as universally received by the Hindus, no doubt originated with the Vedas, and consequently the three

---

[*] [III, 192 ff. Vishṇu Purāṇa p. 320 ff.]

great divinities of their mythology, Brahmá, Vishńu, and Śiva, must have been devised about the same time, as they are nothing more than the personified attributes of the Supreme Being in action, or his powers to create, preserve, and destroy, or, rather, regenerate—manifested. Brahmá is the creator, Vishńu the preserver, Śiva the regenerator. Their invention was probably at first little more than a metaphor, a personification, or allegory. It has been mentioned, that little beyond their names appears in the Vedas regarding them, and it is doubtful how far any definite figures, any images of them, any temples for them, any worship of them, formed part of the ancient religion. It is doubtful if Brahmá was ever worshipped. Indications of a local adoration of him at Pushkara, near Ajmír, are found in one Puráńa, the Brahma Puráńa[*], but in no other part of India is there the slightest vestige of his worship[**]. Of Śiva it is also to be remarked, that he receives worship under one form alone—that of the Linga or Phallus, of which, as before observed, no notice occurs in the Vedas. Some of the continental mythologists, therefore, have been egregiously mistaken in asserting that the primitive worship of India was that of the phallic emblem of Śiva. When this type was introduced is uncertain: it was, probably, prior to the Christian era. The worship was in its most flourishing state at the date of the first Mohammedan invasion, the end

---

[*] [Journal R. As. Soc., Vol. V, 72.]   [**] [Lassen, Ind. Alt., I, 776.]

of the tenth century, when twelve celebrated Lingas were enshrined in as many of the capital cities of India. Somnáth was one of them, the destruction of whose temple by Mahmúd, of Ghizní, is narrated by Gibbon. The worship of the Linga is now in a somewhat dubious condition in different parts of India. In the south, it gives a name and a principle of combination to a particular sect—the Janguinas or Lingáyits[*], whose chief priests are Pariahs, outcasts,— although the votaries include Brahmans, and Brahmans are in some of the temples ministering priests under a Pariah pontiff. In Bengal, although the temples are numerous, they are ordinarily mean and are little frequented, and the worship is recommended to the people by no circumstances of popular attraction. It has no hold upon their affections, it is not interwoven with their amusements, nor must it be imagined that it offers any stimulus to impure passions. The emblem — a plain column of stone, or, sometimes, a cone of plastic mud—suggests no offensive ideas; the people call it Śiva, or Mahádeva, and there's an end. They leave to Europeans speculations as to its symbolical purport. It is enough for them that it is an image, to which they make a prostration or to which they cast a few flowers. There are no secret rites, no mysterious orgies celebrated in its honour.

Vishńu, the preserving power, is a much more popular divinity, not in his own person, however, but

---

[*] [See above Vol. 1, 216 ff. Lassen, Ind. Alt., IV, 623.]

in some of his Avatáras—descents or incarnations, especially as Ráma or Kṛishṅa. I have already stated that it is very doubtful if these incarnations are adverted to in the Vedas, at least in the text*. They are mentioned in some of the Upanishads, supplementary treatises of the Vedas, but these compositions are evidently from their style of later date than the Vedas, and some of them, especially those referring to Ráma and Kṛishṅa, are of very questionable authenticity.

The history of these two incarnations of Vishṅu, Ráma and Kṛishṅa, gives to the adoration paid to them every appearance of Hero worship. They were both of royal descent, and were both born on earth like true knights-errant to destroy fiends, giants, and enchanters, and rescue hapless maids and matrons from captivity and violence. Poetry exaggerated their exploits and mythology deified the performers. The story of Ráma is told in the mytho-heroic poem, entitled the Rámáyaṅa, of the first two books of which a translation in very choice Latin, by the celebrated A. von Schlegel, has been published. No fault is to be found with the character of Ráma as a hero, except the impossibility of his feats; but he is described as a dutiful son, an affectionate husband, an intrepid warrior, and a patriotic prince. His wife, Sítá, is a model of a wife,—gentle, devoted, enduring, and obedient. The worst that can be said of either is, that

---

* [Lassen, Ind. Alt., I. 489. II, 1107 ff. IV, 578 ff.]

their poetic celebrity has been abused, and has given rise to sects of votaries, who think that the repetition of their names is a sufficient substitute for all moral and religious merit. Most of the mendicant orders choose Ráma for their patron.

The worship of Krishńa may be traced to the other of the two great mytho-heroic poems of the Hindus, the Mahábhárata. In the accounts there given of him there is more of mysticism than in the story of Ráma; but even there he does not appear under the character in which he is most popular, that of the infant Gopála, the boy Cowherd, and the juvenile lover of Rádhá. It is in these capacities that he is now most extensively worshipped; and they are no doubt fictions of comparatively modern invention. Vishńu was born as Krishńa for the destruction of Kansa, an oppressive monarch, and, in fact, an incarnate Daitya or Titan, the natural enemy of the gods. Kansa being forewarned of his fate seeks to anticipate his destroyer; but Krishńa is conveyed secretly away from Mathurá, the capital of Kansa, and is brought up as the child of a cowherd at Vrindávan, a pastoral district near Mathurá. It is whilst thus circumstanced that he has been exalted into an object of adoration, and the mischievous follies of the child, the boy, and the lad, are the subject of popular delight and wonder. His male companions are not very prominent in the tale of his youth; but the females, the deified dairy-maids, play a more important part in the drama. Amongst the most conspicuous is the one I have named, Rádhá:

and she receives scarcely less universal homage than
Krishńa himself. The adoration of the forms of Śiva
or Vishńu is advocated not upon the original principle, that worship addressed to them is virtually
addressed to the Supreme, they being merely representations of his power, but upon the novel doctrine,
that one or other of them is himself the Supreme;
and not only this, but in the true spirit of pantheism
that he is all things. This is asserted of Śiva by the
Śaivas; of Vishńu, by the Vaishńavas. This notion,
which is very widely disseminated, seems to have
originated with the next great class of the sacred
writings of the Hindus, the Puráńas.

The Puráńas are eighteen in number: some of them
are voluminous compositions. It is said that they
were the work of the same Vyása by whom the Vedas
were arranged, and they are held in almost equal
estimation. According to a definition* furnished by
many of them, a Puráńa should treat of five topics—
primary creation, secondary creation, the families of
the patriarchs, the reigns of the Manus, and the dynasties of kings. The actual Puráńas conform in no
one instance to this definition: the authors are often
declared to be others than Vyása, and they offer many
internal proofs that they are the work of various
hands, and of different dates, none of which are of
very high antiquity. I believe the oldest of them not
to be anterior to the eighth or ninth century; and the

---

* [Wilson, Vishńu Pur., p. V f.; Burnouf, Bhágav. Pur., I, xlii ff.]

most recent to be not above three or four centuries old. In the present state of Hindu belief the Puráñas exercise a very general influence. Some of them, or portions of them, are publicly read and expounded by Brahmans to all classes of people. Most Brahmans who pretend to scholarship are acquainted with two or more of them, and particular sections, as the Deví Máhátmya, are amongst the most popular works in the Sanskrit language. Prayers from them have been copiously introduced into all the breviaries; observances of feasts and fasts are regulated by them: temples, and towns, and mountains, and rivers, to which pilgrimages are made, owe their sanctity to legends for which the Puráñas or the Máhátmyas, works asserted, often untruly, to be sections of them, are the only authorities; and texts quoted from them have validity in civil as well as religious law. The determination of their modern and unauthenticated composition deprives them of the sacred character which they have usurped, destroys their credit, impairs their influence, and strikes away the main prop, on which, at present, the great mass of Hindu idolatry and superstition relies. That the Puráñas represent in many instances an older, and probably a primitive scheme of Hinduism, is no doubt true; they have preserved many ancient legends; they have handed down all that the Hindus have of traditional history, and they furnish authoritative views of the essential institutions of the Hindus, both in their social and religious organisation. But in their decidedly sectarial character, in their uncompromising advocacy of the pre-eminence of some one deity, or of some one of his manifestations, in the boldness with which they assert his pantheistic presence, in the importance they attach to particular observances, as fasting on the 8th, 11th, and 14th days of each half month, in the holiness with which they invest particular localities, in the tone and spirit of their prayers and hymns, and in the numerous, and almost always frivolous, and insipid, and immoral legends, which they have grafted upon the more fanciful, dignified, and significant inventions of antiquity, they betray most glaringly the purposes for which they were composed, the dissemination of new articles of faith, the currency of new gods. The Hindus are not much disposed to scrutinize with critical suspicion the history of a composition reputed sacred; yet even they have been unable to avoid a controversy amongst themselves respecting the authenticity of the most popular of all the Puráńas, the Bhágavata[*]; and many learned Brahmans maintain that it is the work of an uninspired writer, a celebrated grammarian, named Vopadeva, who flourished in the twelfth century. This is strenuously denied by those with whom it is the textbook for their worship of the infant Kŕishńa; but there is no doubt of the fact. There is equally little doubt that another of these works, the Brahma Vaivartta Puráńa, is still more modern. It is dedicated

---

[*] [Burnouf, Bhágav. Pur., I., p. LIII ff.]

in great part to the juvenile Krĭshńa, and his favourite mistress, Rádhá; and although the worship of Rádhá is now so exceedingly popular, particularly in western Hindustan, yet her person, and even her name, are unknown to all the other Puráńas, to the heroic poems, and even to the popular literature of the Hindus, to the plays, poems, and tales which are not compositions of the last three or four centuries.

It would occupy too much time to enter into any further details upon this subject. The grounds upon which the opinions intimated have been formed may be found in analytical descriptions of the contents of several of the most popular of the Puráńas which have been published in the Journals of the Asiatic Societies of Bengal and Great Britain, and in the preface to the Vishńu Puráńa to which I have previously referred [1].

There seems good reason to believe that the Puráńas in their present form accompanied or succeeded a period of considerable religious forment in India, and were designed to uphold and extend the doctrines of rival sects, which then disputed the exclusive direction of the faith of the Hindus. It began perhaps in the third or fourth century of our æra, having for its object the extermination of the Buddhists, who in

---

[1] Analysis of the Agni Puráńa: Journ. As. Soc. of Bengal, Vol. I, p. 81; of the Brahma Vaivartta P., ib. p. 217; of the Vishńu P., ib. p. 431; of the Váyu P., ib. p. 535; of the Brahma P., Journ. Royal As. Soc. of Great Britain, Vol. V. p. 61; of the Padma P., ib. p. 280.

consequence were driven out of India to Siam, Java, China and Tibet. When the Buddhists, whom all parties considered heterodox were expelled, their enemies began to quarrel amongst themselves, and in the eighth or ninth century a reformer named Sankara Áchárya* is celebrated for having refuted and suppressed a variety of unorthodox professors, and established the preferential worship of Śiva. He instituted in support of his doctrines an order of mendicants which still subsists, and he is in an especial manner regarded as the founder of a system of belief adhered to by Brahmans of learning, particularly in the south of India. The triumph that he obtained for the deity he patronized did not long survive him. Early in the eleventh century Rámánuja**, a follower of Vishńu, undertook to depose Śiva and set up his own divinity, not only in the belief of the people, but in the more substantial benefits of temples and endowments. Tradition records, that the great temple of Triveńí, one of the largest and richest in the Peninsula, now dedicated to Vishńu, was wrested from the rival votaries of Śiva by Rámánuja and his followers. The ascendency of the Vaishńavas was not undisputed in the south, and a new sect of Śaivas, to whom I have alluded, the Lingáyits, sprang up in opposition to them: the contest was carried on with popular violence, and in one of the disturbances that ensued, the

---

* [Lassen, Ind. Alt., IV, 618 ff., 836 ff.]

** [l. l. 608 f. Wilson, Sketch of the Rel. Sects, p. 34-46.]

Rájá of Kalyánpur was killed and his capital destroyed. The Mohammedan invasion of the south crushed both the contending parties, and the predominance of the same power in Upper India prevented the like violence of collision. The Vaishnavas there spread with little resistance under the followers of Rámánand, a disciple of Rámánuja, to whom, or to whose pupils, the greater proportion of the mendicant orders in Hindustan owe their origin, and under two Brahmanical families, one in the west sprung from a teacher named Vallabha, who established themselves as hereditary priests of the juvenile Krishńa, and one in Bengal and Orissa descended from Nityánand and Adwaitánand, two disciples of Chaitanya, a teacher, with whom the popularity of the worship of Jagannáth originated. A particular description of all the different divisions of the popular religion of the Hindus may be found in the sixteenth and seventeenth volumes of the Asiatic Researches[1].

These different orders and families are now almost exclusively the spiritual directors of the people. Some of them are rich and of Brahmanical descent; some are poor and composed of persons of all castes. They are almost all, whether rich or poor, illiterate and profligate. Such literature as they occasionally cultivate—and it is one of the means by which they act upon the people—is vernacular literature, composi-

---

[1] Sketch of the Religious Sects of the Hindus, As. Res. Vol. XVI, p. 1, and XVII, p. 169. [Vol. I. of Wilson's Essays.]

tions in the spoken languages. These are mostly songs and hymns addressed to Vishńu, Krishńa or Rádhá, tales and legends of individuals celebrated amongst them as saints, always marvellous, mostly absurd, and not unfrequently immoral, and vague and dogmatical expositions of elements of belief, which, although in some degree discoverable in the Puránas, have assumed a novel and portentous prominence in the doctrines of the Vaishńava teachers and the practices of the people. These elements are passionate devotion and all-sufficient faith.

Whatever may have been the mistaken veneration entertained by the early Hindus for personified elements and attributes, or even for deified mortals, the language of invocation and prayer, though reverential, is calm and unimpassioned. The hymns of modern fanatics are composed in a very different strain, and breathe a glowing fervour of devotion which might almost be mistaken for sensual love. Something of this may have been borrowed from the Mohammedans, amongst whom the Súfís have always employed the language of earthly rapture, to describe the yearnings of the human soul, to be reunited with that divine spirit from which it is supposed to have originally proceeded. "Oh! the bliss of that day," says a Persian mystic, "when I shall depart from this desolate mansion, shall seek rest for my soul, and shall follow the traces of my beloved." They possibly derived their notions from one branch of the Hindu philosophy, the Vedánta; but they pursued the figure until they had converted it into a gross deformity, and furnished a model adapted to the ardent imagination of irrational enthusiasm. A remarkable specimen of this style has been given to English readers by Sir William Jones, in his translation of the songs of Jayadeva*; where, although to the uninitiated the hero and heroine appear to be actuated by human passions alone, yet the initiated find in the fervent desires and jealous tortures of Rádhá the anxieties, the hopes, the fears, the longings of the soul; and in the steady, though sometimes seemingly inconstant love of Krishńa the affection which the Supreme Being bears amidst all his misgivings and fallings off to man. As a brief and inoffensive specimen of this kind of composition, I will quote a few stanzas attributed to a lady named Mírá Báí, princess of Jaypur, and one of the Sádhwís, or female saints of the Vaishńavas, addressed to Krishńa as Rańa-chhoŕ, a curious title to have been given him, as it means the coward, the runaway from battle.

"O sovereign Rańa-chhoŕ, give me to make Dwáraká my perpetual abode. Dispel with thy shell, discus, and mace, the fear of Yama (the deity of death). Eternal rest is pilgrimage to thy sacred shrines. Supreme delight is the sound of thy shell, the clash of thy cymbals. I have abandoned my love, my pos-

---

* [Works IV. 235 ff. See also Lassen's edition of the Gítagovinda, p. xi–xiii. Ind. Alt., IV, 618. G. de Tassy, Histoire de la lit. hind., II, 54–64.]

sessions, my principality, my husband. Mírá thy servant comes to thee for refuge — O take her wholly to thee. Lord of Mírá, Girdhara her beloved, accept her, and never let her more be separate from thee." Upon which, says the legend, the image opened — Mírá leaped into the fissure — it closed — and the princess disappeared for ever [*].

The other principle which I have specified, and which is closely allied with the preceding, is the absolute sufficiency of faith alone, wholly independent of conduct, to insure salvation. This doctrine is carried to the very utmost of that abuse of which it is susceptible. Entire dependence upon Krishña, or any other favourite deity, not only obviates the necessity of virtue, but it sanctifies vice. Conduct is wholly immaterial. It matters not how atrocious a sinner a man may be, if he paints his face, his breast, his arms, with certain sectarial marks; or, which is better, if he brands his skin permanently with them with a hot iron stamp; if he is constantly chaunting hymns in honour of Vishñu; or, what is equally efficacious, if he spends hours in the simple reiteration of his name or names; if he die with the word Hari or Ráma or Krishña on his lips, and the thought of him in his mind, he may have lived a monster of iniquity — he is certain of heaven.

Now these doctrines and practices, however popu-

---

[*] [Rel. Sects of the Hindus, p. 138. G. de Tassy, t. I. II. 21 - 26.]

lar with the multitude, and although traceable to authorities held in high estimation, are not looked upon, it may be easily imagined, by Brahmans of learning, with any profound deference. Their tendency is in a great degree to supersede all ritual, whether of the Vedas or Puráńas, and to divest the authorized expounders of those works of all influence and control over the acts and thoughts of the people. They will therefore not be indisposed to acknowledge that the objects of this fervour of devotion are wholly unworthy of it, and that its inculcation is calculated to destroy all moral and religious principle.

Whilst most of the existing sects have thus outraged even Hinduism, it is consolatory to find that a few have taken a different direction; and although they have stopped short of the truth, they have displayed a disposition to seek it which may turn to good account. There are several sects that have abandoned all worship of idols, that deny the efficacy of faith in any of the popular divinities, and question the reasonableness of many of the existing institutions: they substitute a moral for a ceremonial code, and address their prayers to one only God. These sects are not numerous, but they are in general respectable. Such however is the want which is felt by the Indian mind of something tangible on which to lean, that they have mostly lapsed into something very like an idolatrous worship of their founder. Still they prove that the people are not all satisfied with the superstitions of their forefathers, and that some among them are inclined to inquire, and think, and determine for themselves. That they offer a favourable soil in which to implant the seeds of Christianity has been lately shewn by the conversion of the inhabitants of several villages in the vicinity of Kṛishṇāgnṛh, who had for some time past seceded from the prevailing practices, and under teachers of their own had adopted a theistical belief.

There is still another and a very important division of the Hindu religion to be noticed, so far is it from being a consistent and homogeneous system. The history of this is very obscure, and the origin of the authorities on which it rests is unknown. Tradition is silent as to the authors of the Tantras—they are mythologically ascribed to Śiva, and are generally in the form of a colloquy between him and his wife Pārvatī. They are very numerous, and some are of considerable volume; but they are not included in any of the ordinary enumerations of Hindu literature, and were, no doubt, composed after that literature was complete in all its parts. They are specified in some of the Purāṇas, to which they must be therefore anterior[*]. They have been but little examined by European scholars, but sufficient has been ascertained to warrant the accusation that they are authorities for all that is most abominable in the present state of the Hindu religion.

The great feature of the religion taught by the

---

[*] (Lassen, Ind. Alt., IV, 633 f. Wilson, Rel. Sects, p. 248 ff.)

Tantras is the worship of Śakti—Divine power personified as a female, and individualized, not only in the goddesses of mythology, but in every woman; to whom, therefore, in her own person religious worship may be and is occasionally addressed. The chief objects of adoration, however, are the manifold forms of the bride of Śiva: Párvatí, Umá, Durgá, Kálí, Śyámá, Vindhyávásiní, Jagannátá, and others. Besides the usual practices of offerings, oblations, hymns, invocations, the ritual comprises many mystical ceremonies and accompaniments, gesticulations and diagrams, and the use in the commencement and close of the prayers of various monosyllabic ejaculations of imagined mysterious import. Even in its least exceptionable division it comprehends the performance of magical ceremonies and rites, intended to obtain superhuman powers, and a command over the spirits of heaven, earth, and hell. The popular division is, however, called by the Hindus themselves the *lefthand* Śákta-faith. It is to this that the bloody sacrifices offered to Kálí must be imputed; and that all the barbarities and indecencies perpetrated at the Durgá Pújá, the annual worship of Durgá, and the Charak Pújá, the swinging festival, are to be ascribed. There are other atrocities which do not meet the public eye. This is not an unfounded accusation, nor a controversial calumny. We have the books—we can read the texts—some of them are in print, veiled necessarily in the obscurity of the original language, but incontrovertible witnesses of the veracity of the charge. Of course no respectable Hindu will admit that he is a Vámáchárí, a follower of the left-hand ritual, or that he is a member of a society in which meat is eaten, wine is drunk, and abominations not to be named are practised. The imputation will be indignantly denied, although, if the Tantras be believed, "many a man who calls himself a Śaiva, or a Vaishṅava, is secretly a Śákta, and a brother of the left-hand fraternity." But what can any Hindu of reason and right feeling say in vindication of a system which has suffered such enormities to be grafted upon it, which could afford any plea, any suggestion, any opening for abuses of which he admits, when he dares not avow them in his own case, the shame and the sin?

For further information on this subject, I must once more refer you to the 16th and 17th volumes of the Asiatic Researches.

From the survey which has thus been submitted to you, you will perceive that the practical religion of the Hindus is by no means a concentrated and compact system, but a heterogeneous compound, made up of various and not unfrequently incompatible ingredients, and that to a few ancient fragments it has made large and unauthorized additions, most of which are of an exceedingly mischievous and disgraceful nature. It is, however, of little avail yet to attempt to undeceive the multitude; their superstition is based upon ignorance, and until the foundation is taken away, the superstructure, however crazy and rotten, will hold together. By what means this object may be best accomplished, admits of difference of opinion; but there can be no disagreement as to the general conclusion, that all means which hold out promise of success, which are honest, rational, and benevolent, should be tried, as far as may be consistent with the most scrupulous regard for the obligations of our political position in India, upon the permanence and integrity of which depends every hope of ultimate success.

The means suggested by the plan submitted to the University, are in every respect unexceptionable: you are invited to employ knowledge and argument in endeavouring to convince intelligent and learned Hindus of the defects and errors of their religion. This is probably not difficult of accomplishment to a certain extent: many, perhaps most, educated Hindus contemplate with indifference or contempt the practices and belief of the majority of their countrymen. There are, however, obstacles of some magnitude to be overcome, before conviction can be hoped for.

The whole tendency of Brahmanical education is to enforce dependence upon authority. In the first instance upon the Guru, in the next upon the books. A learned Brahman trusts solely to his learning; he never ventures upon independent thought; he appeals to memory; he quotes texts without measure, and in unquestioning trust. It will be difficult to persuade him that the Vedas are human and very ordinary writings, that the Puráńas are modern and unauthentic, or even that the Tantras are not entitled to respect. As long as he opposes authority to reason, and stifles the workings of conviction by the dicta of a reputed sage, little impression can be made upon his understanding. Certain it is, that he will have recourse to his authorities, and it is therefore important to shew that his authorities are worthless.

Another serious obstacle is opposed by his temporal interests. Although the learned Brahman does not participate in the profits of religious offices, yet he derives no small share of emolument and consideration from his connexion with religion, as the interpreter of the works in which it is taught. A Pandit, a learned Brahman, although he takes no part in the ceremonial of religious festivals, or marriage feasts, or funeral solemnities, is always invited as a guest, and presents are made to him, of value proportionate to his reputation. They constitute, indeed, his chief, often his sole means of subsistence, as well as of that of his scholars, whom he is obliged by the law to teach, without gratuity or fee, and whom it is his duty also in part to support. The predominance of a foreign government, and one which, notwithstanding the plausibility of its professions, sympathises not at all with any class of its native subjects, excludes a learned Hindu from any hope of the patronage of the state, and we need not wonder, therefore, if he should be reluctant to acknowledge the truth, by which he may starve, and should cling to the error, by which alone he lives.

There is still another and a weighty obstacle to conviction, which arises from the state of the native mind, especially amongst men of learning. Their toleration is so comprehensive, that it amounts to indifference to truth. The Brahmans who compiled a code of Hindu law, by command of Warren Hastings, preface their performance by affirming the equal merit of every form of religious worship. Contrarieties of belief, and diversities of religion, they say, are in fact part of the scheme of Providence; for as a painter gives beauty to a picture by a variety of colours, or as a gardener embellishes his garden with flowers of every hue, so God appointed to every tribe its own faith, and every sect its own religion, that man might glorify him in diverse modes, all having the same end, and being equally acceptable in his sight. To the same effect it is stated by Dr. Mill in the preface to the Khrista Sangítá, or sacred history of Christ, in Sanskrit verse, that he had witnessed the eager reception of the work by devotees from every part of India, even in the temple of Kálí, near Calcutta, and that it was read and chaunted by them, with a full knowledge of its anti-idolatrous tendency, close to the very shrine of the impure goddess. "No one acquainted with India," he adds, "will rate these facts at more than their real worth, and to those who, in ignorance of the genius of paganism, might found erroneous conceptions on them, it may be sufficient to recall to mind, what is the most melancholy trait in the history of this work, the readiness with which these devotees of superstition can assume the ideas of a faith most opposed to it." This indifference is undoubtedly the most formidable impediment with which argument has to contend, but it is not in the nature of things, it is not, we may presume to believe, in the dispensations of Providence, that truth should not ultimately prevail. Its effects may not be confessed, though felt; its influence may not be manifested, though implanted. The seed lies long beneath the soil, but it germinates, though in darkness: and it rises at last into daylight, and ripens into the nutritious grain, blossoms in the beautiful flower, and expands into the vast and majestic monarch of the forest.

In my next lecture I propose to take a view of the opinions of the Hindus on the existence and character of God—the creation of the universe—the nature of the soul—and the destiny of man.

LECTURE II.

We yesterday considered the state of the Hindus in regard to those practices of a religious character which are prevalent in India. The domestic worship which originated with the Vedas, and of which portions are still retained in the daily and occasional observances of individuals in their purifications, their marriage, and their funeral ceremonies, and the public worship of the Divine attributes of creation, preservation, and regeneration, referable to the same works, first engaged our attention. We then adverted to the introduction of Hero worship by the mytho-Heroic poems, its dissemination under new modifications by the Puránas, and its still further alteration and adaptation to the taste of the people by persons and orders of modern date, who had introduced new divinities and new elements of belief in the passionate devotion and all-sufficient faith of which Krishńa was in particular the object, and we lastly noticed the mystical and debasing rites which, founded upon the class of works called Tantras, were exercising at present a most baneful influence upon the manners and principles of the Hindus. These circumstances, although comprehending even the better informed and more learned amongst the natives of India, apply still more particularly to the religious practices of the people at large. We have now to treat of topics which concern the educated and learned more especially — to the opinions which they have been taught, by men whom they consider as little lower than divinities, to entertain on some of the most important subjects of reflexion, which in all ages have exercised and tested the energies of the human mind.

The speculative notions of the Hindus originate, in a great degree, with the same authorities that have enjoined their religious practices. Although in their widest scope familiar only to the learned, and to some only amongst them, yet the subjects of speculation, and the modes in which they are investigated, are not wholly unknown to the literature of the people. The Indian mind, even amongst the least instructed, has a ready tendency to contemplative reflexion, and delights in subtle and metaphysical research. We need not be surprised, therefore, to find the great mysteries of the universe, some attention to which is forced upon the least civilized portions of the human race, favourite objects of inquiry amongst the Hindus from the earliest periods of their traditional history, or that they should from the first have expatiated freely in conjecture and hypothesis, how the universe came to be and whence, what is the nature of man, what his origin, and what his destination. What were at first conjectures only were soon transmuted into dogmas. These were next moulded into systems, and a variety of works have in all ages been composed by Hindu writers, in which it is attempted, with considerable profundity of thought and subtlety of reasoning, and with still more unhesitating positiveness, to solve all the most dark and difficult perplexities of our condition, but leaving them, as all the efforts of human wisdom unassisted by revelation have ever left them, still in darkness and perplexity.

The Hindus boast of six different schools or systems of metaphysical philosophy. They are called the Púrva Mímánsá, Uttara Mímánsá, or Vedánta, the Sánkhya, the Pátanjala, the Nyáyika, and the Vaiseshika: these, although some of them offer irreconcilable contradictions to essential doctrines of their religious belief, are recognised by the Brahmans as orthodox, and attributed to authors of saintly reputation. There are other schools, as those of the Chárvákas, Buddhists, and Jains, which, although in some respects not more at variance with received opinions than the preceding, are stigmatized with the reproach of infidelity and atheism. The cause of this difference is sufficiently obvious, and is characteristic of a state of feeling which prevails as much in the present as in any former period. The orthodox schools of philosophy do not disparage the authority of the Vedas, they do not dissuade the celebration of the acts of formal devotion which the Vedas or Puránas enjoin, although they argue their utter inefficacy as means of final and permanent felicity. They recommend their performance, however, as conducive to that frame of mind in which abstract contemplation may be safely substituted for devotional rites, and even admit of external observances after the mind is in pursuit of true knowledge, as long as such ceremonies are practised from no interested motive, as long as they are observed because they are enjoined, and not because any benefit is either to be expected or desired from their practice. Again, the writings of the orthodox philosophers meddle not with existing institutions; and least of all do they urge or insinuate any consideration to detract from the veneration, or trespass upon the privileges, of the Brahmans. As long as these precautions were observed, the Brahmans did not, nor would they now, object to any form of doctrine having in view the establishment of merely abstract propositions. The case was very different with the heterodox schools. They went from abstractions to things. The Chárvákas condemned all ceremonial rites, ridiculed even the Śráddha, and called the authors of the Vedas fools, knaves, and buffoons*. The Buddhists and Jains denied the inspiration of the Vedas and the sanctity of the Brahmanical character, abrogated the distinction of caste, invented a set of deities for themselves, whom they placed above those of the Hindu pantheon, and organized a regular hierarchy, a priesthood, and a pontiff; an institution still subsisting in the trans-Indian countries, of which the grand Lama of Tibet is the head. It is a remarkable historical fact, that this organization was found too feeble to oppose, in India, the apparently loose and incoherent, the undisciplined, the anarchical authority of the Brahmans. It had, however, the effect of exciting their apprehensions and their hatred to such an extent, that it became proverbial with them to say, "If your only alternative be to encounter a heretic or a tiger, throw yourself before the latter; better be devoured by the animal than contaminated by the man." There may be a few Chárvákas in India, but their opinions are unavowed. The Buddhists have totally disappeared. The Jains are found in some numbers and influence in the west of India, but are little heard of elsewhere.

Besides the acknowledged schools or systems of

---

* [Sarvadarśana Sangraha, p. 6, śl. 10.]

philosophy, there is another, which, without being considered as one of the number, and without claiming the character of a system, is, nevertheless, to be included in the list, as it presents a peculiar scheme of doctrine on metaphysical subjects, and exercises more influence over popular opinion than any of the rest; this is the Paurànik school, the philosophy of the Puránas: it may be termed also the Eclectic school, as it has evidently derived its principles from different systems, and formed them into a miscellaneous combination of its own contrivance. It is not put forward as a new scheme, but is subsidiary to the popularization of particular objects of worship, for which the Puránas, as we remarked yesterday, seem to have been composed.

The Vedas are authority for the existence of one Divine Being, supreme over the universe, and existing before all worlds. "In the beginning," it is said, "this all (this universe) was in darkness." "He (the Supreme) was alone, without a second." "He reflected, I am one, I will become many." Will was conceived in the Divine mind, and creation ensued. This being the doctrine of the Vedas is that also of the Vedánta, the purport of which school is declared to be the same as that of the Vedas—their end (anta) or aim. I mentioned before that the Vedas comprise two portions, one practical, one speculative. The speculative or theological portion of the Vedas is explained chiefly in separate treatises, called Upanishads. These are for the most part short, and are commonly mystical and obscure. The ordinary enumeration of them is fifty-one*. There are some others, but they are probably spurious. The whole fifty-one were translated into Latin, and published by Anquetil du Perron in 1801, under the title of "Oupnekhat, seu, Theologia et Philosophia Indica¹." His translation was made from a Persian version, translated by order of a Mohammedan prince, the elder brother and unsuccessful competitor of Aurengzeb, Dárá Shukoh. Persian translators are not very careful, nor is the Latinity of Anquetil du Perron remarkable for precision. His version, therefore, is almost as unintelligible as the original Sanskrit**. Some of the Upanishads have been rendered into very good English by Rámmohan Roy²; and the whole are in course of translation into French, by a Prussian gentleman, M. Poley***. There will be no difficulty, therefore,

---

* {According to more recent authorities, 108. See Journal As. Soc. Bengal, Vol. XX, 607-19. Weber, Ind. Stud., III, 324-26. Müller, History of ancient Sanskrit Lit., 325-27. Also Dr. Röer's edition of the Taittiriya and Aitareya Upanishads. Calc. 1850, pref. p. v.]

¹ Oupnekhat &c. 2 Vol. 4to. Parisiis (IX.) 1801.

** [An analysis of these Upanishads, by A. Weber, is to be found in his "Indische Studien", Vols. I & II.]

² Translation of several principal books, passages, and texts of the Vedas, by Rájá Rámmohan Roy. 8vo. London, Allen and Co. 1832.

*** [The translation of only two of these, the Mundaka and Káthaka, has been published. In the "Bibliotheca Indica" the following Upanishads have appeared in text and English trans-in acquiring whatever information the Upanishads may afford regarding the Monotheism and the Psychology of the Vedas.

The Vedánta is called also the Uttara-mímánsá—subsequent or supplementary investigation. I have named also a Púrva-mímánsá, or prior school of investigation; the object of this is to teach the art of reasoning, with the express purpose of aiding the interpretation of the Vedas not only in the speculative but the practical portion. As far as concerns the former, it of course adopts the same monotheistic principles. The Pátanjala school teaches also the being of a God; the Nyáyika and Vaiseshika teach the existence of one Supreme Soul—the seat of knowledge and the maker of all things; and the Pauránik or Eclectic school maintains the same doctrine. The Sánkhya denies the existence of a Supreme Being, although it recognises a twofold distribution of the universe, as matter and spirit.

The simple fact, then, of the existence of one supreme spiritual Cause of all things—supreme over and quite distinct from the mythological divinities—is, with one exception, the received doctrine of the Hindus. When they come to particulars, and attempt to define the Divine nature, their notions, as may be

---

lations: The Brihad Áranyaka, Chhándogya, Taittiríya, Aitareya, Swetáswatara, Kena, Ísá, Katha, Prasna, Mundaka, and Mándúkya. The eight last-mentioned were also published by the Tattwabodhini Sabhá, four of these, the Katha, Mundaka, Ísá and Swetáswatara, accompanied with an English translation.]

easily conceived, are exceedingly embarrassed and unsatisfactory. Brahma—not Brahmá in the masculine, but Brahma in the neuter form, the term commonly applied to the supreme first Cause—is for the most part defined by negatives. He is incorporeal, immaterial, invisible, unborn, uncreated, without beginning or end; he is illimitable, inscrutable, inappreciable by the senses, inapprehensible by the understanding, at least until that is freed from the film of mortal blindness; he is devoid of all attributes, or has that only of perfect purity; he is unaffected by emotions; he is perfect tranquillity, and is susceptible therefore of no interest in the acts of man or the administration of the affairs of the universe. Vyása declares that the knowledge of the Supreme Being is not within the boundary of comprehension, that what and who he is cannot be explained*.

These are the most generally adopted sentiments, and conformably to them no temples are erected, no prayers are even addressed to the Supreme. Texts from the Vedas and other authorities, enjoining the worship of God alone, were adduced, as I noticed yesterday, by Rámmohan Roy in support of the reform which he set on foot; but it is generally and consistently enough maintained by his opponents, that they intend spiritual worship, mental adoration, abstract meditation—not formal, practical, or external worship—and that they are applicable only to

---

* [Colebr., Essays, p. 216-38.]

those persons who devote themselves to contemplative devotion, not to those who are engaged in the daily duties of social life. It is, however, undeniable, that in contradiction to these negative descriptions we have affirmative attributes asserted: "God is a Spirit," "the Supreme Spirit;" he is knowledge, he is purity, he is happiness: he sees all, he hears all, he moves whithersoever he will, he takes whatsoever he will, although he has neither eyes, nor ears, nor feet, nor hands; he is omniscient, omnipresent, almighty; he is the maker of all things, and the director and governor of the world; not, however, in his own person, but through the instrumentality of agents, whom he has created for the purpose.

That the Supreme Being exercises an immediate personal providential control over the affairs of the world, is, however, the doctrine of the Pauránik school; but it is the progeny of another doctrine, which is also theirs, and theirs alone, the identity of some one personate and perceptible form—some one present deity with the Supreme. There is no difference of opinion with regard to the character of the Gods of Hindu mythology, of Brahmá, Vishńu, Śiva, and the rest of the thirty-three millions of the host of heaven, at least in their own individualities. The most ignorant Hindu will tell you, that either of these, as considered *per se*, is an imperfect and finite creature; he is mighty, merely in contrast to the weakness of man: he is immortal only in relation to the shortness of human life. The Gods had a beginning, they will have an end; their duration ceases at the period of universal dissolution. The Puránas, however, as I have intimated, have it especially in view to elevate to exclusive adoration some individual of the greater mythological divinities; and they can claim this exaltation for their favourite only by identifying him with that Being of whose supremacy and eternity there is no dispute. Their God, their Vishńu or Śiva, is then no longer a limited and finite Being; he is no longer a God—he is God. The incongruity of attributes and no attributes, of perfect happiness with feelings of affection or animosity, of perfect purity with the human frailties and vices that reduce the Pauránik deities to weak and profligate men, of almighty power and wisdom with the feebleness and fear and folly ascribed to them on various occasions, is too palpable to be denied. The objection is therefore evaded. It is asserted that the Supreme assumes these disguises for his sport or for the manifestation of his power, or that the whole is an illusion and mystery—which the grossness of human conception is unable to penetrate or comprehend. The philosophical writings are, however, free from these contradictions, and they clearly owe their origin to that spirit of sectarian rivalry of which the Puránas are the champions, and were, perhaps, the source. They are foreign also to the tenor of the doctrine of the Vedas; for although texts are frequent which affirm that Brahma is all that exists, and consequently is Brahmá, Vishńu and Śiva, as well as all other persons and things, yet none can be cited affirmative of the converse of the proposition, or sanctioning the doctrine that any one of the inferior divinities is Brahma.

The doctrine of Pantheism — the identification of God and the universe — is another principle which the Puránas most unequivocally and resolutely maintain. Vishńu, Śiva, or Śakti, whatever individual they undertake to glorify, is not only the remote and efficient, but the proximate and substantial cause of the world. Thus, in the Linga Purána, Brahmá addresses Śiva, "Glory to thee, whose form is the universe." In the Vishńu Purána, "This world was produced from Vishńu; it exists in him; he is the cause of its continuance and cessation; he is the world*." In the Kálika Purána, the goddess Kálí is said to be identical with the universe, as well as distinct from it; and in the Brahma Vaivartta, even Rádhá is eulogized as "the mother of the world, and the world itself; as one with primæval nature — with universal nature, and with all created forms; with all cause, and with all effect." Expressions of this tenor occur in every page of the Puránas; and although something may be ascribed to the exaggerations of panegyric, and the obscurities of mysticism, yet the declarations are too positive and reiterated to admit of reasonable doubt. And it cannot be questioned that these writers confound the creature with the Creator, and

---

* [Wilson, Vishńu Pur., p. 6.]

expose themselves justly to the imputation of gross materialism.

Little doubt can be entertained that the materialism of the Puráńas derives some countenance from the Vedas. Universality is there predicated of the Supreme Being directly, without the intervention of any one of his hypostases. Thus it is said, "This whole is Brahma, from Brahmá to a clod of earth. Brahma is both the efficient and the material cause of the world. He is the potter by whom the fictile vase is formed; he is the clay of which it is fabricated. Every thing proceeds from him, without waste or diminution of the source, as light radiates from the sun. Every thing merges into him again, as bubbles bursting mingle with the air, as rivers fall into the ocean, and lose their identity in its waters. Every thing proceeds from and returns to him, as the web of the spider is emitted from, and retracted into itself[*]." These and similar illustrations speak the language of materialism too plainly to be misunderstood, although it may be possible that the full extent of their signification was not intended; that these comparisons are not to be interpreted too literally; that they purpose no more than to assert the origin of all things from the same first Cause; that the authors of the texts may have been in the same predicament as the author of the "Essay on Man", and inculcated materialism without being aware of it.

---

[*] [Transact. R. As. Soc., III, 413.]

The distinction however did not escape the notice of the philosophers; and the schools, which are probably the most ancient, carefully discriminate between spirit and matter, as the two opposite elements by whose temporary association the world is compounded. This is particularly the case with the Sánkhya, the doctrines of which school may be seen in the translation of one of its text-books (the Sánkhya Káriká), printed in Oxford[1]. Matter is by the Sánkhyas subtilized, in its undeveloped state, into a principle, the precise character of which is not very intelligible, but to which the vague denomination of "Nature" may be applied. They do not however question the reality of substance: the various forms of substance, gross material forms, they trace back through others more subtile, which proceed from one imperceptible, indefinable Prakriti or nature. They maintain that causes and effects are essentially the same, and there is no real difference between a product and that which produces it. Consequently, as all substances are products of nature, nature itself is substantial; that is, it is matter. Matter and spirit, then, are the two elements of the universe; both unproduced; the former productive, the latter not; both eternal and independent; subject to change of form and condition, but incapable of destruction; combining, from the influence of a controlling necessity, for a given object

---

[1] Sánkhya Káriká, translated from the Sanskrit, &c. 1 Vol. 4to. 1837. Allen and Co.

and a definite term, but perpetually reverting to a primitive, inert, and reciprocal independence.

It might be supposed that the Vedánta philosophy, professing to carry out the doctrine of the Vedas, would have been next in order of time to those works; but this is questionable: and it seems not improbable that the system originated in the purpose of exonerating the Vedas from the charge of materialism, by founding upon such texts as have already been quoted the refinement of spiritual Pantheism, or idealism, and at the same time controverting the doctrine of the Sánkhyas and the Nyáyikas, which maintained the distinct and independent existence of matter and spirit. The doctrine of the Vedánta is denominated κατ' ἐξοχὴν Adwaita, non-duality; and the very title indicates the priority of a dualistic hypothesis: the main proposition contended for, in opposition to that which affirms two elements of creation, matter and spirit, being the existence of one only element in the universe, which universal element or principle is spirit.

But then comes the question, the solution of which has puzzled the philosophers, not of India only, but of the world; not only of ancient but modern times: not only Vyása and Sankara, but Parmenides and Plato; Mallebranche and Berkeley; Fichte and Schelling. If all is spirit, what is substance? The early teachers of the Vedánta school asserted it was the Sakti, the perceptible power, the active energy, the manifested instrumentality of the Supreme Spirit; and therefore, though not substantially, yet essentially one and the same. As this solution was possibly found too subtle to satisfy the understanding, later teachers went a step farther, and boldly cut the knot, by maintaining there is no such thing as substance. In the spirit of the Berkeleyan theory, they affirmed that matter exists not independent of perception, and that substances are indebted for their seeming reality to the ideas of the mind. They went still farther, and maintained that until our intellects are purified by abstraction, until we have attained a just appreciation of our own nature, and of that of universal spirit, our ideas are all wrong. Until the day of true knowledge dawn upon us, we are asleep—in a dream; we misconceive of all we perceive; we take a rope for a snake; an oyster-shell for mother-of-pearl; mirage for real water. All that we see in our unilluminated condition is Máyá, deception, illusion. There are no two things in existence; there is but one in all. There is no second, no matter; there is spirit alone. The world is not God, but there is nothing but God in the world.

Should it be an object to acquire more precise views of this part of our subject, they are easily attainable. The doctrines of the Vedánta philosophy have been recently the topic of controversy, as similar doctrines of idealism or transcendentalism have ever been and will probably ever be. The different schools of Indian philosophy are described by Mr. Colebrooke in several essays, in the Transactions of the Royal

Asiatic Society*. In speaking of the Vedánta, he indicates the tendency of the illustrations which its teachers borrow from the Vedas towards materialism, and asserts the explanation of Máyá or illusion, to have been an after-thought. Col. Vans Kennedy, also a distinguished Oriental scholar, had maintained in a work which merits to be consulted on a variety of important points—Researches on the Nature and Affinities of ancient and Hindu Mythology¹—that the Hindu philosophers of every school and every period had asserted a spiritual principle alone, and never countenanced materialism. He therefore in defence of his theory controverted Mr. Colebrooke's account of the Vedánta in an essay on the subject, published in the third volume of the Society's Transactions**. Sir Graves Haughton appended to this paper some observations in vindication of Mr. Colebrooke's views, which called forth further comments from Col. Vans Kennedy, a reply from Sir Graves Haughton, and a rejoinder from the colonel. These latter papers were printed in the London Asiatic Journal; whether they have settled the point in dispute may be doubted, but they have had the effect of bringing the principal doctrines of the Vedánta philosophy within the acquirement of European students².

---

* [Essays, London, 1858, p. 143 - 269.]
¹ Published by Longman and Co. 1 Vol. 4to. 1831.
** [p. 412 - 36.]
² Asiatic Journal, October, 1835; November, 1835; January, 1839. London. Allen and Co.

The observations thus made have anticipated in some degree an explanation of the opinions entertained by the Hindus in regard to the creation. The theories that attempt to elucidate its course are more definite and congruous than those which would ascertain its cause. All the schools admit two sorts, or rather stages of creation, one rudimental and primary, the other formal and secondary. They all admit the infinity and eternal succession of creations, their periodical dissolution or disintegration, and their periodical regeneration or reorganization. In the season that precedes creation, all agree that there is no perceptible form—all is without shape. According to the Vedánta philosophy there is no substratum even of form, there is no immaterial substance; the illusion is dissipated, the energy has ceased to act separately; all real, that is, all spiritual existence is concentrated in its supreme source, which is still all that is. All the other schools, theistical or atheistical, are dualistic, and agree in recognising the eternity and indestructibility of the principle or element of the sensible world, the major part of the Indian sages adopting as an axiom the prevailing doctrine of classical antiquity, *ex nihilo nihil*. Whether creation therefore took place from the will of a Creator, or the spontaneous evolution of its principles, it is preceded by a something; by nature, say the Sánkhyas, by simple uncompounded imperishable atoms, say the Nyáyikas. When the evolution of the first imperceptible material principle into perceptible form takes place without the intervention of the Divine will, it proceeds from necessity. Nature is compelled to assume corporeal form that the ends of Spirit may be fulfilled, namely, that it may be embodied, until by a series of bodily migrations it has no longer need of such a state, it has attained knowledge which is the cause of its liberation, and its connection with matter ceases. "Soul desists," says the Sánkhya Káriká*, "because he has seen (or fully understood) nature. Nature ceases (or withdraws) because she has been seen;" that is, fully understood. It is not very intelligible why the soul, which in its independent state is described as already pure, should be allied with body merely to be purified, and so freed from the alliance. But this is a difficulty for the followers of the Sánkhya to explain.

The mode in which the Divine will operates as it is alluded to in the Vedas, is not attempted to be explained. He wills creation to be, and it is. In the systems in which primæval crude matter is the subject of Divine agency, its development is ascribed to an influence communicated to it by the Divine will, by which it receives motion and life. This appears to have been expressed in language originally metaphorical, but some of the Puránas have understood it literally, and abusing the figure of personification, have described the production of the world as if it was analogous to that of animal birth. The abuse is of very old date, and not confined to the Hindus.

---

* [66.]

The mundane egg, the form in which, according to Manu[*], the rudiments of the world are first manifested, was not unknown, as you are well aware, to the ancient cosmogonies of Greece.

In whatever mode movement is imparted to the first inert principle of things, the stages by which it evolves into the actual variety of perceptible forms are much the same in the different systems; the first product is intelligence; thence proceeds egotism, or the consciousness of individuality; thence come the senses; thence the rudiments of the objects of sense or the subtle elements, and from them the gross or perceptible elements ether, air, fire, water, earth are developed, and they are the compound ingredients of all visible and tangible form. A more particular detail may be found in the Sánkhya Káriká and Vishńu Puráńa[**].

The elements of forms thus developed from primary matter remain unaltered for a day of Brahmá: a tolerably long interval, 2,160,000,000 years. At the end of this period, Brahmá sleeps. The material forms which then occupy the world, and the lower spheres of the universe, are then consumed by fire; the fire is extinguished by mighty rains, and the globe becomes a shoreless ocean. The sages, the gods, the elements survive, and when Brahmá wakes and finds what mischief his slumbers have generated, he sets to work to repair it. With the materials ready to his

---

[*] [I, 9. Vishńu Pur. p. 18. A. H. A. Kellgren, Mythus de ovo mundano. Helsingfors.: 1849, p. 9 ff. Weber, Ind. Stud., II, 332.]
[**] [S. K. 22 ff. V. P. p. 14 ff.]

hands, he remanufactures the earth and its inhabitants, and this is what is intended by secondary creation. This kind of creation is repeated daily during the 100 years of Brahmá's existence;—a term which cannot be expressed in mortal years by any of our scales of numeration, but which may be written with fifteen figures, or 311,040,000,000,000 years[*].

At the end of this term Brahmá himself expires, and with him die all the gods and holy sages, and all forms whatever retrograde successively into their constituent elements, until the whole is finally merged into the single or double rudiment of being, universal spirit, or primary matter and primary spirit, according to the theories of the dualistic or non-dualistic philosophers. After a considerable interval, similar causes produce similar effects; nature and spirit are again in movement, the creation is renewed, and the universe thus eternally fluctuates between existence and non-existence, without any motive, without any end, that rational conjecture can guess at.

Upon the subject of the extravagant chronology of the Hindus it may be remarked, that the enormous periods of which it is composed are of a purely mythological character. The attempts that have been made to account for them on astronomical computations have led to no satisfactory results. How far they are analogous to similar extravagancies in the chronology of other nations of antiquity is also undetermined;

---

[*] [Dr. J. Muir's Original Sanskrit Texts, I, 18 ff.]

the subject is only of importance as furnishing an additional argument against the authority of those works in which it is seriously affirmed as truth.

The philosophical systems take no notice of the creation of man except in the abstract: for the origin of the human race we must have recourse to other authorities, and particularly to the Puránas, in which various accounts of the occurrence are narrated. It is not difficult to detect, through all their embellishments and corruptions, the tradition of the descent of mankind from a single pair, however much they have disguised it by the misemployment of the figures of allegory and personification. The embodied creative attribute, the agent in formal creation, Brahmá, is fabled to have divided himself into two creatures—one male, one female; from their union the first man and first woman were born, who married and begot children, and from them sprang not only mankind but all living creatures. This is the general outline of the mode in which it is related that the earth was peopled, and it is probably traceable to the Vedas: but the heroic poems and the Puránas have remodelled the tale in a variety of shapes, until it presents an incoherent and conflicting series of legends—not always very intelligible, and sometimes not very decent. I must refer for details to the Vishńu Puráńa[*].

The description of the phenomena of secondary creation includes an account of the disposition of the

---

[*] [See Dr. J. Muir, Original Sanskrit Texts 1, 13–43.]

universe, of the different spheres or worlds, of the situation and size of the planets, and of the divisions of the earth. As long as the geography of the Hindus is restricted to India, it is sufficiently accurate; but as soon as it extends beyond those limits it is wholly fanciful and absurd. The Puráńas distribute the earth into seven concentric circles or rings, each forming an annular continent, and being separated from the next in succession by a circumambient ocean. These oceans vary also as to their constituent parts; and besides seas of fresh and salt water, we have them of treacle, honey, milk, and wine. The whole is encompassed by a stupendous mountain belt, beyond which lies the religion of darkness; and in the centre of all, which is also the centre of the continent we inhabit, towers Mount Meru, to the height of 64,000 miles[*]. The astronomy is more moderate, but the mythologic or Paurańik astronomy is as incompatible with the scientific astronomy of the Hindus as it is with the Copernican system. Much of the astronomy of the Hindus, properly so called, agrees with that of Europe, and advantage has judiciously been taken of the difference between the inventions of their Puráńas and the facts of their astronomers to convict the former even by native testimony of absurdity and error. It is also through geography and astronomy that the first and strongest impressions have been made upon the minds of native youths who have re-

---

[*] [Vishńu Pur. p. 166 ff. Bhág. Pur. V, 16-20.]

ceived an English education: acquaintance with the extent and divisions of the earth, and with the leading phenomena of the heavens, however superficial, is fatal to all faith in the extravagances of the Puránas, and affixes discredit to whatever they inculcate.

Man being created and provided with a habitation, the next question to be considered is the object of his existence. For what is he designed? Final liberation. What that is understood to be I shall presently endeavour to explain; but it is necessary first to offer a few words respecting the mode in which it is imagined that the purposes of human life may be best effected. The social institutions of the Hindus appear to have originated with the Vedas, and present, as is well known, the characteristic peculiarity of the distinction of castes. The original scheme contemplates but four—the Brahman, whose duties were to study and teach the Vedas, and conduct the domestic worship of the next two classes. The Kshatriya was the warrior and prince, whose duties were to fight and govern. The Vaisya was the merchant and farmer. Both he and the soldier were enjoined to study, though not permitted to teach the Vedas. The fourth caste, that of the Śúdra, supplied artificers, labourers, and servants to the other three. The Śúdras were subjected to much indignity and injustice, but their condition was never so bad as that of the Helot, the bondsman or the serf; they were free, masters of their own property, and at liberty to settle where they pleased. Intermarriages between all four castes took place, and the only check upon them was the degradation of the children. They were not even Súdras; they therefore formed new castes, distinguished according to their mixed descent and the occupation which came to be regarded as peculiarly their own. In the present day the only one of the original castes extant is the Brahman: the Kshatriya, Vaiśya, and Śúdra are extinct; and the innumerable castes which are now met with are in part the representatives of the ancient mixed castes, but in a still greater degree are the progeny of later times, and distinctions unauthorizedly assumed by the people themselves. For it is a great mistake to imagine that caste in India is either a burden or a disgrace. The notion is European, springing like many others out of the belief, that our own customs and feelings furnish an infallible standard by which to measure those of other nations. The fact is, that even with the most abject classes caste is a privilege, not a shame; and in proportion as the scale of society descends, so are the people more tenacious of their caste. Even the Mohammedans, to whose religion such a distinction is as uncongenial as it is to Christianity, imitate in India their Hindu countrymen in this particular, and pique themselves upon their caste. The principle of the distinction is of course indefensible, and in some parts of India, or under particular circumstances, it is oppressively enforced. In practice, however, where European influence predominates, little more inconvenience results from it than from the distinctions of rank in the countries of Europe. The diligent discharge of the duties assigned to each caste is one of the means by which the members are prepared for the attainment of higher grades of perfection.

The period of life, of the three master castes, was divided into four portions or stages. The first, that of the student, was to be devoted to sacred study: the second, that of the householder, to the duties of active life; the third, that of the hermit, to solitude and contemplation; the fourth and last, that of the mendicant, to self-denial and abstraction. This distribution leaves, therefore, but one-fourth of existence for the offices of a householder, the father of a family, the citizen; and this is one respect in which the tendency of the Hindu system to depreciate active, social, and moral obligations is most mischievously manifested. It is not to be imagined that the Hindus are ignorant of the foundations of all morality, or that they do not value truth, justice, integrity, benevolence, charity to all that lives, and even the requital of evil with good. "The tree," says one of their familiar illustrations, "withholds not its shade from the woodman that is cutting it down." "The sandal-tree," says another, "communicates its fragrance to the hatchet that levels it with the ground*."

---

* [छेदनं कार्यमाणिप गुंभावनी ।
छेतुः पार्श्वगता छायां नोपसंहरति द्रुमः ॥
सुजनो न याति वैरं परहितबुद्धिर्विनाशकाले ऽपि ।
छेदं ऽपि चन्दनतरुः सुरभयति मुखं कुठारस्य ॥
Hitopad. I, 52. Bohlen ad Bhartrih. II, 62.]

These duties are all repeatedly enjoined, and Hindu authorities commend as earnestly as those of any other language, and the people practise, in general, as much as most other people, the duties of their social condition, filial piety, paternal tenderness, kindness to inferiors, and obedience to the king. These, however, as well as the duties of caste, and even devotional rites, are held to be only subordinate and preliminary obligations, steps leading towards perfection, but stopping at the threshold, and to be cast away as soon as the interior of the temple is entered. All the obligations of social life do no more than qualify a man to abandon them: they are of no avail, they are impediments in his way when he undertakes to consummate the end of his being, when he would lose himself entirely in imperturbable meditation upon his own nature, by which alone he can know that he himself is one with the Divine nature, by which alone he can be identified with the universal soul, and emancipated for ever from the necessity of future existence.

Now it is true that in the present constitution of Indian society this distribution of the periods of life, beyond that of the student, is never regarded, except by a few, who prefer a life of lazy mendicity, or by some half-crazed enthusiast, who thinks it possible to realise the letter of the law. The great body of the people, Brahmans included, pursue their worldly avocations as long as their faculties permit, spend the decline of life in the bosom of their families, and die peaceably and decently at home. But although the practice is discontinued the doctrine* remains, and influences opinion; and devotional ceremonies, pilgrimage, penance, and abstract contemplation, have an undue preponderance in the estimation of the people, even the best informed amongst them, over active duties and the precepts of morality. As to the common people, they have, as I indicated in my last, a still lower scale, and they find a ready substitute for the inconveniences of all moral restraint in the fervour of that faith which they place in Vishńu, and the unwearied perseverance with which they train a parrot or a starling to repeat his names, to articulate Krishńu-Rádhá, or Sítá-Rám.

What then are the consequences which the Hindus propose to themselves from the fulfilment of any description of prescribed duties or acts of merit? Those who profess devoted attachment to a popular deity expect to be rewarded by elevation to the heaven in which he is supposed to dwell, and to reside there for ever in ecstatic communication or union with him. These notions, however, are innovations; and even the independent establishments, the several heavens of these divinities, are modern contrivances. The heaven of Krishńa, Go-loka, the sphere or heaven of cows, has grown out of the legends of his boyhood, whilst straying amongst the pastures of Vraj. There is no such place in the celestial topography

---

* [Man. 6, 1. 33.]

of the Vedas, or of the most genuine of the Puránas.

According to what appears to be the most ancient and authentic theory of the future state of man, punctual performance of religious rites, with due attention to moral conduct, and entire belief in the holiness of the Vedas, secured for the soul after death a period of enjoyment proportioned to the quantum of moral and religious merit of the deceased, in the heaven of Indra; a kind of Elysium. Neglect of prescribed rites and duties, irreverence for the Brahmans, and disbelief in the Vedas, incurred punishment for a given term, proportionate to the crime, in various hells, or regions of Tartarus. At the expiration of a limited period, the soul, which in either of its destinations had continued to be invested with a subtile and ethereal, but material and sensible body, returns to earth, and is born again, in union with some gross and elemental body, according to the former merits or demerits of the individual, as a reptile, a fish, a bird, a beast, a giant, a spirit, a divinity, until, after sundry migrations, it ascends or descends to man, to undergo a similar career.

Now this, I may remark, is what the Hindus understand by Fate. They do not understand it to depend upon the Divine foreknowledge of what a man will be, or will do, conformably to which he must act and must be; nor is it, in their opinion, an irresistible impulse given to his career, which he cannot choose but obey. It is the result of conduct in a previous existence, the consequences of which are necessarily suffered in a succeeding life. A man is poor, miserable, diseased, unfortunate, not because it was so predestined, not because it was so ordained from the beginning of time, but because he was ignorant, negligent, profligate, irreligious in a former life, and is now paying the penalty of his follies and his sins. He cannot change his actual condition, but he is so far master of his own fate, that by now leading a life of innocence and piety, he will secure his being born again to a better and a happier lot.

The consequences of acts, whether moral or devotional, being thus, in the estimation of all classes of Hindus, temporary and transient, the philosophical schools have made it their especial aim to determine by what means a career so precarious and uneasy may be cut short. For it is a remarkable circumstance in the history of Hindu opinion, that, amidst the many varieties of practice and collisions of belief that have from time to time prevailed in India, it does not seem so have occurred to any individual, learned or unlearned, heterodox or orthodox, to call in question the truth of the Metempsychosis. It is not only the one point on which all are agreed, it is the one point which none have ever disputed. Even the Buddhist, who denies every other essential dogma of the Brahmanical religion, adopts, without demurring, as an article of his creed, the transmigration of the soul. It is, as you know, a doctrine of remote antiquity, and it still reigns despotic, without any sign of decrepitude or decay, over the minds of the nations of the extreme east, over Burman, Chinese, Tartar, Tibetan, and Indian; over perhaps the most numerous portion of the human race; over at least six or seven hundred millions of mankind.

Adopting, then, this unquestioned dogma as the basis of their argument, all the philosophical schools propose for their object the ascertainment of those means by which the wanderings of the soul may be arrested, its transitions through all the painful vicissitudes of corporeal existence be terminated, and its emancipation from bodily imprisonment and degradation be effected for ever. This is what is termed *Moksha*, or *Mukti*—Liberation, emancipation. All the systems agree that this devoutly desirable consummation is to be accomplished only through that knowledge which they profess to teach; not literature, not science, not morality, not devotion, but true knowledge; knowledge, obtained by profound contemplation, of the true nature of the soul, and of the universe; when the contemplatist can say, with perfect conviction, and with truth, I am Brahma, I am all that is, I am one with God. The absolute state of the soul thus liberated is nowhere clearly defined; it ceases to transmigrate; it loses all bodily individuality; it loses all spiritual individuality, as whether, with the Vedánta, we consider it to be reunited with, or absorbed into, the Supreme Spirit, or whether, with the Sánkhyas, we hold it to be commingled with the spiritual element of the universe, individual spirit ceases to exist. Annihilation, then, as regards individuals, is as much the ultimate destiny of the soul as it is of the body, and "Not to be" is the melancholy result of the religion and philosophy of the Hindus.

I have thus attempted to place before you some of the principal features of the religious practices and opinions of the Hindus, to which it is fit that your attention should be directed in engaging in any investigation of their nature. To have entered more fully into detail would have occupied too much of your time, and particulars will be easily multiplied by inquiry. With the minor incidents of the popular superstition it is not necessary to encumber the argument farther than they are countenanced by authorities considerd sacred. That learned Brahmans will readily admit the unauthorized introduction, and the unprofitable and degrading tendency of much of the popular practice, is not unlikely, as I have before stated; and their indifference is likely to be the chief obstacle to their acknowledging the inefficiency and evil of much even of that which is authorized. They are likely to adhere to their speculative tenets, and particularly to those regarding the nature and condition of the soul, with more tenacious obstinacy. Dependence on authority, veneration for antiquity, pride of learning, confidence in argument, and disdain of defeat, will combine with the inherent difficulties of the controversy to oppose the influence of reason in generating conviction in the minds of the

Paṅdits. Still there is no occasion to despair. Besides that encouragement which a firm trust in the omnipotence of truth inspires, we may derive animation and hope from the history of the past.

It will not have escaped your observation, that in all the most important speculations upon the nature of the Supreme Being and man, upon matter and spirit, the Hindus traverse the very same ground that was familiarly trodden by the philosophers of Greece and Rome, and pursue the same ends by the same or similar paths. The result was equally impotent; but what it more concerns us to remark is, that all these speculations—all the specious systems of philosophers, at once acute and profound—all the plausible and graceful illustrations of the most prolific ingenuity—all the seemingly substantial combinations of intellectual powers still unsurpassed, were divested of their speciousness, despoiled of their beauty, deprived of all by which they held reason captive, and shewn to be fallacious and false by the Ithuriel spear of Christian truth. The weapons, which, wielded by the first defenders of that truth, discomfited these delusions, are in your hands. Have they lost their efficacy, or have you not the skill, the courage to employ them?

It is however to be recollected that, agreeably to the invitation of the Bishop of Calcutta, an impression upon the minds of learned natives, that is, upon Paṅdits, Brahmans learned only in Sanskrit learning, is only a contingency. The argument is to be addressed in the first instance to English-reading natives, to natives who have been educated in the language of our country, and in the learning of Europe. There are many such at the chief cities of the British Indian empire. In Calcutta they are in great numbers, perhaps thousands, and they are of various descriptions. The greater number have only such knowledge of English as qualifies them for public employment, and they rarely concern themselves with matters of controversy. Some very good native English scholars continue orthodox, nay even bigoted Hindus. They are generally however men of mature years who studied English in early life, when they were taught little else than words. Some who are familiar with our language are amongst the leading members of the society instituted by Rámmohan Roy, to which I have already alluded; a much greater number consist of young men whose English education is more recent, and has been conducted on an improved and more effective plan, which proposes to give an English tone to their feelings and principles, as well as to communicate parts of speech. Many of these write English, not only with facility but with elegance: they are familiar with our standard authors, are possessed of an extent of general information, which few young men even in England at the same age surpass, and have learned to think and feel on many important subjects more like natives of the west than of the east. These have almost all become Seceders in different degrees from the religion of their fathers. They have not however yet adopted a better. The last description of English scholars is a branch from that just specified, and consists of a few who have read, reflected, reasoned, and believed. One of them, Kristo Mohan Banerji, a young man of very excellent ability and attainments, by birth a Brahman of the most respectable rank, is an ordained minister of the English church in Calcutta.

It is the advantage of those English scholars who halt yet between two opinions, who have no religion at all, that the work to which competition has been invited*, is calculated in the first instance to promote. The feeling with which most of them regard Hinduism is favourable to conviction, and it might be supposed, that as they have already disavowed allegiance to it, they require not to be enlightened as to its errors and evils; but this would be a mistake. Their English education has left them no opportunity of native education, and they know almost as little of what they abandon as what they decline to accept. It is not possible to depend upon the durability of impressions, taken up from a wish perhaps to get rid of inconvenient restrictions, or from the vanity of being thought wiser than others, rather than from a rational estimate of the defects of a system grounded

---

* [In a Convocation, holden on Thursday the 13th of February 1840, the University of Oxford accepted the proposal of a prize of £ 200, made through the Bishop of Calcutta, "for the best refutation of Hinduism in its main systems, both exoteric and esoteric".]

upon a knowledge of that system. By placing those defects clearly before them, they will become more aware of their existence and character, and their conviction will be rational and permanent. They will also be able to defend their conviction, perhaps to communicate it to others. At present truth derives not that benefit even from its professed votaries, which they might easily be in a position to render. The mere native English scholar has no common debateable ground on which to contend with his learned countrymen. The contemptuous answer of the Brahman to his objections is, "You know nothing about the matter—you understand not the language of the Sástras—you are unacquainted with their contents—you are not qualified to impugn them." If his adversary can shew that he is conversant with the system, he will acquire the right of being listened to, and he will possibly not be listened to wholly in vain. When too at the same time that he is supplied with valid reasons for his own departure from the national superstitions, he is furnished with arguments and inducements to seek shelter from his own uneasy undulations of opinion in the harbour of Christian certainty, it may be hoped that he will not only contribute to win his countrymen from their errors, by laying bare their enormity, but that he will afford in his own person an example and a guide to the adoption of a pure and holy system of belief.

It is recommended that, with a view to the translation of the proposed Essay, it should be written in the form of a dialogue. The writers are not to understand by this a mere succession of question and answer, or a keen encounter of wit, or even the more equally maintained discussion of which the works of Cicero and Plato furnish classical models. In the style in which the Puráńas, for instance, are written, a disciple, or one seeking for information, puts a leading question which furnishes a text on which his teacher or instructor dilates, or he suggests a difficulty or hints an objection, which is thereupon attempted to be solved or answered at length.

To those who may undertake the task I have one caution to offer. Let whatever they urge be urged in charity.

It is natural to feel impatient of error—it is difficult not to feel indignant with wickedness; but, in instituting a discussion into the truth or falsehood of a religious creed, with the hope of demonstrating the latter to the assent of those by whom it is professed, we have not in view the expression of our own feelings, but a kindly influence over theirs—we are not contending for victory but for conviction—we seek not to humble or incense our adversaries, but to conciliate their confidence and direct their judgment— we seek to work a salutary change in their principles, and in this we shall most assuredly fail if we commence the operation by disregarding their prejudices and provoking their resentment. The Hindu is not resentful—not unconfiding—not disinclined to discussion—not incapable of appreciating kindness—at the same time he is sensitive and timid. Treat him rudely, harshly, intemperately, it is like touching the leaf of the mimosa; he shrinks from all contest—he adopts the course recommended by his authorities to the man in quest of true knowledge—he imitates the tortoise who retracts his limbs beneath his shell, and is then alike indifferent to the sunshine or the storm. Let the argument, then, be enforced in a spirit of benevolence—let it be a calm and conciliating appeal to the understanding of intelligent men, and, although it may fail of producing any immediate or ostensible effect, it will not in all likelihood have been wholly unprofitable. Important changes in the opinions of nations are not the work of a day. Many and repeated and long continued efforts are necessary for their consummation, and many causes of little apparent magnitude, and of no immediately observable agency, cooperate for their accomplishment. It is not the earthquake or the tempest only that rives asunder the mountain barriers of the Himalaya, and opens its steep recesses to man and to cultivation. The smallest rill that trickles from the eternal snow contributes to swell the torrents, which, bursting through the rocks, transform declivities into valleys, and precipices into paths, and finally descend a stately river to fertilize the plains of Hindustan.

III.

SUMMARY ACCOUNT
OF THE
CIVIL AND RELIGIOUS INSTITUTIONS OF THE SIKHS.

From the Journal of the Royal Asiatic Society, Vol. IX (1846), p. 43.

There have arisen from time to time among what are considered the unlearned classes of the people of India thoughtful and benevolent individuals, who have felt dissatisfied with the religious practices of their countrymen, and with the distinctions of caste and creed by which they are disunited. They have attempted, accordingly, to reform these defects, and to reduce the existing systems of belief to a few simple elements of faith and worship in which the Brahman and the Śūdra, the Mohammedan and Hindu might cordially combine, and from which they might learn to lay aside their uncharitable feelings towards each other.

Although not professing to be deeply versed with the sacred literature of either sect, with the Vedas or the Koran, the Indian reformers have been in general men of respectable attainments, and have been well grounded in the speculative tenets of the two systems which they have sought to amalgamate. Retaining the doctrine of transmigration, they have grafted upon it a philosophy compounded of the Vedánta principle of emanation, or the origin of individual soul from one great pure universal spirit to which the detached portions pine to return, and of the Súfyism of the Mohammedans, in which the language of passion is substituted for that of dogmatism, and the human soul and the divine spirit are typified as the lover and the beloved. These doctrines have been clothed by the reformers alluded to in a popular dress; they have been set forth in short metrical compositions—odes, or hymns, or songs—always in the vernacular dialects, and written in a style addressed to the imagination and feelings of the common people. These are usually chaunted to simple melodies, and even where they have not effected any change of opinion, they have become extensively diffused and have exercised considerable influence over the national character. These compositions gradually accumulated, and, preserved in collections of various extent, constitute the literature and the creed of a large portion of the agricultural population of Upper India.

The teacher whose instructions have exercised, although indirectly, the most durable influence upon any considerable body and, aided by political events, have tended to form a nation out of a sect, is BÁBÁ NÁNAK, or NÁNAK SHÁH, the nominal founder of the religion and nation of the Sikhs. He was born in

1469, at a village now known as Dehrá[1], or the 'village', on the Ravi, about thirty kos from Lahore, and is said to have been at first engaged in trade as a dealer in grain, but to have exchanged in mature age worldly pursuits for a life of meditation and religious instruction. The Panjáb was at that time subject to the Patthán Sovereign of Delhi, Behlol Lodí; but then, as now, the lands were distributed chiefly among Hindu chiefs, who united the character of landlord and ruler, as ráyas or rájás, over districts of different dimensions, paying revenue and rendering military service to the Mohammedan governors. One of these ráyas took Nának under his patronage, and enabled him to disseminate his doctrines without hindrance or danger. According to the legendary biography of Nának, he was a great traveller, traversing not only India but visiting Mecca and Medina, working miracles on his journeys and making numerous proselytes. There is probably little truth in his Arabian peregrinations, although it was consistent with his religious character to have spent some time in wandering over Hindustan, and visiting the places held sacred in the estimation of the Hindus. It is most likely, however, that he passed the greater part of his days in the Panjáb, endeavouring to inculcate his views among

---

[1] Major Leech, J. A. S. B., 1845, p. 394; (but, query) if it is not the same as Kírtipur Dehra, his burial place. Malcolm, As. Res. XI, 207. Malcolm calls his birth place Talwandi, or Rayapur, on the Beyah.

his neighbours and countrymen; several of whom, no doubt, adopted his notions; becoming, as the term Sikh implies, his disciples; the word being the provincial articulation of the Sanskrit word Sishya, a scholar or disciple, the sibilant *sh* being invariably pronounced *kh* in the western provinces. From those disciples he organised a communion, the superintendence of which he bequeathed to one of his principal pupils, named ANGADA, establishing a sort of hierarchy, to which perhaps it was owing that his followers were kept together as a distinct body. The successor of ANGADA, AMARA DÁS, became possessed of some temporal power, and built the fort of Kajaráwal. It would appear, however, that secular aggrandisement was not regarded as altogether orthodox, and the Sikhs, who restricted their views to purely religious objects, separated from Amara Dás and attached themselves to DHARMCHAND, the grandson of Nának, as their 'Guru' or spiritual head. They then became known as *Udásis*, or persons estranged from worldly hopes or fears, or as *'Nirmalas'*, individuals free from soil or sin. It is chiefly from these classes of Sikhs, the Udásis, and Nirmalas, that teachers of the theism of Nának are to be found in almost every considerable city of Hindustan, sometimes singly or sometimes assembled in Sangats or convents. They have nothing of a political or military character, but devote their time to daily prayers and observances addressed chiefly to the memory of Nának and the perusal and adoration of the sacred volume which contains illustrations of his doctrines by various hands, in different dialects of Panjábí and Hindí.

This exposition of the Síkh faith, if anything so vague deserves the appellation of a faith, is known as the Ádi Granth, the 'First Book' to distinguish it from another scriptural authority of the Síkhs of a later date. It is a large volume but contains no systematic exposition of doctrines—no condensed creed—no rules for ritual observances. It is an unconnected compilation of verses of a mystical or a moral purport, ascribed mostly to Nának, but comprehending the writings of other persons, many of whom had nothing in common with Nának, except a general accordance in a sort of spiritual quietism and the acknowledgment of one divine cause and essence of all things. The Ádi Granth was put together by Arjunmal—the fourth Síkh Guru or pontiff in descent from Nának—who flourished in the reign of Jehángír, towards the end of the sixteenth century. The bulk of the materials are attributed to the predecessors of Arjunmal, but it is admitted that thirteen other persons contributed to its contents—or, as the Síkhs say, twelve and a-half, intending, most ungallantly, by the half, a female author. The copies of the Ádi Granth, however, found in different parts of India, vary considerably as to the subordinate contributors[*]; the greater number of the poems bear the name of Nának, but the rest are by different hands, as Kabír,

---

[*] [Comp. also Garcin de Tassy, histoire de la littérature Hindoui et Hindoustani, I, 385 ff.]

Sheikh Ferīd-ad-dīn, Rāmānand, Mīrā Bāī, and other well known sectarian or Vaishṅava teachers. The following are specimens of the poems ascribed to Nának:

My holy teacher is he who teaches clemency;
The heart is awake within, who seeks may find.
Wonderful is that rosary, every bead of which is the breath;
Lying apart on its recess it knows what will come to pass:
The sage is he who is merciful, the merciless is a butcher.
Thou wieldest the knife, and recklessly exlaimest,—
"What is a goat? What is a cow? What are animals?"
But the Sahib declares that the blood of all is one:
Saints, prophets, seers, have passed away in death;
Nának, destroy not life for the preservation of the body.

Again—

Love and fix thy whole heart upon him,
The world is bound to thee by prosperity:
While it endures many will come and sit with thee and surround thee;
But in adversity they will fly, and no one will be nigh thee:
The woman of the house who loves thee, and is ever in thy bosom,
When the spirit quits the body, will fly with alarm from the dead.
Such is the way of the world;
The frailty of human affections.
Do thou, Nának, at thy last hour, rely alone upon Hari.

Or again—

Thou art the Lord, to thee be praise;
All life is with thee:
Thou art my parents; I am thy child;
All happiness is from thy mercy:
No one knows thy end.
Highest Lord among the highest,
All that is from thee obeys thy will,
Thy movements, thy pleasure: thou alone knowest
Nának, thy slave, is a free-will offering unto thee.

Under the tolerant reigns of the first princes of the

house of Timur the propagators of the doctrines of Nának were unmolested, and seem to have risen rapidly in temporal as well as spiritual consideration. Rámdás, the third Guru, enjoyed the favour of Akbar, and settled himself in an ancient city in the Panjáb, which he so much enlarged and improved that it was called after him Rámdáspur. Among his improvements was the construction of a large tank which was called by the people the lake of Ambrosia or Amritsar, and this has, in modern times, given its designation and sanctity to the town so denominated, Amritsar. The wealth and consequence attained by the Sikh Gurus had, however, the effect of drawing upon them the jealousy and persecution of the Mohammedans, and ARJUNMAL, the fourth Guru after Nának, was seized and thrown into prison, where he either died or was put to death. The act was resented by the Sikhs of the province, who took up arms under HAR GOVIND*, the son of Arjun, and exacted vengeance from all whom they regarded as hostile to their religion. Their rising, however, seems to have been regarded as a mere local disturbance, involving no political crisis, much less as indicating the future development of an independent state.

This persecuting spirit continued through several successions of Sikh Gurus, and in some cases, it might be more correctly termed retribution; for the Sikhs, dispossessed of their acquisitions or inheritance

---

* [According to the Dabistán, II, p. 273, Arjunmal was followed by his brother Bharata. See Troyer's note.]

in the plains, and compelled to secrete themselves in the hills, collected into bands of plunderers and robbers, and by their depredations provoked the fate they suffered. Dissensions among themselves also exposed them to the cruelty of their Mohammedan governors, and their ninth Guru, TEGH BAHÁDUR, was publicly put to death in 1675, according to the Sikh authorities, at the instigation of a competitor for the Guruship; according to the Mohammedan writers, however, he was executed for his offences against the law by a life of predatory violence. At his death the Sikhs had almost disappeared except as a few inoffensive sectarians, or as scattered gangs of banditti.

The succession of the son of Tegh Bahádur—GURU GOVIND—constitutes the most important era in the political progress of the Sikhs. He, in fact, changed the whole character of the community, and converted the Sikhs of Nának, the disciples of a religion of spirituality and benevolence, and professors of a faith of peace and good will, into an armed confederacy, a military republic. The worship of "steel" was combined with that of the "book", and instead of attempting to unite Mohammedans and Hindus into one family fraternity, he made his disciples vow implacable hatred to the followers of Mohammed. He finally abrogated the distinction of caste, and opened his ranks to every description of persons, even to the very lowest Hindus, assigning to all his military adherents the name of Sinh—or lion—a term peculiar o the Rájput Hindus. His followers were enjoined always to have steel about their persons, to wear blue dresses, to let their hair grow, and to use as phrases of salutation, as a war-cry, or as responses in prayers, the sentences "Wah! Guru ji ká khálsa: Wah! Guru ji ká fatteh." "Hurra! for the unity of the Guru: Hurra! for the victory of the Guru;" expressions that have been since in use even among the more genuine descendants of Nának, the Udásís, and Nirmalas.

Guru Govind was an author as well as a soldier, and has left a record of his own exploits, in a work called the Vichitra Nátak, forming the first portion of a larger compilation which shares with the Ádi Granth the reverence of the Síkhs. It is called the Daśama Pádsháh ká Granth*, the Book of the 10th King, or more correctly speaking, Pontiff; and like the Ádi Granth it is a compilation of contributions by various writers, but they are more of a martial and narrative than of a moral or speculative complexion. This as well as its predecessor, the Ádi Granth, is composed chiefly in the Hindi dialect of the Panjáb, written in the Gurumukhí character, a singular perversion of the Devanagari alphabet, retaining the forms but altering the sounds of the letters.

To Guru Govind also is ascribed the first attempt at the political organization of the Síkhs by the institution of the Guru matá, or federal council of chiefs, which assembled periodically at Amritsár, as long as

---

* [See Vol. 1, 270 f. It is called in Panjábí *Dasvín pátsáhí dá granth*.]

the city was in the possession of the Síkhs, to consult on measures in which the community was interested, and to concert military operations whether offensive or defensive. It does not clearly appear of whom these councils were at first composed, but no doubt they were of a popular character, and every one who, through his hereditary landed property, or his influence in a village, or his reputation as a bold and fortunate leader, could command the following of a band of armed adherents, however few in number, was admissible to the conclave, and had a voice in its deliberations.

After making head for some years against the generals of Aurangzeb and the hill Rájás, whose enmity Guru Govind provoked by his indiscriminate ravages as much as by his religious tenets, he was reduced to great distress, and after the loss of his friends and his children became a solitary fugitive almost bereft of reason. Much obscurity hangs over the close of his career; but it seems probable that he was expelled from the Panjáb by the Lieutenants of the Emperor and led the life of a mendicant wanderer: he is said to have been killed in the Dekhan in 1708.

Guru Govind was the last of the religious teachers, or Gurus, of the Síkhs; but the temporal command of his followers was assumed, after his death, by BANDA, a bairágí, or religious mendicant, who inflicted a ferocious vengeance for the discomfiture and the death of his friend and teacher. The Síkhs rallied under Banda's guidance, defeated the Mohammedan governor of the province, took and demolished Sirhind, and crossing the Jamná spread desolation to Súháranpur, giving no quarter to the Mohammedans except on condition of their adopting the Sikh faith. Their progress was at last arrested by Abd-us-sámad Khán, a general in the service of Farokhseir. The Sikhs were completely routed and hunted from one stronghold to another until Banda and his most devoted followers who had been shut up in Lohgarh, a fort about 100 miles N.E. of Lahore, were compelled to surrender. According to some accounts they were sent to Delhi and put to death, with circumstances of great ignominy and cruelty; but there is a sect of Sikhs, called Bandá-í, who believe that Banda escaped from the fort and settled in Sindh, where he died peaceably and left his sons to propagate his peculiar doctrines. These do not seem to have been of any essential importance, one of them being the abolition of the blue vesture — an innovation acceded to by the Sikhs in general, but stoutly resisted by the Akális, a class of fanatics calling themselves Immortals, and who are also known as Govind-sinhís, as being in a particular manner the disciples of Govind Sinh. These are still distinguished by the blue colour of their garments and by carrying steel in the form of the chakar or discus always about their persons.

So rigorous a persecution of the Sikhs followed the defeat and death of Banda that they were almost exterminated in the plains. Some, however, again found refuge in the hills, and after a period of thirty years re-appeared amid the confusion which followed the invasion of Hindustan by Nádir Sháh. Their necessities made them plunderers, and their policy suggested their forming fixed settlements by constructing forts, and compelling the cultivators to pay to them the government revenues. They were occasionally repressed by the energy of the viceroys of Lahore, but the distracted state of public affairs during the repeated incursions of Ahmed Sháh of Kabúl was propitious to their growth in numbers and independence, and from this period they continued to gather strength and audacity, until they gradually established themselves in Sirhind and the eastern portion of the Panjáb, between the Ravi and the Setlej. The death of Ahmed Sháh, the dissensions among the Afgháns on the one hand, and the total prostration of the sovereignty of Delhi on the other, enabled them to appropriate to themselves the resources of the country, to confirm their authority over the inhabitants, and to complete a kind of national organization.

The Sikh constitution grew naturally out of their political situation. During the period of recovery from the depression to which they had been reduced by the vigour of the Mohammedan officers, they issued from their retreats, for the sake of the plunder on which they depended for subsistence, in bodies of various strength under a leader who, from his personal character or his family influence, could gather a party round him. He was assisted by his relations, or by companions also enjoying consideration among the fugitives, and bringing contributions to the force of the leader. When they were successful, the party remained located in the country which they had ravaged, and divided it among them; a larger portion of the conquered territory was set apart for the leader, but portions were distributed to every one who had taken a prominent share in the expedition. It might sometimes happen that the land itself, where left desolate and waste, constituted the allotments, but the usual plan was to leave the Rayats, whether Hindus or Mohammedans, unmolested, on consideration of their acknowledging allegiance and paying the government revenue to their new lords. In the fluctuating fortunes of the Panjáb these lordships were at first of but ephemeral duration, but as some expired or were extinguished they were replaced by others, and some of them taking permanent root survived the dependencies of the Mohammedan Governments, upon whose ruin they had risen. This was the origin of the various petty Sikh chiefships which, in the beginning of the present century, spread over the eastern portion of the Panjáb, from the Jamná to the Ravi, comprising in their subjects different races both Mohammedan and Hindu, the hereditary occupants and actual cultivators of the soil who constituted, as they still constitute, the majority of the population[1].

---

[1] M. Jacquemont repeatedly observes that the Mohammedans and Hindus much outnumber the Sikhs. According to Captain Lawrence, the population of the Panjáb may be loosely estimated at 1,500,000, of whom 750,000 are Hindus, 500,000 Musal-

The partition of the lands among the relatives and confederates of the leader led to another peculiarity in the Sikh constitution. The portions varied in extent and value according to the power and influence of each member of the confederacy, and the larger allotment as well as a predominating influence was assigned to the leader of the party; but each member of the confederacy, who considered that he had accompanied the leader as his friend and companion, claimed to exercise independent authority over his own share, and to be exempt from every kind of subordination or control. He was willing to be regarded as voluntarily connected with the chief, and with the other members of the original confederacy, and, in general, was prepared to make common cause with them, but he disdained to be fettered by any kind of allegiance either to an individual or the association. In this manner sprang up the several Misals, or voluntary associations of the Sikhs, acknowledging a common designation and a common head, and combining with each other on particular occasions, or in times of emergency to form the Guru matá, the national council or diet, in which every member of each Misal, however limited his resources, had an equal vote. Twelve such Misals existed in the palmy days of the Sikh confederacy; but those on the north and west of the Setlej were annihilated by the all devouring

---

mans, and only 250,000 Sikhs. Captain Burnes made the population larger, but the proportions much the same.

ambition of Ranjit Sing, and those between the Setlej and the Jumná spontaneously dissolved under the protection of the British Government. The last general diet of the Sikhs was held in 1805, when the fugitive Holkar, and his pursuer Lord Lake, penetrated into the Panjáb.

This notion of a unity of interests, or national identity among the Sikhs, as forming part also of a community of religion, was designated as the Khálsa, the Church Militant, if it might be so interpreted, for it expressed a vague notion of the Sikhs being under one spiritual guidance in temporal as well as spiritual affairs—a sort of abstract theocracy. The term has since come to be applied to the temporal government alone, and the late Mahárája deposed Guru Govind, Nának, and the Supreme Being, whom the Sikhs professed to look up to, from even their abstract or typical participation in the Khálsa. At no time, indeed, was this imaginary unity so well maintained as by Ranjit, whose elevation was in a great degree ascribable to the disunion which prevailed among the several Misals, and the conflicting pretensions of their members: a sketch of his rise will best illustrate the characteristics of the Sikh confederacy.

The first of the family of the late Mahárája Ranjit Sing, of whom any record has been preserved, was a Ját farmer, whose patrimony, it is said, consisted of three ploughs and a well. His son was a convert to the Sikh faith, and abandoning agriculture enlisted as a private horseman in the service of a Sikh chief.

His son Charat Sing became a petty chief himself, and levied a small troop of horse with which he plundered the country. Being successful in his incursions he built a fort near Gajrauli, at no great distance from Lahore, and compelled the villages in the vicinity to pay to him the government assessments. The Afghán governor of Lahore attempted to dislodge him, but the Sikhs flocked to his succour in such numbers that the Afghán was glad to desist from the enterprise and shelter himself in Lahore. These events enabled Charat Sing to extend his acquisitions, and while reserving to himself the Sirdárí portion he distributed among his principal associates the remainder of the districts whose revenues he had appropriated. He was thenceforward the head of a Misal, that of Sukarchak, the name of the village in which his ancestors had resided. His Misal was one of the least considerable of the twelve, being able to send but 2500 horse into the field, while several of the others furnished 10,000 or 12,000.

The son and successor of Charat Sing, Mahá Sing, distinguished himself by his military and political talents, and greatly extended the power of the confederacy of which he was the leader, although he died in 1792 at the early age of twenty-seven.

He was succeeded by his only son Ranjit, then in his twelfth year, under the regency of his mother, but at the age of seventeen he put her to death for alleged misconduct, and assumed the direction of affairs. His resources were much improved by his marriage with the daughter of Sadá Kunwar, who had been left by her husband the regent of the Ghani Misal, whose possessions extended east of Lahore and included Amritsar. He became possessed also of the city of Lahore under a grant from Sháh Zemán, the king of Kabúl, on his retreat from the Panjáb. The city, it is true, was not Sháh Zemán's to give, being in the actual occupation of three other Sikh Sirdárs. The grant, however, was held to confer a title and had an influence with the Mohammedans, by whom Lahore was chiefly inhabited. Their ready assistance placed Ranjit in possession of Lahore, important from its situation and extent, and still more from its ancient reputation as the capital of the vice-royalty of the Panjáb.

It would be incompatible with the object of this sketch to follow Ranjit through the steps by which he rose to the supremacy over the rest of the Sikh chiefs, and transformed an ill-defined and precarious combination of independent military leaders into a compact and despotic monarchy. His first great accession was the annexation of the Bhangí Misal, one of the most powerful of the whole, to his own, upon the death of the Sirdár, by the unjustifiable expulsion of the infant chief and his mother-regent. Taking advantage of hostilities with the Rájá of Káhlúr, Sansár Chand, he compelled various Sikh chiefs in the Jalandhar Doáb to yield him allegiance and to pay tribute, being assisted in his operations by the resources of the Ghani confederacy, under the direction of his mother-in-law, and by the Sikh Sirdár of Aluwálá, who became in early life and continued to be for many years his personal friend. These proceedings were confined to the east of the Ravi; but in 1804 Ranjit was emboldened by the distracted state of the Afghán monarchy to invade the dependencies of Kabúl, lying between the Ravi and the Indus, and, although he did not permanently establish his supremacy, he succeeded in enforcing its acknowledgment in the shape of gifts and tribute from the Mohammedan chiefs who had hitherto held the Afghán kingdom. In 1805 he first became known to the British Government by the advance of Lord Lake's army into the Panjáb. No great opinion was then entertained of his power or prospects. Sir J. Malcolm observes, his force did not amount to 8000 horse, and part of that was under chiefs who had been subdued from a state of independence, and whose turbulent minds ill brooked an usurpation which they deemed subversive of the constitution of the commonwealth.

The principal efforts of Ranjit for the next few years were directed to the extension of his authority to the eastward, and several of the possessions of the original Misals were either wholly or in part incorporated with his own territories. He repeatedly crossed the Setlej, appropriated lands on its left bank, and interfered in the quarrels of the Sikh chiefs so obviously for his own advantage alone, that they became alarmed and had recourse to the British Government for protection as having succeeded to the power of

Delhi, of which they acknowledged themselves to be the subjects, as in truth they as well as all the Sikhs in the Panjáb originally were, rising to independence only when the descendants of Baber were too weak to reclaim their allegiance. The appeal was admitted, but Ranjit, although he relinquished his menacing attitude only upon the approach of a military force, was leniently dealt with: he was allowed to keep the places on the left bank of the Setlej, of which he was in actual possession, however unwarrantable the means by which they had been acquired; but the Sikh chiefs who had so far escaped his grasp were thenceforth protected from his violence or his craft: he thence returned to the westward and there sought more promising fields for the employment of his growing power and the gratification of his ambitious designs. In the prosecution of this policy he took Multán, reduced the districts between the Ravi and the Indus to his absolute dominion, crossed the latter river and conquered a considerable portion of the country of the Afgháns, ascended the mountains on the north of the Panjáb, and compelled the hill Rájás to pay him heavy tribute or to fly from their ancient seats to avoid his tyranny, occupied and ruined Kashmir, and subjected to his will the unoffending princes of Little Tibet, encircling to the north the Himalayan dependencies of British India, and approaching the confines of the Celestial Empire, with which his lieutenants finally came, not very successfully, into collision. To the whole of these possessions he had no other title than the sword, and his conquests, unchecked by the necessity of devising any pretext for them whatever, were the rapid growth of little more than twenty years. A kingdom composed of such heterogeneous materials could be held together only by the means by which it was acquired, and an overpowering military force was necessary to preserve the ascendancy which it had been employed to attain. As long as he preserved a good understanding with the only power in India whom he had cause to dread, as long as the British Government favoured his aggrandisement by turning a deaf ear to the urgent appeals made to its protection by the victims of Ranjit Sing's ambition, he confidently prosecuted his system of aggression, and trampled with impunity upon the rights of his neighbours, whether Mohammedans or Hindus. The transactions that have taken place since his decease have sufficiently shewn the rottenness of his system; the instability of a dominion based upon military violence and individual ambition; the certain consequences of relying upon an army as the main instrument and stay of a government. The successors of Ranjit have perished under the presumption of the military chiefs, and the chiefs themselves have been the victims or the puppets of a mutinous and insolent soldiery. That soldiery has now been pretty well destroyed, but the Khálsa has been left in a state of utter imbecility which will ensure its spontaneous extinction at no distant period, if it be not kept alive by the undeserved protection of the British Government.

Whatever may have been the political organization of the original Sikh confederacy, it is obvious that it had ceased to exist; it had received its death-blow from Ranjit Sing, and was latterly a monarchy of a despotic character, tempered by the necessity of conciliating powerful military leaders, or of holding them in check chiefly through the agency of their mutual jealousies and conflicting pretensions. The Misals were destroyed, the Guru-matá was forgotten, nor has the Sikh religion preserved much more of its primitive character. Its original elements were deism of a mystical tendency, contemplative worship, peace and good-will, and amalgamation of Mohammedan and Hindu. There was not much of dogma or precept, and its doctrines were inculcated through the channel of mystical and moral verses in a popular style. Nának Sháh appears to have sought the amelioration of the principles and feelings rather than an alteration of the creed or usages of the people; he does not seem to have formally abolished caste although he received proselytes from every order, and while he treated the Korán with reverence he acknowledged the whole scheme of the Hindu mythology; so do his followers to the present day, that is, such of his followers as profess the pure Sikh faith. They do not worship images, they worship the visible type of the Khálsa in the book; but they do not question the existence of Brahmá, Vishńu, and Śiva; and the legends relating to them, to Vishńu especially, as popularized from the Puráńas in vernacular compositions, constitute much of their favourite literature; except in the mode of performing public worship, and in the profession of benevolent sentiments for all mankind, there is little difference between a Nirmala Sikh and an orthodox Hindu of the Vaishṅava sect.

Neither are the Govind Sinhís, the disciples of Guru Govind, to be considered as unbelievers in the Hindu mythology. They receive all the Paurâńik legends as true, but they appear to be most partial to those of the Śaiva sect, as harmonizing best with their fierce and martial character. It is affirmed of their teacher Guru Govind himself, that he was directed to loosen his hair and draw his sword by the Goddess Bhavání, of whom he was an assiduous worshipper. He says of himself, "Durgá Bhavání appeared to me when I was asleep, arrayed in all her glory. The goddess put into my hand the hilt of a bright scymetar which she had before held in her own. 'The country of the Mohammedans,' said the goddess, 'shall be conquered by thee, and numbers of that race shall be slain.' After I had heard this I exclaimed, 'This steel shall be the guard to me and to my followers, because in its lustre the splendour of thy countenance, oh Goddess! is always reflected.'" In the account, also, which he gives of his mission, he says that in a preceding life he performed severe penance, meditating on Mahákála and Káliká (or Śiva and Durgá), in consequence of which he was sent into the world by Parameswara, the supreme god, to establish a perfect system, to teach virtue, and exterminate the wicked.

The last—understanding by the term 'wicked' the followers of Mohammed—is the part of his mission which he most laboured to fulfil, and which was the whole spirit of his reform. Hatred of the Mohammedans is evidently the ruling principle of all Guru Govind's institutions. His injunctions were, "It is right to slay a Mohammedan wherever you meet him. If you meet a Hindu, beat him, and plunder him, and divide his property among you. Employ your constant effort to destroy the countries ruled by Mohammedans; if they oppose you, defeat and slay them." The necessity, inseparable from this state of perpetual hostility, of filling his coffers and recruiting his bands, compelled him to have recourse to indiscriminate plunder, and to admit of the proselytism of Mohammedans; but deadly enmity to the latter is the ruling element of his system. To this he has sacrificed the benevolent spirit of the teaching of Nának, and the sacredness of the distinction of caste. As far, however, as is allowable by the institutions of Nának or Govind, the Sikhs observe the domestic usages of the Hindu tribes or castes from which they separated; and, in consequence, those tribes, particularly the Játs or Gújars* in the Panjáb or on the Jamná, do not refuse to eat or intermarry with those of the same races who have become converts to the Sikh religion. The Mohammedan converts are not permitted the

---

* [H. M. Elliot, Supplement to the Glossary of Indian terms. Agra: 1845, pp. 345 ff. and 411 ff.]

same indulgence, and are obliged to eat the flesh of swine, and to abstain from the rite of circumcision. The flesh of the cow is the only article of food prohibited to the Sikhs: and on this head their prejudices are almost stronger than those of the Hindus. Smoking is also prohibited, but there is no restriction upon the use of bhang, opium, or spirituous liquor, and drunkenness, from one source or other, is a common vice. Nor is this the only one to which the Sikhs are addicted. The verses of Nának and his fellow moralists inculcate a pure code of ethics, but this is a portion of his reform to which no reverence is paid; and no race in India is more flagrantly demoralized than the Lions of the Panjáb.

We do not derive from the travellers in the Panjáb any description of the public or private worship of the Sikhs, who are probably more jealous in their own country of admitting strangers to be present at their ceremonies than they are in other parts of India[*]. Although several persons have been admitted into the city of Amritsar, it is only recently that it was allowable or safe to visit the sacred tank and temples in its vicinity. The only description that has yet been published is to be found in the Travels of Baron Hügel. According to him, the tank is about 150 paces square, and apparently fed by a natural spring. It is surrounded by a pavement 20 or 25 paces in breadth, skirted by houses on one side, and having several

---

[*] [See, however, "Das Ausland", 1861, p. 1165.]

flights of steps to the water on the other. In the centre is the Hari Mandir, or Temple of Hari, in which a copy of the Ádi Granth, said to be written by Nának himself, is preserved — a tradition rather at variance with the assertion that the Adi Granth was compiled by Arjunmal. The temple is connected with the embankment on the west side by a bridge. The temple is described by Baron Hügel as a handsome building inlaid with marble, having a golden roof, and a door of gold; and surrounded by small vestibules, the ceilings of which are supported by richly-ornamented pillars. Before the entrance to the bridge are two large banners of red silk, the "Wah! Guru ji ká fatteh" on one, and "Rám Dás" on the other, in white letters. Opposite to the bridge are several small structures, in which the Sikh Udásis and Nirmalas are seated, to receive the gifts and reverences of the people. Fronting this tank was the chief gathering-place of the Akális, whose insolence made it dangerous to approach the holy precincts; but they are not noticed by Baron Hügel. The sacred tank and temple of Amritsar were also visited by our noble President[*], when Governor-General, in company with Rañjit Sing. Whatever may have been the obstructions heretofore in the way of a personal acquaintance with the observances of the Sikhs in their own country, they seem to have had no objection, when out of the Panjáb, to the presence of European visitors; and one of

---

[*] [Lord Auckland.]

the earliest notices of them is the account given by Mr. Wilkins, in the first volume of the Asiatic Researches, of his visit to the Sikh college at Patna. He was civilly treated, and allowed not only to see the place, but to be present at the public reading of the Granth, which constitutes the public ceremonial of the Sikhs. They have for their private use prayers composed by Nának, of which those called Arthí are recited on going to bed, and those entitled Jap are repeated the first thing in the morning. Their public worship, in imitation of the Hindu ritual, takes place three times a day, at the three Sandhyás — morning, mid-day, and sunset. I had an opportunity, when at Benares, of assisting at the latter, at the house of a Nirmala Sikh priest, who readily allowed myself and a friend to witness the ceremony. It was very simple. He occupied a lower-roomed house, inclosed in a small court or compound, and having a covered verandah in front. One end of the verandah was shut in, so as to form a small chamber or chapel, in which, upon a table covered with a white cloth, and decorated with lights and flowers, lay the Ádi Granth. As the people entered, they went singly into the room, and made a reverential salute to the book, with the exclamation, "Wah Guru ji:" and placed upon the table any small offering they might have to make. They then came forth, and seated themselves on the ground fronting the verandah, where sat the Guru on a chair, and his two guests on either hand of him. When the whole party, amounting to some thirty or forty, had assembled, the Guru recited, in a sort of chaunt, several hymns from the Granth, similar to those already quoted, repeating at the end of each, twice or thrice, "Meditate on the Sáheb of the Book, and exclaim Wah Guru!" being answered on each occasion by all present, "Wah Guru—Wah Guru ji ká fatteh." The assistants then brought from the chapel trays of sweetmeats, which were handed to every one, and were eaten on the spot. The visitors were not forgotten. This concluded the service; but the party assembled did not immediately disperse. Individuals among them, accompanying themselves with the small drum or native lute, sang Hindi rekhtas and padas (moral and religious songs) in succession. We departed, as did several of the natives, when two or three had been sung; but the party did not finally break up until it was time to retire to rest. The persons present were of respectable appearance and decorous manners, being mostly shop-keepers, dealers in cloth or in grain, and bankers; some were natives of the Panjáb, settled in Benares, others inhabitants of the city from different quarters, who had adopted the Sikh ritual, or had grafted it upon Vaishṅava tenets. Hari and Rám were as familiar in their invocations, as the Sáheb of the Book, or as the teacher or Guru.

Besides sacred shrines, connected with the history of the Sikhs, as the places where their Gurus were born or died, the Sikhs share the veneration of the Hindus for several of the holy cities, as Benares, Mathurá, Haridwár. They also observe many of the same holidays, as the Holí, the Dasahará, the Dewáli. The latter is the favourite season of pilgrimage to Amritsar.

The initiation of a Sikh convert is termed the Páhul, and is thus described by Captain Murray. "The candidate and the initiator wash their feet in the same water, which they then drink, having put some sugar into it, and stirred it with a dagger; repeating several moral stanzas, and taking a sip between each, exclaiming, 'Wah, wah Govind Sikh. Áp hi Guru chelá!' Govind Sikh hail, himself teacher and disciple! It should be performed in the presence of at least five Sikhs. It is ascribed to Guru Govind, who, when he had only five followers, went through this form with them, drinking of the water which had washed their feet, and they drinking that which had washed his." Sir John Malcolm gives a somewhat different[*] and more dilated account of the ceremony, and says nothing of the previous use of the water, which is administered to the convert by the initiator with this injunction, "This sherbet is nectar: it is the water of life; drink it." Having obeyed, the disciple is told to abstain from all association with five classes of men: the Mína Dhírmal, who, though of the family of Nának, attempted to poison Arjun; the Musandiá, a set of Sikh heretics; the Rám Ráyís, the descendants of Rám Ráya, who caused the death of Tegh Sinh; the Kuḍi-már, or daughter-slayers, or the Rájputs; and the Bhadaní, who shave their heads

---

[*] [See also the Panjábí Dict. Lodiana: 1854, s. v.]

and beards. He is then enjoined to be kind and charitable, to reverence Amritsar, to devote himself to the Khálsa, and to study the sacred books. The children of the Sikhs all pass through this form of initiation.

From this sketch, imperfect as it must necessarily be, it will be seen that the Sikh religion scarcely deserves the name of a religious faith. A vague notion of a Creator and source of all things, and of a divine guardian and protector, pervades the poetry of Nának and his fellow bards, but it is little else than a poetical acknowledgment of a deity who is defined by negatives — who is without form — without time — without attributes. The only worship of him, if it can be called such, consists in the allusions that occur in the odes and hymns which are chaunted at the daily services, to a benevolent and powerful being, designated sometimes as Parameśwara — the supreme being; Sat Nám — the true name; Tat-kartá — the maker of that which is; Ádi-purusha — the first spirit; Bhagaván — the lord; but still more frequently as Rám or Hari, the popular names of Vishńu. Belief in the intervention of a providence in mundane affairs exercises very little influence upon Sikh practice. There is no public adoration of any of the Hindu divinities, nor, as far as is known, are any temples erected to them; but their existence is not disputed, and the characters given them by the Hindus and the legends told of them are devoutly credited; and there are probably some esoteric rites in which the worship of the Tantras is privately practised. The great distinction between the Sikhs and the other Hindus is the abolition of the distinction of caste, and consequent extinction of many of the restraints which, in the more orthodox system, supply, however imperfectly, the want of a purer code of faith and practice. The experiment has not been very successful; and the worship of the Book and of the Sword, and the moral declamations of the contributors to the sacred Granth, have led to as great, if not a greater, laxity of conduct, and as utter a disregard of both religious and moral obligations, as the superstitious belief and multiplied ceremonial of the Brahmans[1].

---

[1] The above summary has been drawn up in compliance with a wish expressed by some of the Members of the Society to be possessed of a brief notice of the institutions of the Sikhs which distinguish them from the Hindus in general. It is of course little more than a compilation from the accounts of the Sikhs already in print, especially those of Sir John Malcolm and Captain Murray, as prepared by Mr. H. T. Prinsep; recourse has been also had to the observations of recent travellers in the Panjáb—particularly Messrs. Moorcroft, Burnes, Jacquemont, and Baron von Hügel, and to the amusing and characteristic work of Major Lawrence—Adventures of an Officer in the Panjáb.

IV.
THE RELIGIOUS FESTIVALS OF THE HINDUS.

From the Journal of the R. Asiatic Society, 1848, Vol IX, p. 60—110.

Among all the nations of the ancient world a considerable portion of the year was devoted to the solemnization of public festivals, at which the people found in the assemblage of multitudes, in the exhibition of games, and in religious pageants and ceremonies, a compensation for the want of those more refined entertainments which are created by the necessities and the luxury of a more advanced stage of civilization. Some of these primitive celebrations have retained their hold upon national tastes and feelings long after their origin and meaning were forgotten, and become interwoven with new conditions of society, with altered manners and institutions, and with a total change of religion. In all the countries of Europe they have left at least traces of their former prevalence in the nomenclature of our calendars, and many of the holidays which are appropriated to the saints of the Christian Church have been borrowed from the public festivals of ancient paganism. In proportion also as nations, or as different classes of the same nation, retain their primitive habits, the observances of olden times enjoy their veneration, and interest their affections. They are, however, fast fading in the Western world, even from the faith of tradition, before the extension of knowledge and refinement, and before the augmented demands for toil which the present artificial modes of life impose, when holidays are denounced as an unprofitable interruption of productive industry, and a festival or a fair is condemned as a wasteful expenditure of time and money. It is only, therefore, in regions remote from the reach of the task-master, where exemption from work is occasionally the equal right of all classes of the community, that we may expect to find the red letters of the Calendar significant signs — importing what they designate — public holidays — days on which the artificer and the peasant rest from physical exertion, and spend some passing hours in a kindly communion of idleness with their fellows, in which, if the plough stands still and the anvil is silent, the spirit of social intercourse is kept alive, and man is allowed to feel that he was born for some nobler end than to earn the scanty bread of the pauper by the unrelaxing labour of the slave.

It is in the remote East, and especially in India, that we may expect to find the living representation of ancient observances, and the still existing solemnizations which delighted the nations of antiquity, and we shall not be altogether disappointed; although even here they begin to languish under the influence of a foreign government, under the unsympathizing superiority which looks upon the enjoyments of a different race with disdain, under the prevalence of the doctrine which regards public holidays as deductions from public wealth, and under the principles of a system of religious faith which, although it might be indulgent to popular recreations, cannot withhold its disapprobation of them when their objects and origin are connected with falsehood and superstition. From the operation of these causes, the Hindu festivals have already diminished both in frequency and in attraction; and they may become, in the course of time, as little familiar to the people of India as those of European institution are to the nations of the West. They will then, perhaps, become also objects of curiosity and interest; and in anticipation of that period, and in order to secure an account of them whilst it is still possible to learn what they are, I propose to offer to the Society some notices of the religious Fasti of the Hindus and Calendar of their public festivals.

The different celebrations of the Hindus are specified in their Almanacs, and are described at length in different works, such as the Tithi Tattwa, Tithi Kṛitya, Vratárka, Kála Nirńaya, the Kalpa Druma of Jaya Sinha, and others, and also in passages of several of the Puráńas, particularly in the Bhavishyottara, which, as it usually occurs, treats exclusively of the festivals. The observances are, for the most part, the same in the different provinces of India, but there are some peculiar to peculiar localities; and even those which are universally held, enjoy various degrees of popularity in different places, and are celebrated with various local modifications. The periods also vary within certain limits, according as the lunar month is reckoned to begin from the new moon, or from the full moon; the former mode of computation prevailing in Bengal and in Telingana, whilst in Hindustan and in the Tamil countries of the South the latter is followed[*]. My opportunities of personal observation have been in a great degree limited to Bengal, and for the rest of India I can speak but imperfectly of any existing practices which may not exactly conform to those enjoined by original works, or of which no account has been published by actual observers. One object of communicating these notices to the Society is, therefore, the supplying of this deficiency. Amongst the Members of the Society are many who, in the course of their public services, must have witnessed the celebration of the Hindu festivals in different and distant places: their better knowledge will enable them to furnish correct information respecting those local peculiarities with which I am unacquainted; and I hope that they may be induced to favour the Society with the results of their experience, and contribute to render the description of the popular festivals of the Hindus as complete and authentic as those who may take an interest in the topic have a right to expect from us.

---

[*] [Prinsep's Useful Tables, ed. E. Thomas, p. 154 f.]

Upon examining the Fasti of the nations of antiquity, it is obvious that many of their festivals originated either from the same or similar motives. They all bear a religious character, inasmuch as religious worship formed part of the celebration; but that was the spirit of the time. However erroneously directed, the feelings of the multitude in the heathen world associated the powers of heaven, real or imaginary, with all their transactions; but the sources to which I more especially refer, however closely linked with this common sentiment, are in some degree varieties of it: they constitute the species, and are obviously reducible to two principal distinctions, which may be regarded as universal or particular. The universal festivals, which are probably traceable among all nations elevated above barbarism, and which may have been handed down by tradition from the earliest periods in the history of the human race, are manifestly astronomical, and are intended to commemorate the revolutions of the planets, the alternations of the seasons, and the recurrence of cyclical intervals of longer or shorter duration. The particular festivals are those arising out of national forms of religious worship, out of the different mythological creations of priests or poets, or out of imperfect narratives, transmitted orally through succeeding generations, of occurrences anterior to historical record. In as far as these traditions may have related to the great mass of mankind, before it was broken up into detached communities, or as the mythological fictions may typify real personages or events of the same era, or may embody objects likely to be presented to the imaginations of men under similar aspects, we need not be surprised to meet with analogies of deep interest, even in the festivals which are of particular institution. It is, however, in those which relate to the course of time and the phenomena of the planetary sphere that analogies are most likely to occur, and do, in fact, present themselves in the practices of distant and apparently unconnected races.

The coincidences that may be discovered between the universal or particular festivals of the various nations of antiquity, form a subject that well deserves careful and patient investigation. It would, in all probability, tend to confirm the remarkable results which comparative philology has of late so unanswerably demonstrated, and furnish corroborative testimony of that relationship of races, which, however dissimilar now, in physical configuration, social condition, and national character, are proved to be of kindred origin by the unequivocal affinities of language. In like manner as the Greek, Latin, Teutonic, Celtic, Slavonic, and Sanskrit tongues have been shown to be allied by principles common to them all, so in all probability it would be found that the festivals and holidays which once animated the cities of Athens and Rome, the forests of Germany and the steppes of Russia, are still continuing to afford seasons of public recreation to the dark complexioned tribes that people the borders of the Indus and the Ganges. The full development of these identifications is, however, a work of time and of research exceeding what I can bestow upon it; and I must be content with contributing only that portion of the materials requisite for its investigation which relates to the Fasti of the Hindus, briefly suggesting, as I proceed, one or two of the most obvious points of apparent similarity.

The subject of the Festivals of the Hindu year was introduced to the Asiatic Society of Bengal by Sir William Jones, who published a paper on it in the third volume of the Researches. What he thought of the inquiry is evident from the manner in which he speaks of the authority whence his information was derived, and which he calls a wonderfully curious tract of the learned and celebrated Raghunandana. It was no doubt this Tithi Tattwa, a standard text-book, as are all the works of the same author, in Bengal. Sir William Jones, however, has taken from this work only the heads of the descriptions, and omits all the particulars into which it enters, with the exception of a few brief notes: and his details are neither sufficiently full nor interesting to inspire others with the sentiments with which he contemplated the subject. Some years ago I collected materials for its fuller elucidation, and published in one of the Calcutta papers brief notices of the festivals as they occurred; but the notices were merely popular, and were necessarily short and unconnected, and they have never been presented in a collective form. The topic is one, therefore, which, if destitute of other recommendation, possesses, even in these latter days, that of some degree of novelty, and may on this account be further acceptable to the Society.

As remarked by Sir William Jones, although most of the Indian fasts and festivals are regulated by the days of the moon, yet the most solemn and remarkable of them have a manifest reference to the supposed motions of the sun. An attempt is usually made to adjust the one to the other; but the principles on which the adjustment of the solar to the lunar year is based, are of a somewhat complicated character, and are not essential to a knowledge of the periods at which the festivals are held, and which, with a few exceptions, are sufficiently determinate. They will be specified as we proceed.

UTTARÁYAṆA.—*First of (solar month) Mágha, first lunation dark half or Moon's wane of Pausha or Mágha, 12th - 13th of January.*—The Roman poet Ovid, in the opening of his "Fasti"*, inquires of Janus why the new year is considered to begin in January instead of April, in winter instead of spring; as the latter is the true season of the renovation of nature, when flowers bud, birds carol, and animals rejoice.

> Dic, age, frigoribus quare novus incipit annus,
> Qui melius per ver incipiendus erat—
> Omnia tunc florent: tunc est nova temporis ætas.

The same question seems to have suggested itself

---

* [v. 149.]

to the reformers of the Hindu calendar, and accordingly the new year of the luni-solar computation now in use begins with the first of Chaitra, which falls somewhere in the course of March, and in solar reckoning is said to agree with the entrance of the sun into the sign Mesha, or Aries. There was, however, a period at which a different principle was followed[1], and one that coincides with the peculiarity that puzzled the poet; the new year then commenced on the first of the solar month Mágha, the date of the Makara-Sankránti, or sun's entrance into the sign Capricornus[2], identical with the Uttaráyaṇa, or return of that luminary to the regions of the North, or, in fact, to the winter solstice; a very important era to the nations north of the equator, amongst whom no doubt were the primitive Hindus, as bringing back to them the genial warmth of the sun and the resuscitation of vegetable life, and deservedly, therefore, held to be the beginning of a new year.

The Uttaráyaṇa, or winter solstice, although no longer considered as occurring on the first day of the

---

[1] According to Bentley, this was 1181 B.C. [Historical View of Hindu Astronomy, p. 30.]

[2] The term Makara denotes an aquatic non-descript animal: the more ancient name of the sign seems to have been Mṛiga, a deer मृगकेन्द्रहरिणी हि "The two Sankrántis, the deer and the crab."—Tithi Tattwa. The same work explains the application of the term, the type of the constellation having the head, not of a goat, but of a deer मृगी मृगास्यासिन अजर: [See Weber, "Indische Studien", II, 299, 415.]

year, and which, even in olden times, as we shall see, was thrown back a fortnight, to the first of the light half of Paush̀a, retains the veneration attached to it originally as the renovator of animal and vegetable existence, and is one of the great festivals of the Hindus. It commences, as in our own calendars, with the entrance of the sun into the sign Capricornus; but, although the astronomical period is the same, the actual dates present a considerable deviation. According to our Ephemerides, the sun enters Capricorn on the 21st of December; according to those of the Hindus, on the 1st of their solar month Mágha; and this, in actual practice, is identified with the 12th of January or thereabouts. I have already observed that the adjustments of the Hindu calendar are very difficult matters to deal with, and an explanation of the difference between the 21st of December and the 12th of January is to be found only in astronomical calculations. Thus Colonel Warren observes, the dates of the equinoctial and solstitial points, as far as they are regulated by the solar and lunar moveable zodiac, are fixed, but their relation to the sidereal zodiac depends upon the precessional variation[1]. For our present purpose, however, it is sufficient to know that the essential elements of the celebration are the Makara Sankránti, or sun's entrance into Capricorn; the Uttaráyaṅa, or commencement of the sun's return to

---

[1] Kála Sankalitá, p. 4, note. [Journal of the American Oriental Soc., VI, 249.]

a northern declination; and the actual observance on the 1st of the luni-solar month Mágha falling on the 12th of January, or occasionally a day before or after it.

The observances enjoined on this occasion are partly of a private, partly of a public character. The first consist of offerings to the Pitrís, or progenitors, whether general, as of all mankind; or special, as of the family of the worshipper; to the Vástu devas, the Dii Lares, or domestic genii; the guardians of the dwelling, or the site on which it is erected; and to the Viśwa devas, or universal gods. The ceremonies addressed to all these are performed within the abode of the householder, and are conducted by the family priest. The principal article of the offering is tila, or sesamum seeds, either separately, or, as is more usual, mixed with molasses, or the saccharine juice of the fruit of the date-tree, and made up into a kind of sweetmeat, called Tilñá. Pishtakas or cakes also are offered, composed of ground rice, mixed with sugar and ghee; whence the festival has the denomination of Tilñá Sankránti and Pishtaka Sankránti, the solar conjunction of the sweetmeat or the cake.

The good things prepared on this occasion are not intended exclusively for those imaginary beings who are unable to eat them. They are presented merely for the purpose of consecration, and that they may be eaten with greater zest by the householder and his family; nor is that all, for a portion of them is sent to friends and relations, as memorials of regard, inclosed in fine linen, silk, or velvet, according to the means of the presenter, and the station of those to whom they are presented.

In many places in Bengal a curious practice is observed, called Báwanna bandhana, particularly by the females of the family. In the evening, one of the women takes a wisp of straw, and from the bundle picks out separate straws, which she ties singly to every article of furniture in the house, exclaiming "Báwanna pauti", implying, may the measure of corn be increased fifty-two fold,—pauti denoting a measure of grain. In the villages similar straws are attached to the Golas, or thatched granaries, in which the grain of the preceding harvest has been stored[*].

Besides these private ceremonies, which expressively typify the feelings of satisfaction with which the re-approach of the sun was hailed by a people to whom the principal phenomena of the heavens were familiar, there are also public celebrations of the same event, expressing similar sentiments, but deriving a more local and peculiar complexion from the physical circumstances of the country, and the superstitions of its inhabitants.

According to the Kalpa Druma of Jayasinha, upon the authority of the Padma Puráńa, the whole month of Mágha is especially consecrated to Vishńu, to whom and to the Sun also prayers should be daily addressed,

---

[*] [A similar custom is met with in some parts of Germany; see A. Kuhn und W. Schwartz, "Norddeutsche Sagen", Leipzig: 1848, p. 407. A. Wuttke, "Der deutsche Volksaberglaube", Hamburg: 1860, p. 13 f.]

and offerings or arghyas presented. The introduction of Vishńu is a modern interpolation[1]. The same work prescribes daily bathing before sunrise. The Bhavishyottara[*] also directs daily bathing in Mágha, with mantras or prayers by the three first classes, silently by Śúdras and women, and affirms that the practice is enjoined by the Vedas, a rather questionable assertion. The same may be said of the Vaishńava formulae, given by Raghunandana; according to whom the person performing his ablutions is to invoke various personifications of Vishńu. Thus the Saukalpa, or previous prayer, is, "By this bathing, when the sun is in Makara, be thou, oh Mágha, oh Govinda, oh Achyuta, oh Mádhava, oh God, the giver of the promised reward to me[**]." He is then to bathe, calling to mind Vásudeva, Hari, Krishńa, Śridharu, and to say, "Salutation be to thee, oh Sun, lord of the world, giver of light, do thou make perfect this great worship, this bathing in Mágha[***]."

Whatever may be the date of this mixture of tenets, the ablution is no doubt an ancient portion of the rite.

---

[1] The ablution is to be preceded by a fast and followed by a feast and gifts to Brahmans. पूर्वं व्रताहि्के कुर्यात्परेद्यु: जान-
ह्राजयी: Tithi T.

[*] [c. 107.]

[**] [मकरस्थे रवौ मा‍घे गोविन्द्राच्युतमाधव ।
कामनानेन मे देव यथोक्तफलदो भव ॥]

[***] [चो दिवाकर जगन्नाथ प्रभाकर जलोऽषु मे ।
परिपूर्णं कुरुष्वेदं माघस्नानं महाव्रतम् ।
Śabdakalpadruma s. v. mágba, p. 3394. The Nirńayasindhu (71, b, 8, Benares edition) reads उचयति instead of महाव्रतम्.]

Bathing in sacred streams constitutes an indispensable part of most of the ceremonial observances of the Hindus; and where such rivers are not within access, their place is supplied by other pieces of water of less lofty pretensions; a dirty puddle may take the place of the holy Gangá. At the winter solstice, bathing at the confluence of the Ganges with the ocean is particularly meritorious, and accordingly a vast concourse of people is annually assembled at Gangá Ságar, or the mouth of the Hugli branch of the Ganges, at the period of the Makara Sankránti, agreeably to the limitations above assigned to it; that is, its identification with the 1st of Mágha or the 12th of January. Wherever such assemblages take place, objects of a secular nature are now, as they have ever been, blended with those of devotion; and the Melá, which originates in purposes of pilgrimage, becomes equally or in a still greater degree a meeting of itinerant merchants, or a fair[*].

The number of persons who assemble at Gangá Ságar is variously estimated. Some years ago they were considered to average about one hundred thousand; but I have been informed by high authority that latterly the number has increased to double that amount. They come from all parts of India, the larger proportion, of course, from the contiguous provinces of Bengal and Orissa; but there are many from the Dekhan and from Hindustan, and even from

---

[*] [G. de Tassy, Mémoire sur les particularités de la religion Musulmane dans l'Inde. Paris: 1831, p. 26 ff.]

Nepal and the Panjáb. They are of both sexes and of all ages; many come with small pedlery for petty traffic; many from idleness or a propensity to a vagrant life, not uncommon in India; and there is a very large proportion of religious mendicants of all sects. The Śaivas usually predominate.

The place at which the Melá is held is, or perhaps it were more safe to say, was, some years ago, a sand bank, on the southern shore of the island of Ságar, immediately to the west of the inlet called Pagoda Creek, from a small pagoda or temple, also on the west of the creek, nearer to the sea than the bank of sand, and separated from the latter by a smaller creek running inland. South from this to the sea-shore, extended a thick jungle, with a pathway leading into the interior, where was a large tank for the supply of the people with fresh water. Tigers lurked in the jungle, and not unfrequently carried off the pilgrims. Along the sea-side, for more than a mile, extended rows of booths, shops, and small temporary temples, with the travelling gods of the religious mendicants, who received the adoration and contributions of the pious. Besides the numerous shops for the supply of provisions and sweetmeats, a brisk traffic was carried on in small wares, especially in betel-nuts, black pepper, and the red powder that is scattered about at the vernal festival of the Huli. A Pańdit in my employ, who had visited the Melá, asserted that an impost was levied by the custom officers of Government, of four ánás per oar on each boat; but no such charge appears to have been authorized, except in the case of the Ságar Island Society, who were permitted to make some such charge in consideration of the clearings and tanks made by them. The mendicants, however, petitioned against this privilege, and it was withdrawn from the Society. The petition was not disinterested, as the Sannyásis claimed a right to levy the charge on their own account; a practice that seems to have grown up from long use, and to have been silently acquiesced in by the pilgrims. The total amount was inconsiderable, having been farmed by a native contractor from the Society, whilst in their possession, for 1200 rupees in the first year, and 2000 in the second.

The Melá lasts several days, but three days are the limit of the religious festival. The first ceremony is the propitiation of the ocean, by casting into it various offerings, with short ejaculatory prayers; the oblations are commonly cocoa-nuts, fruits, or flowers; the most appropriate gift is that of the five gems, Pancha ratna, consisting of a pearl or diamond, an emerald, a topaz, and a piece of coral, along with a cocoa-nut, an areca-nut, and the thread worn by Brahmans. These are wrapped up in a cloth, and cast into the branch of the river which communicates with the sea, at a place called Dholá Samudra, and also at the confluence. The jewels are, in general, of the smaller size, not worth more than a rupee or two. There was a time when the offerings were of a less innocent description, and children were cast into the sea. This horrible and unnatural practice was wholly unsanctioned by anything in the Hindu ritual; and its suppression, by the Government of Bengal, had the cordial concurrence of the Brahmans. The act was not, like the oblation of fruits or jewels, intended to obtain the favour of the deified ocean, but in satisfaction of a vow; as where a woman had been childless, she made a vow to offer her first-born at Gangá Ságar, or some other holy place, in the confidence that such an offering would secure for her additional progeny. The belief is not without a parallel in the history of antiquity, sacred or profane, but it was the spontaneous growth of ignorance and superstition, not only unprompted, but condemned by the Hindu religion, and was confined to the lowest orders of the people. It will easily be credited, that the occurrence was rare, and that no attempt has ever been made to infringe the prohibition.

On the first day, bathing in the sea is to be performed; it takes place early in the morning, and is repeated by some at noon; some also have their heads shaved after bathing; and many of those whose parents are recently deceased celebrate their Śráddha, or obsequial ceremonies, on the sea-shore. After ablution, the pilgrims repair to the temple, which is dedicated to a Muni, or divine sage, an incarnation of Vishńu, named Kapila. Vishńu became incarnate in his person for the destruction of the sixty thousand wicked sons of King Sagara. He is said to have stationed himself at this place, which was then upon the brink of a vast chasm leading to the infernal regions. When the sons of the king, who were in search of a horse intended for the solemn sacrifice of the Aswamedha, arrived here, they found the Muni absorbed apparently in meditation, while the steed was grazing near him. Accusing him of having stolen it, they approached to kill him, when fire flashed from his eyes, and instantly reduced the whole troop to ashes. In order to expiate their crime, purify their remains, and secure paradise for their spirits, Bhagíratha, the great-grandson of Sagara, brought down by the force of his austerities the Ganges from heaven; and led her from the Himálaya, where she had alighted, to this spot. The sons of Sagara were sanctified, and the waters of the river, flowing into the chasm, formed the ocean. The Ganges is called Bhágírathí, from King Bhagíratha; and the sea is termed Ságara, after his great-grandsire. The legend is told, in its most ancient and authentic shape, in the Rámáyaña[*].

The temple of Kapila is under the alternate charge of a Bairágí and Sannyásí, mendicants of the Vaishñava and Śaiva sects; the latter presides at the Melá held at this place in the month Kártik, the former at the Melá of Mágha. They exact a fee of four ánás from each person who comes to the temple. The aggregate collection of Mágha was divided amongst five different establishments of mendicants of the Rámánandí order, in the vicinity of Calcutta. In front of the temple was

---

[*] [I, 42 – 45.]

a Bur tree, beneath which were images of Ráma and Hanumán, and an image of Kapila, of the size nearly of life, was within the temple. The pilgrims commonly write their names on the walls of the temple, with a short prayer to Kapila; or suspend a piece of earth or brick to a bough of the tree, with some solicitation, as for health, or affluence, or offspring; and promise, if their prayers are granted, to make a gift to some divinity.

Behind the temple was a small excavation termed Sítá kuṅd, filled with fresh water, of which the pilgrim was allowed to sip a small quantity, on paying a fee to the mahant or head manager of the temple. This reservoir was probably filled from the tank, and kept full by the contrivances of the mendicants, who persuaded the people that it was a perpetual miracle, being constantly full for the use of the temple.

On the second and third days of the assemblage, bathing in the sea, adoration of Gangá, and the worship of Kapila, continue as on the first; after which the meeting breaks up. During the whole time the pilgrims, for the most part, sleep on the sand; for it is considered unbecoming to sleep on board their boats.

This is the great public celebration of the recurrence of the winter solstice in Upper India. In the south there is an equally popular commemoration of the same event, but of which the ceremonies are peculiar, consisting principally of marks of public reverence for cattle, but comprehending also the preparation and distribution of food; whence, indeed, its appropriate appellation, in the Tamil language, *Pongal*, which according to a native authority, Tiruvákádu Muthia, signifies literally boiled rice, and metaphorically, prosperity or rejoicing[1]. The word is therefore another denomination of the festival of the *Makara Sankránti*, or sun's entrance into Capricorn; or, in the words of the same writer, the first day of the Indian January, corresponding, agreeably to the mode of computation followed in the Dekhan, with the 1st of Tye or Taishya, the Paushya of Hindustan, which (as in the latter) falls about the 12th of January. The following particulars of the festival are from a paper published in the Asiatic Annual Register for 1807 by the intelligent native already named, Tiruvákádu Muthia.

"On the day on which the sun enters Capricorn, which is the beginning of the auspicious period of the Uttaráyana, the Hindus offer libations of water, mixed with tila and kuśa, or sesamum seeds and sacred grass, to the manes of their ancestors. They then boil rice with milk and sugar; and when they see it bubble up, they cry aloud 'Pongal, O pongal!' meaning, Let the world be prosperous and rejoice. The boiled rice, along with esculent fruits, is offered to the sun, invoking him for the general good, and the production of abundance. Early the next morning, the husband-

---

[1] Pongal, according to Rottler, Tam. Dict., means "a bubbling up"; in Telugu [and Canarese] Pongali denotes a dish of rice mixed with boiled milk and sugar and other articles.—Campbell, Tel. Dict.

men sprinkle water upon corn sown or grown in fields, crying aloud, 'Pongal, pongal!' meaning, Let the corn grow in plenty, by the grace of the glorious sun, who has begun his northern course (the Uttaráyańa), which is a day of the gods. At noon rice and milk are again boiled, and are presented to Indra, praying him to bestow abundant rain, and by thus favouring pasture, cause cattle to increase and multiply. In the afternoon, cows and bulls are washed, and fed with part of an oblation first offered to Indra; and being also painted and adorned with leafy and flowery chaplets, are brought in herds, attended by bands of music, to the public place of the village; there the cow-keepers dress victuals, and provide fresh perfumes and flowers, wherewith to decorate their animals; and sprinkle saffron water with mango leaves upon them, as a preservative from evil, crying aloud, 'Pongal, pongal!' meaning, Let cattle be cherished and multiplied, by the grace of Indra, as well as of Gopála (or Krishńa the cow-herd). Then the Hindus, with joined hands, are to walk round the cows and bulls, and particularly round the Brahmans, and to prostrate themselves before them. This done, the cow-keepers, with their herds of kine and oxen, return home to their several houses[1]. Hence this day is termed Máttu Pongal; that is, the feast of cattle."

---

[1] The Abbé Dubois adds the following particulars of this part of the ceremony. "On peint de diverses couleurs les cornes des vaches et on leur met au cou une guirlande de feuillages verts entremêlés de fleurs à laquelle on suspend des gâteaux,

"So the day of the Makara Sankránti, or Perum Pongal, is dedicated to the sun, and the day of Máttu Pongal to Indra; they are both comprised in the term Pongal, which is an anniversary festival of a week's duration. During this term the Hindus visit and compliment each other, wishing a happy pongal or many returns of it. Sons and daughters prostrate themselves before their parents, servants before their masters, disciples before their teachers. Some people give alms to the poor, some make presents to their friends and relations, some sport and amuse themselves with diversions of different kinds. This ceremony is said to be a practice of very ancient standing, which the former kings of Madura, of the Pándya dynasty, introduced upon the authority of the Sástras and and Puránas[1]."

des cocos, et autres fruits, qui se détachant bientôt par le mouvement de ces animaux sont ramassés et mangés avec empressement par ceux qui les suivent. Après avoir conduit les vaches en troupe hors de la ville ou du village, on les force à s'enfuir de côté et d'autre en les effarouchant par le bruit confus d'un grand nombre de tambours et d'instrumens bruyans. Ce jour là ces bêtes peuvent paître par tout sans gardien, et quelques dégats qu'elles fassent dans les champs où elles se jettent, il n'est pas permis de les en chasser."—II, 387.

[1] This authority acknowledges, therefore, a principal festival of but two days, but we have that of the Madras calendar for three; the first being called the Bhoga Pandikei, the second the Perum (or great) Pongal, and the third the Máttu (or cattle) Pongal. So the Abbé Dubois, "La fête dure trois jours;" the first of which is called Bhoga Pongal (pongal de la joie, from Bhoga, enjoyment), the second Súrya Pongal (pongal du soleil),

There can be no doubt that the remark of Muthia, that the observance of the Uttaráyaña is a practice of high antiquity, is perfectly true; and there can be equally little doubt that it was of like universality amongst, at least, the Indo-Teutonic races. The analogies are so obvious, that they must instantly occur to every one's mind; and the offerings and distribution of food and sweetmeats and presents, the sports and the rejoicing, and the interchange of mutual good wishes, which characterize the Uttaráyaña amongst the Hindus, are even yet, though to a less extent than heretofore, retained by Christian nations at the same season; beginning with the plum-puddings and mince-pies of Christmas, passing through the new year's gifts and happy new years, the strenæ of the Romans, quæ omnia simul strenas appellarunt; and terminating with Twelfth-night. Whatever modifications these types of rejoicing may have undergone, and however changed in their present purport, by their connexion with our religious faith, they are evidently of the same general character as the observances of the Hindus; and designate the commencement of a period, in which the northern hemisphere

---

and the third the Pongal des vaches.—II, 335. In Rottler's Tamil Dict. [III, 432] we have the three days: the first Pogipañdikei, dedicated, it is said, to Indra; the second Perum pongal, sacred to the sun; and the third the Máttu pongal, sacred to Krishña. [See Wilson's Glossary of Indian Terms, p. 421. The same Bhogi is given, in Telugu and Marathi, to the even of some particular feasts, vide Brown's Telugu Dict., and Molesworth's Marathi Dict. s. v.]

is again to be gladdened by the proximity of the fountain of light and heat.

In looking for the more striking points of coincidence between the observances of the East and West at this particular season, it is not necessary to be restricted to dates, beyond approximate limits. Our own calendar has been subjected to different reforms, which have, even within a recent term, advanced, by twelve days, the enumeration of the days of the month; and alterations of an astronomical nature have also been alluded to, which may perhaps explain further deviations in this respect. The main point of agreement is unaffected. It is not the recurrence of any precise day of the week or month that constitutes the occasion of the celebration; it is the recurrence of the commencement of the sun's northward course, the Uttaráyaña, or winter solstice, from which all the manifestations of gladness derive their origin; and whether this be fixed accurately or inaccurately — whether the period at which the phenomenon was first noticed has in the course of ages undergone a change — is immaterial. Little doubt can be entertained that the same event gave rise to the same feelings; and that they have been expressed by actions, varying in form, but not in spirit, by very distant nations, through a very long succession of the generations of mankind.

It has already been seen that the Romans connected the beginning of the year with the sun's entrance into Capricorn, and that they then celebrated the renovation of nature. Their mode of celebrating it seems to have had many things in common with the usages of the Hindus, particularly in the interchange of sweetmeats; only substituting for the rice, cakes, and molasses of the Hindus, figs, dates, and honey. These articles they sent, at this season, to their friends and relations: they were intended, according to Janus, to be ominous of an agreeable year to follow.

> Omen sit, causa est ut res sapor ille sequatur,
> Et peragat cœptum dulcis ut annus iter[*].

They also interchanged læta verba, good wishes and congratulations;—et damus alternas accipimusque preces[**]. The presents made at this season were called strenæ; and the word, as well as the practice, subsists in the Etrennes of new year's day in France. Strenam vocamus quæ datur die religioso ominis boni gratiâ. According to Festus, the practice is referred by Symmachus to an early period of Roman history, the reign of Tacitus; but it was no doubt much older. How far it prevailed among the Greeks does not fully appear. The Greeks had a festival in the month Poseideôn, or January, in which they worshipped Neptune, or the Sea, in like manner as the Hindus worship the ocean; but no other particulars are recorded; and it is remarkable how little of the Greek calendar is of an astronomical origin. It is almost entirely legendary and mythological, arguing

---

[*] [Ovid. Fast. 1, 187.]   [**] [l. l. 176.]

a people shut up by themselves in very ancient times, and comparatively late in their observations of planetary phenomena. However, it would seem that the sending of good things to one another was not limited to the Romans, as it is said that the Fathers of the Church rigorously condemned the observances of this season, not because of the exchange of civil missives and mutual pledges of regard, but because of the idolatrous worship. "In calendas Januarii antiqui patres vehementius invehebantur, non propter istas missitationes adinvicem et mutui amoris pignora, sed propter diem idolis dicatum."—Montacut. Orig. Eccles. pars prior, p. 128. As the "Fathers" are named so generally, it may be inferred that the observances which they condemned were known wherever the primitive church was established.

The Christmas and new year's festivities, which have left traces amongst the Teutonic nations, were transferred to them from their German forefathers, in the time of Paganism. Thus Bede observes of the Anglo-Saxons, "they began their year on the eighth of the calends of January, which is now our Christmas-day." So the yule clog, log or block, which was burnt on the eve of Christmas-day, is considered to have been used as an emblem of the return of the sun, and the lengthening of the days; for, according to Bede, both December and January were denominated Giuli or Yule, upon account of the sun's returning and augmenting the duration of the days: "December Giuli—eodem quo Januarius nomine vocatur. Giuli a conversione solis in auctum diei nomen accepit."—Beda de Ratione Temporum. Again, Bishop Stillingfleet states, in his Origines Britannicæ, "that the ancient Saxons observed twelve days at this period, and sacrificed to the sun." And Mallet states, "that all the Celtic nations worshipped the sun, and celebrated his festival at the winter solstice, to testify their joy at his return to the northern sky. This was the greatest solemnity in the year."—North. Ant. 2, 68. Identifications too palpable to be denied, with the Uttaráyaña of the Hindus, and the worship by them also of the sun, at the same season, and on the same account. A like analogy may be suspected in the Yule dough, or cakes of flour and water, which, after the introduction of Christianity, were kneaded into little images; but were originally, in all probability, nothing more than the rice cakes of the Hindus. The extension of the period of festivity, so as to include the new year, brings us also to the interchange of presents and good wishes which, amongst the Saxons, as well as the Romans and Hindus, was thought peculiarly appropriate at this season.

Mention is made by Mr. Brand, to whose work on Popular Antiquities* I am indebted for most of the preceding statements, that it was enjoined in the ancient Calendar of the Roman church, to present on

---

* [ed. Sir H. Ellis, 1, 17 ff., 467-78. Compare also: "Calendrier Belge." Bruxelles: 1861, 1, 3-11. "Fest-Kalender aus Böhmen." Wien: 1861, p. xi and 2-7. Pfeiffer's Germania, II, 228-38.]

Christmas eve, sweetmeats to the Fathers, "In Vaticano dulcia patribus exhibentur." Of course the Fathers of the Christian church are intended; but it is scarcely possible to avoid a suspicion that something was originally meant, that the practice was, in fact, a relique of heathenism, and that the "Fathers" were in their primitive character, the Dii Manes of the Romans, the Pitris of the Hindus.

Whatever may be thought of this coincidence, there can scarcely be a doubt that we have some community of origin between the Pongal and the blessing of the cattle at Rome, on the day dedicated to St. Anthony. According to the legend[*], the Saint once tended a herd of swine, and hence possibly his connexion with other animals. A much more intelligible relation subsists between them and the Hindu Indra, or Jupiter pluvius, as provender is plentiful and nutritive in proportion as rain is abundant. The following account of this ceremony is taken from "Rome in the Nineteenth Century", and it will be observed that the time of the year, the decorating of the cattle, the bringing them to a public place, the sprinkling of them with holy water, and the very purport of the blessing, that they may be exempt from evils, are so decidedly Indian, that could a Drávira Brahman be set down of a sudden in the Piazza, before St. Mary's church at Rome, and were he asked what ceremony he

---

[*] [See J. F. Wolf. "Beiträge zur deutschen Mythologie", 1857, II, 86.]

witnessed, there can be no doubt of his answer; he would at once declare they were celebrating the Pongal.

"*January 18th, 1819.*—We were present to-day at one of the most ridiculous scenes I ever witnessed, even in this country. It was St. Anthony's blessing of the horses, which begins on that Saint's day and lasts for a week. We drove to the church of the Saint, near the Santa Maria Maggiore, and could scarcely make our way through the streets, from the multitudes of horses, mules, asses, oxen, cows, sheep, goats, and dogs, which were journeying along to the place of benediction; their heads, tails, and necks decorated with bits of coloured ribbon, on this their unconscious gala-day. The Saint's benediction, though nominally confined to horses, is equally efficacious and equally bestowed upon all quadrupeds. The priest stood at the door of the church, holding a brush in his hand, which he continually dipped into a large bucket of holy water, and spirted at the animals as they came in unremitting succession, taking off his little skull cap and muttering every time, 'Per intercessionem Sancti Antonii abbatis hæc animalia liberantur a malis'."

There can be no doubt that this ceremony is much older than St. Anthony, and it probably is a relique of the Latin village festival of the Paganalia or the Feriæ Sementinæ*, which took place about the middle

---

* [L. Preller, "Römische Mythologie", 1858, p. 404 f.]

of January, when, after the seed had been sown, the
ploughs were laid up in ordinary, and the cattle were
decorated with garlands.

> —— nunc ad præsepia debent
> Plena coronato stare boves capite.—Tib. lib. xi, El. i, l. 8.

A palpable relique of which rite is also traceable in
the Plough Monday of our calendar (13th January),
and the games with which it was celebrated.

The long course of ages which has elapsed has necessarily impaired the evidence of a perfect concor-
dance between the ceremonies with which the nations
of antiquity commemorated the sun's northern journey; yet no reasonable doubt can be entertained that
they did agree in celebrating that event with practices,
if not precisely the same, yet of a very similar character; and that traces of such conformity are still
to be discovered in the unaltered ritual of the Hindus,
and the popular, though ill-understood and fast-
expiring practices of the Christian world,—affording
a curious and interesting proof of the permanency of
those institutions which have their foundation in the
immutable laws of nature, and in the common feelings
of mankind.

The important character of the Uttaráyańa festival,
and the remarkable analogies which, whether indisputable or not, it unavoidably suggests, have led to a
more copious detail, perhaps, than the subject deserves. It is only, however, in such cases that pro-
lixity will admit of apology. The greater number of

the festivals will receive briefer notices in proportion as they are more or less of a purely local description, and of inferior interest.

MÁNSÁSHTAKA.—*Eighth lunar day of the dark half of the lunar month Mágha, about the 20th of January*[1].—The denomination of this day defines its occurrence, *ashtaka* meaning eighth; it also indicates its purport, *mánsa* signifying flesh. Accordingly, on this day, the Śráddha, or obsequial offerings of flesh, should be made to the pitris or manes. According to the Pauránik authorities[2], there are three days of this nature, in the months severally of Ágraháyaṅa, Mágha, and Phálguna; which is also the specification of Gobhila, as quoted by Raghunandana. But according to the Mitákshará, there are four such ashtakás in the course of the year; there being one on the eighth of the moon's wane of each of the two months of the two seasons of Hemanta and śiśira, or the four winter months, when śráddhas are positively enjoined (nitya[3]). The former authorities direct that different offerings shall be made on the three days, or severally, cakes,

---

[1] The specification of the date is to be understood as applicable to Bengal, and even there it is subject to occasional variation.

[2] The Vishńu Puráńa [III, 14] specifies three altogether—Aghan, Mágha, and Phálguna. Raghunandana quotes the Brahma P. for the same. [In the Śráddhaviveka (12, r, l. 2) Pausha takes the place of Aghan.]

[3] यस्माद्यतस्तः हेमन्तशिशिरयोर्मासेष्वष्टमीषु कर्त्तव्यानि श्राद्धानि इत्यस्मादवचनोक्तात्: Mitákshará, 33, r, l. 16 [ad Yájnav. I, 217].

flesh, and vegetables, as will be noticed. The institution appears to have been part of the ancient ritual, and to have fallen into comparative neglect. The Brahmans of Upper India, who maintain a perpetual fire, and are thence called Agnihotras, are said to observe the Mánsáshtaka; so do the orthodox Śaivas and Śáktas, and the disciples of Raghunandana in Bengal; but it is usual to substitute cakes of boiled rice flour[1], mixed with milk and sugar for the meat which was anciently presented, not only at the Ashtaká śráddhas, but, as Manu enjoins, at the periodical śráddhas in general. "Let the Brahman who maintains a household fire, who has performed the funeral ceremonies of his own family, repeat the subsequent general śráddha at the conjunction of the moon every month. The wise have called the monthly śráddhas the subsequent, or periodical śráddha, and that is to be offered diligently with excellent flesh." (B. III, 122. 123.) The time is specified in the Mitákshará, upon the authority of an ancient lawgiver, Áswaláyana[2]. The flesh should be that of a goat or a deer, King Ikshwáku having commanded a large deer to be brought to him for the śráddha at the Athtaká[3].

---

[1] Boiled in a pot, sthálipáka, as Gobhila says, चपि वा स्थालीपार्क कुर्वीत ।

[2] [Grihya S. II, 4. cf. Páraskara's Gŕ. S. III, 2.]

[3] इक्ष्वाकुष्ठ विदुषिं ये पञ्चबाणमचाहिदन् ।
मांसमानय चाचाय मृगं हत्वा महावलम् । [Vishṇu Pur. IV, 2.]

RATANTI CHATURDAŚÍ.—*Fourteenth lunar day of the dark half of Mágha (26th January).*—In Sir William Jones's description of this festival, he merely explains it by the sentence, "The waters speak", the word "ratanti", meaning "they speak"; being the first part of an ancient text importing, "The waters say, We purify the sinner who bathes in the month of Mágha, when the sun is scarcely risen, although he be a cháṅdála, or the killer of a Brahman[1]." Accordingly the essential rite on this day is bathing in some sacred stream or piece of water; which should be performed before dawn, whilst the stars are yet visible. As in many parts of India the temperature of the atmosphere is at this season almost cold, bathing at such an hour in the open air may easily be conceived to be no trifling penance. Offerings should also be presented on this occasion to Yama, the judge of the lower regions; for he who worships Yama at this period, it is said, shall not see death[2]. Besides the usual libations of water to deceased progenitors, a śráddha should be celebrated, and Brahmans and the family should be fed with rice mixed with pulse, accompanied by a particular Mantra[3].

---

[1] Harivaṅśa, as cited by Raghunandana. The text, as quoted by Raghunandana, is —

माघे माघि रटन्त्याप: किंचिद्भ्युदिते रवी ।
मज्जनमपि चाण्डालं न पतन्तं पुनीमहे ॥

[2] [Śabdakalpadruma s. v. Mágha, p. 3395, a.]

[3] As in the Nirṇayámṛita, from the Brahma Purána. माघ-

These appear to be the ancient directions for a religious rite on the 14th of the dark half of the Mágha; but later days have changed both its time and object. According to the present practice, in Bengal at least, ablution is performed, not before sunrise, but after sunset; and instead of Yama one of the terrific forms of Deví is worshipped, Muṅḍamáliní, she with the chaplet of skulls, or Syámá, the black goddess; particularly when any cause has prevented the adoration of the latter in the month of Kártik. The authority for this modification of the ceremony is that of the Tantras; and, except by the Sáktas, is not held in much estimation. The day is little observed anywhere.

VARADÁ CHATURTHÍ.—*Fourth lunar day of the light half of Mágha (30th January—1st February).*—According to some of the authorities[2] followed in Hindustan, Siva is to be worshipped on this day in the evening, with offerings of jasmine flowers, whence it is also called Kunda Chaturthí; but the more usual designation Varadá Chaturthí implies a goddess, the giver of boons, who in some of the Puráńas is identified with Gaurí, or more especially with Umá, the bride of Siva. She is on this day to be worshipped with offerings of flowers, of incense, or of lights, with

---

चयोत्सवम् । The Kalpa Tauwa has शाङ्गवेध: कचरासं भो-
जनं दला ।

[2] Hemádri, Nirńayámŕita, Padma Puráńa.

platters of sugar and ginger, or milk or salt, with
scarlet or saffron-tinted strings and golden bracelets.
She is to be worshipped by both sexes, but especially
by women; and women themselves, not being widows,
are also to be treated with peculiar homage. In the
Devī Purāṇa it is enjoined, that various kinds of grain,
and condiments, and confections, and plates made of
baked clay, should be given on this day by maidens
to the goddess. The due observance of the rite is
said to secure a flourishing progeny. The worship of
Gaurī, at this season, seems to be popular in the South
of India, as the Calendar specifies the 2nd, 3rd, and
4th of Mágha to be equally consecrated to her. In
Bengal little regard is paid to this celebration, although
worship is sometimes offered to Umá, on behalf of
unmarried females, in reference to the means adopted
by Gaurī or Umá, whilst yet a maiden, to propitiate
Śiva, and obtain him for her husband[1]. This last
circumstance renders it not unlikely, that the epithet
Varadá ought to be differently interpreted, and that
it means the giver of a husband, a bridegroom being
one sense of Vara, and the part which is assigned in
it to unmarried girls, the presents to be made by and
to them—the offerings to be made for them—and the
reward of the rite—a family of children, leave little
doubt of the correctness of the interpretation. Now
this festival, it is to be observed, occurs in the last

---

[1] See Sir Wm. Jones's Ode to Bhavání; also translation of Kumára Sambhava, by Dr. Mill, Journal As. S. B., Vol. II, p. 329.

days of January or beginning of February, and is not far from that time, when "quisque sibi sociam jam legit ales avem". What St. Valentine had to do with the choosing of mates has perplexed antiquaries; the interposition of Umá, in the selection of a bride or bridegroom, is more intelligible, as she may well be disposed to encourage that of which she set the example. The Romish Church, however, furnishes us with a somewhat nearer approximation in the festival of St. Agnes*, which occurs on the 21st January, for on the eve of her day, many kinds of divination are practised by virgins to discover their future husbands. Although the festival is accounted for by a legend** of the martyrdom and canonization of the virgin Agnes, it is not impossibly a relict of Paganism, like St. Valentine's day***, which has been supposed to derive its origin from the Roman Lupercalia. These festivals may possibly, however, be merely an ill-understood record of ancient usages with regard to seasons of the year when marriages were most suitably solemnized†. This seems to be indicated by the Hindu worship of Varadá, although, even amongst them, the precise import of the festival is forgotten.

---

* [Brand's Popul. Antiqu. I, 34-39. F. Nork's "Festkalender". 1847, p. 116.]

** [Legenda Aurea, ed. Graesse, p. 113 ff. Fornsvensk Legendarium, ed. G. Stephens, p. 370 f.]

*** [Brand, I, 53-62. J. W. Wolf, Beiträge zur deutschen Mythologie, II, 102 f.]

† [Festkalender aus Böhmen, Wien: 1861, p. 32. Calendrier Belge, I, 72.]

That this season was considered propitious for marriages amongst the Greeks, is evident, from the name of the month corresponding with January-February, *Γαμηλιών*, from marriages (*γαμός*) being frequently celebrated in it; and what is very curious, although very possibly no more than an accidental coincidence, the fourth from the new moon—the Hindu Chaturthí—is especially recommended by Hesiod: *Ἐν δὲ τετάρτῃ μηνὸς ἄγεσθαι ἐς οἶκον ἄκοιτιν·* "Let him (the bridegroom) take home his bride on the fourth of the moon."

Śrí Panchamí.—*Fifth lunar day of the light half of the month Mágu (2nd February)*,—The designation Srí indicates the bride of Vishńu, the goddess of prosperity and abundance; and the text quoted from the Samvatsara Pradípa, in the Tithi Tattwa, confirms the identification by stating, that upon this day, Lakshmí, the Goddess of Fortune, (who is also the bride of Vishńu,) is to be worshipped with flowers, perfumes, food, and water: probably the day was originally dedicated to her. The same text, however, proceeds to direct, that pens, and ink, and books, should be reverenced upon this day; and that a festival should be observed in honour of Saraswatí, the goddess of learning—hence it is inferred, that by Śrí, in the first part of the rubric, Saraswatí also is intended, especially as Śrí had various significations, one of which may be Saraswatí.

Saraswatí, by the standard mythological authorities,

is the wife of Brahmá, and the goddess presiding over letters and arts. The Vaishńavas of Bengal have a popular legend, that she was the wife of Vishńu, as were also Lakshmí and Gangá. The ladies disagreed, Saraswatí, like the other prototype of learned ladies, Minerva, being something of a termagant, and Vishńu, finding that one wife was as much as even a god could manage, transferred Saraswatí to Brahmá, and Gangá to Śiva, and contented himself with Lakshmí alone. It is worthy of remark, that Saraswatí is represented as of a white colour, without any superfluity of limbs, and not unfrequently of a graceful figure wearing a slender crescent on her brow, and sitting on a lotus.

On the morning of the fifth lunar day of Mágha, the whole of the pens and inkstands, and the books, if not too numerous and bulky, are collected—the pens, or reeds, cleaned, the inkstands scoured, and the books, wrapped up in new cloth, are arranged upon a platform or a sheet, and are strewn over with flowers and blades of young barley; no flowers except white are to be offered. Sometimes these are the sole objects of adoration; but an image of Saraswatí stands, in general, immediately behind them; or, in place of the image, a water-jar; a not uncommon, although a curious substitute for a god or a goddess, amongst the Hindus.

After performing the necessary rites of ablution, Saraswatí is to be meditated upon, and invited to the place of worship, with some such mental prayer as the following: "May the glorious goddess of speech, she who is of a white complexion and graceful figure, wearing a digit of the moon upon her brow, and carrying an inkstand and a pen in her lotus-like hands, —may she, sitting on her lotus throne, be present for our protection[1], and for the attainment of honours and wealth." Water is then to be offered for the washing of her feet; food for her refreshment; flowers, or more costly articles, as pearls and jewels, for her decoration; and three salutations are to be made to her with the mantra, "Reverence to Saraswatí, reverence to Bhadrakálí, reverence to the Vedas, to the Vedángas, to the Vedánta, and to all seats of learning[2]." Of other mantras addressed to her, the following are given in the Matsya Puráńa[3]: "As

---

[1] Śáradá Tilaka [6, quoted in the Śabdakalpadruma s. v. Saraswati, p. 5975, b, as follows (see also p. 1824, b and 3395, b):

तवच्चक्रसंगिनीर्विभ्रती मुघ्यकान्ति:
कुच्चभरनमितांगी बद्धिरमा चिताम्ने ।
निजकरकमलोदहेजनीपुच्चमश्री:
सकलविभववृद्धि पातु वारिदेवता न: ॥].

Sir W. Jones translates this prayer somewhat differently.

[2] Brahma Puráńa:

[भद्रकाली नमो नित्यं सरस्वति नमो नम: ।
वेदवेदान्तवेदाङ्गविद्यास्थानेभ एव च । स्वाहा ॥]

[3] [c. 65. Śabdakalpadruma, l. l. (comp. p. 3396, a):

यथा न देवी भगवान्नहा लोकपितामह: ।
त्वां परित्यज्य सन्निष्ठा भव परमहा ।
वेदा: शास्त्राणि सर्वाणि नृत्यगीतादिकं च यत् ।
न विहीनं त्वया देवि तथा मे सन्तु सिद्धय: ॥]

Brahmá, the great father of all, never, oh Saraswatí! lives without thee, so do thou ever be my benefactress." Or, "As the Vedas and all inspired writings, as all the sciences and the arts, are never, oh goddess! independent of thee; so, by thy favour, may my wishes be fulfilled." "In the forms of thy eight impersonations, Lakshmí, Medhá, Dhará, Pushtí, Gaurí, Tushtí, Prabhá, and Dhṛiti, do thou, oh Saraswatí! be ever my protectress."

At the end of the ceremony, all the members of the family assemble and make their prostrations—the books, the pens, and ink, having an entire holiday; and should any emergency require a written communication on the day dedicated to the divinity of scholarship, it is done with chalk or charcoal upon a black or white board.

After the morning ceremony, the boys and young men repair to the country for amusement and sport, and some of these games are of a very European character, as bat and ball, and a kind of prisoner's base. School-boys also used to consider themselves privileged, on this day, to rob te fields and gardens of the villages, but this privilege was stoutly opposed, and was all but extinct some years ago. In the evening there are entertainment according to the means of the parties.

कमलेनैषा भरा पुस्तिकीरी तुष्टि: मभा पूर्ति: ।
एताभिः पाहि मजुभिरहाभिर्मा सरस्वति ॥

See also the Brahmavaivartapuráṇa, Prakṛitikhaṇḍa, c. 4.]

The regular celebration of this festival here terminates, but of late years a supplementary observance forms a plea for a second day's holiday in Bengal. The Bengalis have a great passion for throwing the temporary images of their female divinities into the Ganges. It is a rite especially appropriate to Durgá, at the end of the Durgá Pújá; but it has been extended to other goddesses, and amongst them to Saraswatí, at this season. Accordingly, on the sixth lunar day, the image, which is commonly of plastic clay painted, is conveyed in procession to the river side, stripped of its ornaments, and tossed rather unceremoniously into the stream.

There are some remarkable varieties regarding the seasons of this festival, in different parts of India, whether it be considered as dedicated to Saraswatí or to Lakshmí. The Śrí panchamí, when applied to the former, is observed in Hindustan in Áświn (August-September), and when to the latter, in Márgaśírsha (October-November), as we shall have future occasion to notice, or the present, the fifth of Mágha, is held to be the proper Śrí panchamí, and dedicated, not to Saraswatí, but to Lakshmí. There is, however, both in Upper India and in the Dekhan, a festival on the fifth of the light half of Mágha, which is no doubt the original and ancient celebration, — the Vasanta Panchamí, or the vernal feast of the fifth lunar day of Mágha, marking the commencement of the season of Spring, and corresponding, curiously enough, with the specific date fixed for the beginning of Spring in the Roman calendar, the fifth of the ides of February.

> Quintus ab æquoreis nitidum jubar extulit annis,
> Lucifer, et primi tempora veris eunt.—Ovid, II, 149. 150.

After the Vasanta Panchamí, Káma the god of love, and his bride Ratí, pleasure, are to be worshipped with offerings of fruits and flowers[1]. In general observance, however, Vishńu and Lakshmí now take their places, as there are no temples to Kámadeva; nor indeed are the celebrations, which probably once occurred at this season, very particularly observed. The day is retained in the calendars, and constitutes a nominal fixed point, from which festivals, which become conspicuous enough a few weeks afterwards, are still said to commence.

Śítalá Shashťhí.—*Sixth lunar day of the light half of Mágha (3rd of February).*—This ceremony is of a strictly private character, and is limited to married women who have children. The object is, in the present day, especially to protect them from the small-pox. The observance, however, seems to

---

[1] Ratí is personified as a young and beautiful female, richly attired and decorated, dancing and playing on the Víńá; and Káma is represented as a youth with eight arms, attended by four nymphs,—Pleasure, Affection, Passion, and Power,—bearing the shell, the lotus, a bow and five arrows, and a banner with the Makara,—a figure composed of a goat and a fish, or, as before mentioned, the sign Capricorn.

have had originally no such specific application, but to have been intended to secure, generally, the healthiness of infants*, by the propitiation of a goddess termed, apparently at the original institution of this rite, Shashṭhí, but now more commonly Śítalá. According to the legend, the ceremony was instituted by King Priyavrata, in gratitude to Shashṭhí for restoring his dead son, Suvrata, to life[1]. It should be celebrated on the sixth day of the light fortnight in every month, but this frequent repetition of it has fallen into disuse. Shashṭhí is said to be so named because she is a sixth part of the goddess Prakṛiti, but she evidently derives her name from the day of the fortnight of which she is a personification. She is the daughter of Brahmá, and wife of Kúrtikeya, the general of the hosts of heaven, and is to be meditated upon as a female dressed in red garments, riding on a peacock and holding a cock. Śítalá, in its ordinary sense, means cold, and is here used as an epithet, in reference, perhaps, to the occasional coolness of the day at this time of the year, as distinguished from the sixth lunar days in other months. The word seems also to have suggested the principal observance on this occasion. Cooking on this day is interdicted, victuals must be dressed on the day preceding, and on this eaten cold. Images of Shashṭhí are rarely made, but sometimes a small doll represents the god-

---

* [See A. K. Forbes, Rás Málá. London: 1856, II, 326 ff.]

[1] From the Brahma Vaivartta Purāṇa.—Prakṛiti Khaṇḍa, s. 40.

dess, or she is typified by the stone on which condiments are ground. This is covered with a yellow cloth and placed upon a platform; or in villages, at the foot of the Indian fig-tree. Fruits and flowers are offered to it, with this prayer, "Oh, Shashíhí! as thou art cold, do thou preserve my children in health."

The worship of Śítalá, as identical with Shashíhí, seems to be retained only in Bengal. In Hindustan, upon this day, the sun is worshipped with fasting and prayers, and with offerings of Akand or Mandára leaves, whence it is called the Mandára Shashíhí. There is, however, a Śítalá Pújá on the eighth of the dark half of Chaitra (or Phálguna), in which case the two minor goddesses are of course distinct.

BHÁSKARA SAPTAMÍ.—*Twenty-second of Mágha, seventh day of the light fortnight (4th of February).*—This day is in an especial degree sacred to the sun. Abstinence is to be practised on the day preceding; and in the morning before sunrise, or at the first appearance of dawn, bathing is to be performed until sunrise; a rigid fast is to be observed throughout the day, worship is to be offered to the sun, presents are to be made to the Brahmans, and in the evening the worshipper is to hold a family feast; one of the observances of the day is abstinence from study, neither teacher nor scholar being allowed to open a book.

At the time of bathing, certain prayers are to be mentally recited, during which the bather places upon his head a platter holding seven leaves of the arka plant (calotropis gigantea), or śatávarí (asparagus racemosus), or the jujube, or a little oil and a lighted wick, and stirs the water around him, according to some, with a piece of sugar-cane; after his prayers, he removes the articles from his head, and sets the lamp afloat on the water. He then makes the usual libations to the Manes, and having gone home, presents food, and money, and clothes, according to his means, to the Brahmans. One of the formulæ of meditation given is, "Glory to thee, who art a form of Rudra, to the lord of Rasas, to Varuńa, oh Hárivása, be salutation to thee."

The Káśí Khańda, as quoted in the Kalpa Druma, gives a different prayer: "Of whatever sin committed by me during seven lives, may this Mákarí Saptamí remove both the sorrow and the shame*, and whatever sin has been committed by me in this life, through the influence of time, whether in mind, spirit, or body, wittingly or unwittingly, may every such sin, involving the fruit of seven diseases, be effaced by this bathing, oh thou who art identical with the sun, do thou efface it, oh Mákarí Saptamí!" The repetition of this prayer purifies a person from all sin, and the whole rite is considered as securing him from sickness and premature decay.

As appears from these latter mantras, the day is

---

* [Śabdak.d., p. 3291, a, and Nirńayasindhu, c. II, p. 73, b:

यदज्मजड़त पाप मया सप्तसु जन्मसु ।
तच्चे शोकं च शोकं च माकरी हन्तु सप्तमी ॥

also termed Múkarí Saptamí, the seventh lunar day of the sun in Capricornus. It may be doubted if the term Múkarí is rightly understood, even by the original authorities. Raghunandana considers it to designate the whole month of Mágha, which, regarded as a solar month, should commence with the sun's entrance into the sign. There may, however, be something more in it, and it may originally have been identical with the Uttaráyaṇa, when the sun is equally an especial object of adoration, and either a change of computation depending on astronomical periods, or the purpose of multiplying festivals, has detached it from its primitive position.

In Upper India, the day is also called Achalá Saptamí, the fixed or immovable seventh, because it is said it is always to be held sacred. In the South it is better known as the Ratha Saptamí, or Seventh of the Chariot; for it is also the first day of a Manwantara, or period of the reign of a Manu, being that of Vivaswat, when the sun comes abroad in a new carriage. Agreeably to the directions given in the Kalpa Taru, for the proper observance of this rite, the sun should be worshipped in his own temple—a temple it would now be difficult to discover in any part of India—with prayers and offerings upon the sixth; during which abstinence is to be practised, and at night the worshipper is to sleep on the ground. He is to bathe and fast on the seventh, as before described, but he is also to construct a car of gold, or silver, or wood, with horses and driver; and after the mid-day ablutions, to decorate it, and with prayers from the Vedas invite the sun to take his place in it. Worship is then to be addressed to the sun, and the worshipper is to prefer whatever desire he may have formed, which the sun will assuredly grant him. The night is to be spent with music, singing, and rejoicing, and in the morning ablution is to be repeated; presents are to be made to the Brahmans, and the car with all its appurtenances is to be presented to the Guru or spiritual preceptor. This is probably an ancient rite, coeval with the development of the institutions of the Vedas.

Various other appellations are specified as belonging to this same lunar day, as the Jayantí Saptamí, the victorious seventh; the Mahá Saptamí, the great seventh, and others; but the characteristic observance is the same, and whatever the designation, the worship of the sun is the prominent ceremony of the seventh of the light half of Mágha.

The same may be said, however, of the seventh lunar day throughout the year, chiefly of one seventh in each fortnight, that of the moon's increase; but also of the seventh day of the wane. Besides which, there are particular sevenths to which the concurrence of other circumstances, such as its falling on a Sunday*, or when the moon enters certain mansions,

---

* [मुक्तपक्ष सप्तम्यां सूर्यवारी यदा भवेत् ।
सप्तमी विजया नाम तत्र हन्ति महापतकम् ॥]
From the Bhavishyapurána, quoted in the Śabdakalpadruma p. 5891, a.]

as Rohiní[*], gives extraordinary sanctity, and renders the worship of the sun more than usually efficacious. The specification of the days of the week by the names of the seven planets is, as it is well known, familiar to the Hindus. The origin of this arrangement is not very precisely ascertained[**], as it was unknown to the Greeks and not adopted by the Romans until a late period. It is commonly ascribed to the Egyptians and Babylonians, but upon no very sufficient authority, and the Hindus appear to have, at least, as good a title as any other people to the invention[1].

[*] [See Journ. As. Soc. Bengal, 1, 227.]

[**] [See, however, A. Weber, "Indische Studien", II, 167, and Burgess' translation of the Súrya Siddhánta, p. 176–8.]

[1] It has been thought that Herodotus alludes to the custom, when he observes, lib. II, c. 82, that the Egyptians assign their months and days to different deities. Pliny also has an obscure intimation that the sovereignty over each day was attributed to the planets in the order of their revolution. In the time of Dion Cassius, or in the beginning of the third century, the nomenclature had come into general use, and he is the authority for its Egyptian origin. As in the Latin version, quod autem dies ad septem sidera illa, quos planetas appellarunt, referuntur id ab Ægyptiis institutum.—Lib. 3ª, c. 18, Christmannus, a modern Latin writer (de Kalendario Romano), attributes the nomenclature to the Babylonians: Sane apud Romanos, nulla tunc erat distinctio temporis in hebdomades dierum; ea tamen apud Babylonios et Ægyptios statim a regno Nabonassari in usu fuit cum septem planetarum nominibus dies septimanæ appellarentur. He does not give his authorities. It was not impossibly of Chaldæan invention, but was very generally diffused throughout the East at a remote date.

Aditya-vára, Ravi-vára, or Rabi-bár in the barbarized vernacular, Dies Solis, or Sunday, is one of every seven. This is somewhat different from the seventh Tithi or lunar day, but a sort of sanctity is, or at least was, attached even to Sunday, and fasting on it was considered obligatory or meritorious[1]. But the religious Fasti of the Hindus confine their instructions to the Tithi, and declare, that whoever worships the sun, on the seventh day of the moon's increase, with fasting, and offerings of white oblations, as white flowers and the like, and whoever fasts on the seventh of the moon's wane, and offers to the sun red flowers and articles of a red colour, is purified from all iniquity and goes after death to the solar sphere[2]. The worship of the sun, on the seventh of the dark fortnight, seems to have gone out of use, but that on the seventh of the light fortnight is strongly recommended in various authorities, beginning with this seventh of Mágha and continuing throughout the year. In connexion with this observance, different modes of abstinence are enjoined for each succeeding lunar day, such as taking, during the day, small quantities only of milk, or ghee, or water, or acrid leaves; or fasting wholly from sunset on the sixth till after morning ablutions on the eighth; thence this day is

---

[1] The jackall declines touching the sinewy meshes of the noose, because it is Sunday.—Hitopadeśa [I, p. 21, l. 21, ed. Lassen et Schlegel].

[2] Commentary on Tithi Tattwa.

also termed Vidhâna Saptamí—the seventh of observance—as being the first of the series. On all these occasions Arghyas, or offerings, are presented to the Sun; but the arghya, more peculiarly appropriated to him, consists of eight articles. These slightly vary in different specifications, but they are usually water, milk, curds, ghee, sesamum and mustard seeds, grains of rice, and the blossom of the kuśa grass. Perfumes and flowers, especially of a white or a red colour, are also most fit to be presented to the sun, according to some authorities. Gifts of fuel, and the lighting of a large fire on the morning of the seventh lunar day of Mágha, are also meritorious acts. The following are two other prayers[1] usual on these occasions, in which it will be noticed that the number "Seven" makes a conspicuous figure.

Upon presenting the Argha, the day itself personified as a goddess is thus addressed; "Mother of all creatures, Saptamí! who art one with the lord of the seven coursers and the seven mystic words, glory to thee in the sphere of the sun;" and on prostration before the sun or his image, the worshipper utters, "Glory to thee, who delightest in the chariot drawn by seven worlds; glory to thee on the seventh lunar day—the infinite, the creator[*1]!" It is impossible to

---

[1] From the Narasinha Purâna.

[*] [जननी सर्वभूतानां सप्तमी सप्तसप्तिके ।
सप्तव्याहृतिके देवि नमस्ते रविमण्डले ॥]

avoid inferring, from the general character of the prayers and observances, and the sanctity evidently attached to a recurring seventh day, some connexion with the sabbath, or seventh, of the Hebrew Heptameron.

BHISHMÁSHTAMÍ.— *Twenty-third of Mágha, eighth lunar day of the light half (7th February)*.—This is a festival which, at first sight, appears to be of special and traditional origin, but which has, probably, its source in the primitive institutes of the Hindus, of which the worship of the Pitŕis, the patriarchs or progenitors, the Dii Manes, constituted an important element. According to the Tithi Tattwa, this day is dedicated to Bhíshma, the son of Gangá, and great uncle of the Páńdava and Kaurava princes; who was killed in the course of the great war, and dying childless left no descendant in the direct line, on whom it was incumbent to offer him obsequial honours. In order to supply this defect, persons in general are enjoined to make libations of water on this day to his spirit, and to offer him sesamum seeds and boiled rice. The act expiates the sins of a whole year: one of its peculiarities is, that it is to be observed by persons of all the four original castes, according to a text of Dhavala, an ancient lawgiver, quoted by Raghunan-

वसवमिवदमीष वसजोकामदीपन ।
वसमां हि नमचुर्य नमो ऽमताय वेधसे ॥

Śabdakalpadruma s. v. Saptamí p. 5896, *b* (comp. p. 3396, *b*) and, with some various readings, Nirńayasindhu, I. L] dana, "Oh twice-born! persons of all the Varṅas should on the eighth lunar day offer water, sesamum seeds, and rice, to Bhīshma. If a Brahman, or man of any other caste, omit to make such offerings, the merit of his good deeds during the preceding year is annulled." According to a different reading of the text, however, it should be rendered: "Let all the twice-born castes make the oblations*." This excludes Sūdras, but extends the duty to the Kshatriyas and Vaiśyas as well as Brahmans. The intention of the rite, as now understood, is expressed in the formulæ uttered at the time of presenting the offerings: "I present this water to the childless hero Bhīshma, of the race of Vyāghrapada, the chief of the house of Sankṛiti. May Bhīshma the son of Santanu, the speaker of truth and subjugator of his passions, obtain by this water the oblations due by sons and grandsons**." The simple nature of the offerings which are sufficient on such occasions, water and se-

---

* [वैशाख्यां तु सिते पक्षे भौमास्य तु तिलोदकम् ।
वर्षे च विधिवद्दद्युः सर्वे वर्णा द्विजातयः ।
सर्वे वर्णा रघुपादाणां ब्राह्मक्षमूढयोरधिकारः ।
ब्राह्मणादानां ये वर्णा द्विजभर्मिमाय नो अमम् ।
संवत्सरकृतं पुण्यं तत्त्वत्नादैव नश्यति ।
Śabdak.d., p. 2980 f. Hemādri ap. Nirṅayasindhu, c. II, 74, a.]

** [वैवाखपक्षगीयाच ब्राह्मवष्यराच च।
वपुषाय वृद्धार्क्षिततद्विषं भीषवर्मथै ।
भीष्म: ग्रान्तनवो वीर: सत्यवादी जितेन्द्रिय: ।
अभिरद्भिरवाप्नीतु पुचपौत्रोचितां क्रियाम् ॥
Śabdak.d., p. 2981, a. Nirṅayasindhu, c. II, p. 74, a. Prāṇatoshanī, f. 172, b, 2.]

samum seeds, justifies the remark made by Ovid on the Feralia, that the Manes are easily satisfied,—
Parva petunt manes.

The observance of this ceremony is almost obsolete in Bengal, and in the principal authorities of Hindustan it is not noticed. The Bhavishyottara Puráṅa* has a Bhíshma panchakam,—a solemn rite which begins on the 11th of Kártik (light half), and continues to the 13th, which has something of the character of the Feralia, being a period of mortification and fasting, and expiatory of sin, which is worshipped in an effigy made for the occasion, placed upon a measure of sesamum, and invoked by the appellations of Dharmarájá or Yama, the judge of the dead. The ceremony is said to have been ordained by Bhíshma, when mortally wounded, and is to be practised by all castes, and even by women. The rite is not found, however, in any of the calendars, and it is probably an expiring relique of the once general and public worship of the Manes.

BHAIMYEKÁDAŚI.—*Eleventh lunar day of the light half of Mágha (10th February).*—This is also a festival of traditional origin, said to have been first observed by Bhíma, one of the Paṅdu princes, in honour of Vishṅu, according to the instructions of Vásudeva.

---

* [c. 63. See also Padmapuráṅa, Uttarakhaṅda, c. 132, and Garudapuráṅa, c. 123, as quoted in the Śabdak.d. s. v. Bhíshmapanchakam.]

Every eleventh lunar day, it may be observed, is held in extravagant veneration by the Hindus, but more particularly by the Vaishṅavas. Fasting on the eleventh is declared to be equally efficacious with a thousand aswamedhas, and eating during its continuance as heinous a sin as parricide, or the murder of a spiritual teacher. This extravagance demonstrates its sectarian character, and consequently its more modern origin. The notion may have grown, however, out of particular appropriations of the lunar day, when the eleventh was set apart, as in the present case, to the adoration of Vishṅu.

According to the ritual, the worshipper on this occasion is to fast on the tenth, and bathe at sunset. He is to bathe at dawn on the eleventh, and having previously constructed a temporary temple in the court-yard of his house, he is to cause burnt-offerings to be made to Purushottama and other forms of Vishṅu, by Brahmans acquainted with the Vedas; he himself going through a rather complicated series of prayers and gesticulations. There is no image of Vishṅu, and he is invoked by formulæ derived from the Vedas. The worshipper observes a strict fast throughout the day, and keeps a vigil at night with music and singing. On the morning of the twelfth he dismisses the Brahmans with presents, bathes, and then takes a meal, of which flesh forms no part. The performance of this ceremony expiates the sin incurred by omission of any of the prescribed fasts during the preceding twelvemonth.

Some differences of date and nomenclature occur, in various authorities, regarding this day. The Kalpa Druma calls it Jayá, but enjoins fasting and watching, and the worship of Vishńu; and attributes to it the same expiatory efficacy, calling it the purifier, the destroyer of sin, the bestower of all desires, and the granter of emancipation to mankind.—Pavitrí, pápa-hantrí cha, kámadá, mokshadú nŕińám. The same work, however, has a day named from Bhíma, and refers to the same legend for its origin; but it places it on the following day, as Bhíma dwádasí. The Bhavishyottara Puráńa* also removes the day to the twelfth, and tells a different story to account for it, describing it as taught by the sage Pulastya to King Bhíma, the father of Damayantí, in reply to his anxious inquiry how sin was to be efficaciously expiated. Like the preceding, its essence is the domestic worship of Vishńu, with the Homa or oblations to fire, and ceremonies and prayers of Vaidika origin. One part of the ceremony consists in the administration of a sort of shower-bath to the institutor of the rite, as towards evening water is dropped upon his head from a perforated vessel, whilst he sits meditating upon Vishńu. The evening is to be spent in music and singing, and the reading of the Harivanśa, or Śánti parva of the Mahábhárata. The ceremony expiates all possible wickedness. The rite is held in

---

* [c. 65. See also Garudapuráńa, c. 127, quoted in the Śabda-kalpadruma s. v. Bhaimí.]

little esteem, and is evidently compounded of the observances of various eras,—all of which are equally little understood,—although the compound is manifestly of a purificatory or expiatory character.

Shat́ Tila Dánam.—*Twenty-seventh Mágha, twelfth day of the light half (11th February).*—This may be considered as in some sort a continuation of the Bhaimyekádasí, and is intended for the same object—the removal or expiation of sin. As the name implies, six different acts are to be performed, in all which Tila, or sesamum seeds, are an essential ingredient. The person who observes the rite is to bathe in water in which they have been steeped—to anoint himself with a paste made of them—to offer them with clarified butter upon fire—to present them with water to the manes of his ancestors—to eat them—to give them away[*]. The consequences of so doing are purification from sin, exemption from sickness and misfortune, and a sojourn in Indra's heaven for thousands of years. According to the Brahma Puráńa, Yama, the deity of the infernal regions, created Sesamum after long and arduous penance upon this day, whence its sanctity. The same title and the same virtues are sometimes attributed also to the twelfth of the dark fortnight of the month, as was explained

---

[*] [तिलोद्वर्त्ती तिलस्नायी तिलहोमी तिलप्रदः ।
तिलभुग्तिलवापी च षट्तिली नावसीदति ॥
Tithitattvam, quoted in the Śabdakalpadruma, p. 5655, a.]

by Agastya to Dattátreya, when he asked by what means the effects of sin would be obviated, and sinners saved from hell without great effort or munificent donations[1]. The ceremonies to be performed with Tila seeds are the easy means of accomplishing the object. The importance attached to the use of Sesamum in most of the offerings, but especially in those to the Manes, is very remarkable and not very explicable. The legend of their being generated by Yama is rather the consequence than the cause of such appropriation. Sesamum seeds did form an ingredient in the offerings of the Greeks, but not with the same frequency, nor apparently with the same object. Cakes of sesamum were distributed by them at marriages, as the grains were considered typical of fertility. Perhaps some such opinion may have prevailed amongst the Hindus, and hence their use in obsequial offerings, the great end of which is not merely the satisfaction of the dead, but the perpetuation of progeny, and the prosperity of the living.

Another festival is observed on this day, in some parts of India, in honour of Vishńu, as the Varáha, his descent as a boar to lift up the earth from beneath the waters being supposed to have occurred on this day; hence it is termed also the Varáha Dwádasí.

YUGÁDYÁ.—*Thirtieth Mágha, fifteenth day, light half, or full moon of Mágha (14th February).*—

---

[1] Kalpa Druma.

Bathing and fasting, and the offering of sesamum seeds to the Manes, are enjoined on the full moon of Mágha, and it is also held in additional honour as the anniversary of the commencement of the Kali Yug, or present age of the world, the age of impurity. According to some authorities the anniversaries of the Yugas occur not on the days of opposition, or full moon, but on those of conjunction or new moon, and this is more consonant to the character of the rites principally practised, as bathing and libations of water and sesamum to the Dii Manes. Thus the Vishṅu Puráṅa observes, the fifteenth of Mágha in the dark fortnight is one of the days called by ancient teachers the Anniversaries of the first day of a Yuga or Age, and are esteemed most sacred; on these days water mixed with sesamum seeds should be regularly presented to the progenitors of mankind; and again, the Pitṛis are described as saying, "After having received satisfaction for a twelvemonth we shall further derive it from libations offered by our descendants at some holy place at the end of the dark fortnight of Mágha."

SÁKÁSHTAMÍ.—*Ninth of the solar month Phálguna; Eighth day of lunar month Phálguna, dark half (22nd February).*—This is another of the eighth lunar days dedicated to the Manes, when their worship is to be performed with the usual accompaniments of bathing and abstinence, and offerings to the Viśwadevas or universal gods. On this occasion the offerings presented to the Pitṛis are, as the name imports, restricted to vegetable substances, Śáka signifying any potherb.

VIJAYAIKÁDASÍ.—*Eleventh Phálguna, dark half (24th February).*—A celebration little known or observed. A water jar, decorated with the emblems of Vishńu, and considered as a type of him, is worshipped with the usual oblations; bathing in the morning and a vigil at night are to be observed. This is considered as a purificatory ceremony, first performed by Ráma to secure his passage across the ocean to Lanká: according to the authority, the Skanda Puráńa, quoted by the Kalpa Druma, it is an old ceremony of a purificatory tendency, removing sin and conducing to virtue.

Before taking leave of the period which has been latterly described, and which corresponds with the greater portion of the month of February, it is impossible not to be struck with the peculiar character of the ceremonies. From the time of the Vasanta panchamí, which ushers in the spring with indications of festivity, all the observances partake more or less of a lustral or purificatory purport; some of them have no other aim than the expiation of sin, whilst this in others is mixed up with the worship of the Manes. Purification from, or expiation of wickedness is, however, the predominating design of the ceremonies; and ablution and fasting, and abstinence of all kinds are the practices considered essential to the attainment of this object. Such are the chief intentions of the Makara Saptamí, Bhíshmáshṭamí, Bhaimyckádaśí, Shaṭ-tila dánam, Yugádyá, and Śákáshṭamí, all occurring within this interval. Now the spirit of the time is precisely that which marked a great part of the month of February among the Romans, and the name of the month itself is said to have been derived from its dedication by Numa to Februus, the god of lustrations, for in that month it was necessary to purify the city and pay to the Dii Manes the oblations that were their due: "Nomen habet a Februo deo lustrationum cui a Numa erat dicatus. Lustrari autem eo mense civitatem necesse erat; quo statuit ut justa Diis manibus solverentur[1]." According to some, the name is derived from the verb "februor", to be cleansed or purified. The connexion between lustrations and obsequial rites is another analogy, and consonantly with this opinion, the Feralia, or worship of the manes were celebrated for several days in February, ending with the 17th, or according to some with the 23rd. The month was thence called also the Feralis Mensis. This similarity of time and of purposes can scarcely have been accidental, and there can be no reasonable doubt that the Feralia of the Romans and the Śrádḋha of the Hindus, the worship of the Pitris and of the Manes, have a common character and had a common origin.

Śivarátri.—*Fourteenth of the lunar month Phál-*

---

[1] Macrobius, Saturn. 1, 13.

guna; dark half (27th February).—This, in the estimation of the followers of Śiva, is the most sacred of all their observances, expiating all sins, and securing the attainment of all desires during life, and union with Śiva or final emancipation after death. The ceremony is said to have been enjoined by Śiva himself, who declared to his wife Umá, that the fourteenth of Phálguna, if observed in honour of him, should be destructive of the consequences of all sin, and should confer final liberation. According to the Íśána Sanhitá, it was on this day that Śiva first manifested himself as a marvellous and interminable Linga, to confound the pretensions of both Brahmá and Vishńu, who were disputing which was the greater divinity. To decide the quarrel, they agreed that he should be acknowledged the greater, who should first ascertain the limits of the extraordinary object which appeared of a sudden before them. Setting off in opposite directions, Vishńu undertook to reach the base, Brahmá the summit; but after some thousand years of the gods spent in the attempt, the end seemed to be as remote as ever, and both returned discomfited and humiliated, and confessed the vast superiority of Śiva. The legend seems to typify the exaltation of the Śaiva worship over that of Vishńu and Brahmá, an event which no doubt at one time took place.

There is some difference of practice in respect to the day on which this festival is observed; according to some authorities, it is held on the fourteenth of the dark half of Mágha, according to others on the fourteenth of that of Phálguna; but this is a mere nominal difference, arising from the modes of reckoning the beginning of the month from the new or the full moon. Another difference, which is less easily adjusted, is that of date; some considering the festival as properly commencing on the thirteenth instead of the fourteenth; which appears to be the case in the South, according to the published calendars. This arises from the circumstance of the chief part of the ceremony being observed by night, as the name of Sivarátri denotes, and of a variety in the apportionment of the hours of the night to the series of observances. According to some, the ceremony should begin on the evening of the thirteenth Tithi, or lunar day, if it extends to four hours after sunset; according to others, it should begin on whichever of the two tithis or lunar days comprises the larger proportion of the hours of the night; according to some, it should be held on the Tithi, which comprises both evening twilight, and midnight; and according to others, that which includes midnight without the evening. These are knotty points, which are not very intelligible without reference to an almanac, but they are not the less important in the eyes of the worshippers of Siva. When the Tithi coincides with the solar day, or lasts from sunrise, it is called Śuddha, or pure, and the rite begins with the morning of the fourteenth and closes on the morning of the fifteenth.

The three essential observances are fasting during the whole Tithi, or lunar day, and holding a vigil and worshipping the Linga during the night; but the ritual is loaded with a vast number of directions, not only for the presentation of offerings of various kinds to the Linga, but for gesticulations to be employed, and prayers to be addressed to various subordinate divinities connected with Śiva, and to Śiva himself in a variety of forms. After bathing in the morning, the worshipper recites his Sankalpa, or pledges himself to celebrate the worship. He repeats the ablution in the evening, and going afterwards to a temple of Śiva, renews his pledge, saying, "I will perform the worship of Śiva, in the hope of accomplishing all my wishes, of obtaining long life, and progeny, and wealth, and for the expiation of all sins of whatever dye I may have committed during the past year, open or secret, knowingly or unknowingly, in thought, or act, or speech*." He then scatters mustard-seed with special mantras, and offers an argha; after which he goes through the mátríká nyása,—a set of gesticulations accompanied by short mystical prayers, consisting chiefly of unmeaning syllables, preceded by a letter of the alphabet: as, A-kaṃ, Á-srín, salutation to the thumb; I-chan, Í-srín, salutation to the forefinger; U-stan, Ú-stún, salutation to the middle-finger; and so on, going through the whole of the alphabet with a salutation, or namaskár, to as many parts of the body, touching each in succession, and adding, as the Mantras proceed, names of the Mátrís, female

---

* [See Prāṇatoshaṇī, f. 173, b, l. 2.]

Śaktis, or energies of Śiva, who, by virtue of these incantations, are supposed to take up their abode for the time in the different members of the worshipper. Other objects are supposed to be effected by similar means; impediments are obviated by stamping thrice, and repeating as often the Mantra "Haun, to the weapon, phat;" next, with the same mantra, and by thrice snapping the finger, the ten quarters of the sphere, or universal space, are aggregated in the Linga; and the purification of all beings is to be effected by thrice clapping the hands together, and uttering the same Mantra each time. The repetition of nyása, or touching parts of the body whilst repeating mystical ejaculations, accompanies every offering made to the Linga, as fruits, flowers, incense, lights, and the like, during the whole ceremony.

When the rite is performed, as it most usually is, in the performer's own residence, a Linga, if not already set up, is consecrated for the purpose; and this is to be propitiated with different articles in each watch of the night on which the vigil is held. In the first watch, it is to be bathed with milk, the worshipper, or the Brahman employed by him, uttering the Mantra "Haun—reverence to Íśána." An offering is then made with the prayer: "Devoutly engaging in thy worship, oh Íśwara, and in repeating thy names, I celebrate the Śivarátri rite according to rule, do thou accept this offering*!" Incense, fruits, flowers,

---

* [शिवरात्रिव्रतं देव पूजाजपपरायणः ।
करोमि विधिवद्यत्नं गृहाणार्घं महेश्वर ॥]

and articles of food, as boiled rice, or sometimes even dressed flesh are offered with the customary prostration, and with the repetition of other Mantras.

A similar course is followed in the other three periods, with a modification of the formulae, and the articles used to bathe the Linga with. Then in the second, it is bathed with curds, with the Mantra, "Haun—reverence to Aghora;" and the mantra of the Argha is "Reverence to the holy Śiva, the destroyer of all sins; I offer this Argha at the Śivarátri, do thou with Umá be propitious*." In the third, the bathing is performed with ghee, with the Mantra "Haun, reverence to Vámadeva;" and the Argha-mantra is, "I am consumed by pain, poverty, and sorrow: oh Lord of Párvatí, do thou, oh beloved of Umá, accept the Argha I present thee on this Śivarátri**!" In the fourth watch the Linga is bathed with honey, with the Mantra "Haun, reverence to Sadyojáta;" and the Argha-prayer is, "Oh Śankara! take away the many sins committed by me, accept, beloved of Umá, the oblation I present thee on this the night of Śiva***." At the end of the watch, or daylight, the ceremony is to be concluded with the radical mantra, "Śiváya

---

* [नमः शिवाय घोराय सर्वपापहराय च ।
शिवरात्रौ दुग्धार्घ्यं गृहीद् उमया सह ॥]

** [कुक्षदारिद्र्यशोकेन दग्धो ऽहं पार्वतीवर ।
शिवरात्रौ दुग्धार्घ्यमुमाकान्त गृहाण मे ॥]

*** [मया ज्ञात्वाऽनेकानि पापानि हर शङ्कर ।
शिवरात्रौ दुग्धार्घ्यमुमाकान्त गृहाण मे ॥]

namah", and some such prayers as these: "Through thy favour, oh Iswara! this rite is completed without impediment; oh look with favour, oh lord of the universe, Hara, sovereign of the three worlds, on what I have this day done, which is holy and dedicated to Rudra! Through thy grace has this rite been accomplished. Be propitious to me, oh thou most glorious! Grant to me increase of affluence: merely by beholding thee I am assuredly sanctified*." Oblations to fire are then to be made, and the ceremony concludes with further offerings to the Linga, and with the Mantra, "By this rite may Sankara be propitiated, and coming hither, bestow the eye of knowledge on him who is burnt up by the anguish of worldly existence**." Brahmans are to be entertained, and presents are to be made to them by the master of the house and his family holding a feast.

Those modes of adoration which are at all times addressed to the different forms of Siva, and those articles which are peculiarly enjoined to be presented to the Linga, form, of course, part of the observances of the Sivarátri. Amongst the forms is the Japa, or

* [यविघ्नेन व्रतं देव तत्प्रसादात्समर्पितम् ॥
कमलं जगतां नाथ त्रैलोक्याधिपते हर ।
यथायाच हरं पूर्वं तद्रुद्रख निवेदितम् ॥
तत्प्रसादात्तवाज्ञया देव ब्रतमव समर्पितम् ।
प्रसन्नो भव मे श्रीमन्मूर्तिं प्रतिपद्यताम् ॥
तवालोकनमात्रेण पवित्रोऽस्मि न संशय: ।]

** [संसारक्लेशदग्धख प्रतिमानेन शङ्कर ।
प्रदीह मुमुक्षो नाथ ज्ञानदृष्टिमहो मय॥]

muttered recitation of his different names as the worshipper turns between his fingers the beads of a rosary, made of the seeds of the Rudráksha, or Eleocarpus. The fullest string contains one hundred and eight beads, for each of which there is a separate appellation, as Śiva, Rudra, Hara, Śankara, Íśwara, Maheśwara, Śúlapáńi, Paśupati, and others. Amongst the latter are certain leaves and flowers, and fruits, and especially those of the bel-tree, as in the text—"The Vilwa is the granter of all desires, the remover of poverty; there is nothing with which Śankara is more gratified than with the leaf of the Vilwa*." The flower of the Dhattúra is another of his favourites, and a single presentation of it to a Linga is said to secure equal recompense as the gift of a hundred thousand cows. At the Sivarátri worship, the Linga may be crowned with a chaplet of Ketakí flowers, but only on this occasion. According to the legend, a Ketakí blossom fell from the top of the miraculous Śiva-linga, already alluded to as having appeared to Brahmá and Vishńu, and being appealed to by the former, falsely affirmed that Brahmá had taken it from the summit of the Linga. Vishńu, knowing this to be untrue, pronounced an imprecation upon the flower, that it should never more be offered to Śiva.

---

* [सर्वकामप्रदं विल्वं हारिद्राख महापापनम् ।
विल्वपत्रादरं नाकि येन तुष्यति शङ्कर: ॥

The preceding quotations are from the Tithitattwa. See Śabdakalpadruma p. 5359. 60 and 63, b.]

He was moved, however, by the penitence of the flower, so far to remit the penalty, as to allow its decorating the Linga worshipped at the Sivarátri pújá.

The worship of Śiva at this season is permitted to all castes, even to Chándálas, and to women, and the use of the Mantras seems to be allowed to them; the only exception being the mystical syllable "Om". This they are not to utter; but they may go through the acts of worship with the prayer "Śiváya namah". The same rewards attend their performance of it with faith, elevation to the sphere of Śiva, identification with him and freedom from future birth, and these benefits accrue even though the rite be observed unintentionally and unwittingly, as is evidenced by the legend of a forester which is related in the second part of the Śiva Purána, ch. XXXIV. Being benighted in the woods on the Sivarátri, the forester took shelter in a Vilwatree. Here he was kept in a state of perpetual wakefulness by dread of a tiger prowling round the foot of the tree. He therefore observed, though compulsorily, the Jágarańa or vigil. The forester had nothing with him to eat, consequently he held the fast. Casting down the leaves of the tree to frighten the tiger, some of them fell upon a deserted Linga near the spot, and thus he made the prescribed offering. On the ensuing morning the forester fell a prey to the tiger, but such was the fruit of his involuntary observance of the rites of the Sivarátri, that when the messengers of Yama came to take his spirit to the infernal regions they were opposed by the messengers of Śiva, who enlisted him in their ranks, and carried him off in triumph to the heaven of their master.

Notwithstanding the reputed sanctity of the Śivarátri, it is evidently of sectarial and comparatively modern, as well as merely local institution, and consequently offers no points of analogy to the practices of antiquity. It is said in the Kalpa Druma, that two of the mantras are from the Ṛig veda, but they are not cited, and it may well be doubted if any of the Vedas recognise any such worship of Śiva. The great authorities for it are the Puráṅas and the Tantras; the former—the Śiva, Linga, Padma, Matsya, and Váyu, are quoted chiefly for the general enunciations of the efficacy of the rite and the great rewards attending its performance: the latter for the mantras: the use of mystical formulæ, of mysterious letters and syllables, and the practice of the Nyása and other absurd gesticulations being derived mostly, if not exclusively, from them, as the Iśána Sanhitá, the Śiva Rahasya, the Rudra Yámala, Mantra-Mahodadhi, and other Tántrika works. The age of these compositions is unquestionably not very remote, and the ceremonies for which they are the only authorities, can have no claim to be considered as parts of the primitive system. This does not impair the popularity of the rite, and the importance attached to it is evidenced by the copious details which are given by the compilers of the Tithi Tattwa and Kalpa Druma regarding it, and by the manner in which it is observed in all parts of India.

The performance of the ceremonies of the Śivarátri is possessed of enhanced efficacy when conducted at those places which are in an especial manner dedicated to Śiva, particularly at the shrines which were known to have been celebrated seats of worship of the Linga before the Mohammedan invasion. Such is the temple of Vaidyanáth in Bengal, about 110 miles w. by s. from Murshedúbád. The Linga worshipped there is one of the twelve great Lingas which were worshipped in India at least ten centuries ago, and still retains its reputation. In consequence of the establishment of the Mohammedan rule, and its position in a rugged and mountainous country overrun with thickets, the shrine fell for a season into neglect and decay, but it was repaired and restored to popularity by a Maithila Brahman about two centuries since. An annual Melá takes place at Vaidyanáth[*], at the Śivarátri, when more than a hundred thousand pilgrims assemble. The meeting lasts three days, and the offerings made to the temple ordinarily exceed a lakh and a-half of rupees. The shrine has some credit as an oracle, and a course of worship and fasting on the spot is productive of dreams, which are believed to convey the answers of Śiva to the prayers and petitions that have been preferred to him.

A still more numerous concourse of pilgrims occurs annually on the Śivarátri at the temple of Mallikárjuna[**] in the Dekhan, also one of the twelve ancient

---

[*] [Śivapurána, c. 55.]   [**] [ib. c. 44.]

Lingas, the temple of which is situated in a country quite as difficult of access as Vaidyanáth. An account of the Melá held here is given by the late Colonel Mackenzie, in the fifth volume of the Asiatic Researches. He calls the place Śrí-parvatham—properly Śrí Parvata, or Śrí Śaila, the holy mountain—he specifies the name of the Linga, however, as Mallikarja, that is to say Mallikárjuna.

According to the Bombay Calendar, there is a numerous assemblage of Hindus at the Śivarátri on the Island of Elephanta, the great cave temple of which place contains the well known three-headed image of Śiva.

GOVINDA DWÁDAŚÍ.—*Twenty-seventh solar Phálguna; twelfth day, light half (13th March).* This is a festival, which, as observed in Bengal, is held in honour of Krishńa, who is worshipped in his juvenile form as a cowherd. In Hindustan it is termed the Nrisinha dwádaśí, and is dedicated to Vishńu in his Avatára of the Nrisinha, or man-lion. In neither is it an observance held in much repute*.

GHAŃTÁ-KARŃA PÚJÁ.—*Twenty-ninth solar Phálguna; fourteenth day, light half (14th March).* This is also a minor festival, and apparently confined to Bengal. Ghańtá-karńa, one of Śiva's gańas, or attendants, is to be worshipped under the type of a water-

---

* [Bhavishyottarapuráńa, c. 67.]

jar: the object of the rite is expressed in this prayer, which accompanies the presentation of fruits and flowers to the jar: "Oh Ghaṅṭā-karṅa! healer of diseases, do thou preserve me from the fear of cutaneous affections*." Ghaṅṭā-karṅa is described in the Siva Purāṅa as endowed with great personal beauty, and is, therefore, reputed to sympathise with those who suffer any disfigurement. In Hindustan there are directions for worshipping Maheśwara, or Śiva himself, on the fourteenth of the light half of Phálguna.

DOLA YÁTRÁ, or HOLI.—*Thirtieth solar Phálguna, or first of Chaitra; fifteenth day, light half, or full moon of Phálguna (16th March).*—Although named together, and in various parts of India, especially in Bengal, confounded with each other, yet in other places these festivals are still, as they no doubt were originally elsewhere, distinct[1]; the Dolotsava, or Swinging Festival, taking place at a date something later, and this period belonging, most appropriately, to the Holí. It will be convenient to notice them here together however, for the Holí, as a distinct celebration, is not known in Bengal, although many of the observances which are there practised at the Dola Yátrá are in many respects the same, are influenced

---

* [ब्रह्माण्डं महावीर सर्वव्याधिविनाशन ।
विस्फोटकभये घोरे रख रख महाबल ॥ Tithitattwa.]

[1] The Kalpa Druma does notice a Dolotsava,—the swinging of Kṛishṅa on the Phálguní púrṅimá.

by the same spirit, and express in the like style of language and deportment the feelings of exuberant gladness which hail the return of spring.

When India was governed by native princes, and the institutions of the Hindus were in full vigour, there is reason to believe, that at this time of the year a series of connected and consistent festivities spread through a protracted period of several weeks, and that the whole constituted the Vasantotsava, the feast of Vasanta or Spring. The proper commencement of this period was, perhaps, the Vasanta Panchamí, the fifth of the light half of Mágha, which, as we have had occasion to notice, was regarded as the beginning of Spring. After this, however, ensued the gloomy succession of lustral and purificatory rites which have been described, and which suspend the season of festivity until the period now under consideration, when the Holí takes the place of the initiatory Vasanta Panchamí, and is followed by celebrations in honour of Spring, and the friend of Spring, Love. Whether there has been any dislocation of times and observances here—whether the lustral days did not at one time precede the vernal rejoicings, we have no means of determining; but it is somewhat remarkable, that such was the case with the February of the Romans, which, in the days of Numa, when their year consisted of but ten months, was the last of the year, and therefore, was fitly enough the season for expiating the accumulated iniquities of the preceding months. However this may be, such is now the case, and the vernal festival is broken in upon and interrupted by observances of a different complexion — the effect of which may, perhaps, have been to heighten by the contrast the sense of exhilaration when the time for it recurred.

It is also to be remarked, that although traces of the original purport of the festival are palpable enough, yet that Love and Spring have been almost universally deposed from the rites over which they once presided, and that they have been superseded by new and less agreeable mythological creations; new legends have also been invented to account for the origin and object of the celebration, having little or no obvious relation to the practices which are pursued. Thus, in Bengal, the divinity worshipped at the Dola Yátrá is the juvenile Kríshńa, whilst in Hindustan the personified Holí is a female hobgoblin, a devourer of little children.

As publicly commemorated in Bengal, the Dola Yátrá, or swinging festival, begins on the fourteenth day of the light half of Phálguna (about the middle of March). The head of the family fasts during that day. In the evening fire-worship is performed; after which the officiating Brahman sprinkles upon an image of Kríshńa, consecrated for the occasion, a little red powder, and distributes a quantity of the same among the persons present. This powder, termed Phalgu, or Abíra, is made chiefly of the dried and pounded root of the Curcuma Zerumbet, or of the wood of the Cæsalpinia Sappan, which are of a red colour, or in some places the yellow powder of Turmeric is substituted. After this ceremony is concluded a bonfire is made on a spot previously prepared, and a sort of Guy Fawkes-like effigy, termed Holiká, made of bamboo laths and straw, is formally carried to it and committed to the flames. In villages and small towns the bonfire is public, and is made outside the houses. The figure is conveyed to the spot by Bruhmans or Vaishńavas, in regular procession, attended by musicians and singers. Upon their arrival at the spot, the image is placed in the centre of the pile, and the ministering Brahman, having circumambulated it seven times, sets it on fire. The assistants should then immediately return to their homes. The remainder of the day is passed in merriment and feasting.

Before daylight on the morning of the fifteenth, the image of Kŕishńa is carried to the swing, which has been previously set up, and placed in the seat or cradle, which, as soon as the dawn appears, is set gently in motion for a few turns. This is repeated at noon, and again at sunset. During the day, the members of the family and their visiters, who are numerous on this occasion, amuse themselves by scattering handfuls of red powder over one another, or by sprinkling each other with rose-water, either plain or similarly tinted. The place where the swing is erected is the usual site of the sport, and continues so for several days. Boys and persons of the lower orders sally forth into the streets and throw the powder over the passengers, or wet them with the red liquid thrown through syringes, using, at the same time, abusive and obscene language. In the villages, the men generally take part in the mischief, and persons of respectability and females are encountered with gross expressions, or sometimes with rough usage, and rarely, therefore, trust themselves out of their houses whilst the license continues.

The people of Orissa have no bonfire at the Dola Yátrá, but they observe the swinging and the scattering of the abíra; they have also some peculiar usages. Their Gosáins, Brahmans, followers of Chaitanya, carry in procession the images of the youthful Krishńa to the houses of their disciples and their patrons, to whom they present some of the red powder and atr of roses, and receive presents of money and cloth in return.

The caste of Gopas, or cowherds, is everywhere prominently conspicuous in this ceremony, and especially so amongst the Uriyas; and at the Dola Yátrá, or Holí, they not only renew their own garments, but all the harness and equipments of their cattle; they also bathe them and paint their foreheads with sandal and turmeric. They themselves collect in parties, each under a leader or choragus, whom they follow through the streets, singing, and dancing, and leaping, as if wild with joy. A curious part of their proceeding, suggesting analogies, possibly accidental, with some almost obsolete usages amongst ourselves, is their being armed with slender wands; and as they go along, the leader every now and then halts and turns round to his followers, and the whole clatter their wands together for an instant or two, when they resume their route, repeating their vociferations and songs, chiefly in praise of Kŕishńa or in commemoration of his juvenile pastimes.

Although the Holí is considered in some parts of Hindustan to begin with the vernal fifth, or Vasanta Panchamí, yet the actual celebration of it, even in Upper India, does not take place till about ten days before the full moon of Phálguna. The two first days of this term are of preparation merely; new garments, red or yellow, are put on, and families feast and make merry together; on the eighth day, the work proceeds more in earnest: images of Kŕishńa are set up and worshipped, and smeared with red powder, or sprinkled with water, coloured with the same material. In the villages and towns, where there is no Anglo-Indian police to interfere, the people, having selected an open spot in the vicinity, bring thither gradually the materials of a bonfire,—wood, grass, cowdung, and other fuel. The head men of the villages, or the chiefs of the trades, first contribute their quotas; the rest collect whatever they can lay hands upon,—fences, door-posts, and even furniture, if not vigilantly protected. If these things be once added to the pile, the owner cannot reclaim them, and it is a point of honour to acquiesce—any measures, however, are allowable to prevent their being carried off. During the whole period, up to the fifteenth day, the people go about scattering the powder and red liquid over each other, singing and dancing, and annoying passengers by mischievous tricks, practical jokes, coarse witticisms, and vulgar abuse. In the larger towns, which are subject to British authority, the festival is restricted to three days, and the celebrants are not permitted to attack indifferent passers by of any degree. In Calcutta little of the festival is witnessed, except among the palankin bearers, who are generally permitted by their masters to devote a few hours of the forenoon, for two or three days, to amuse themselves by staining each others' faces and clothes, and singing and dancing, and sometimes getting tipsy. They do not venture to throw the powder over their masters, but they bring a small quantity with some sweetmeats on a tray, and the courtesy is acknowledged by those who do not despise national observances and the merry-making of their dependants by placing two or three rupees upon the platter. In the native regiments a little more licence is allowed, and the officers are gently bepowdered with the abīra; and at the Courts of Hindu princes, when such things were, the British Resident and the officers of his suite were usually participators in the public diversions of their Highnesses. An amusing account of the proceedings at the Court of Mahárâj Dowlat Rao Sindhia is given by Major Droughton, in his letter from a Marhatta camp.

We have, however, in this digression rather anticipated matters, and must return to the fourteenth day, by which time the pile of the bonfire is completed.

It is then consecrated and lighted up by a Brahman, and when the flames break forth, the spectators crowd round it to warm themselves, an act that is supposed to avert ill-luck for the rest of the year; they engage also in some rough gambols, trying to push each other nearer to the fire than is agreeable or safe, and as the blaze declines, jump over and toss about the burning embers; when the fuel is expended and the fire extinct, which is not until the fifteenth or full moon, the ashes are collected and thrown into the water. Such of the celebrants as are Śaivas take up part and smear their bodies over with them in imitation of Śiva. According to Colonel Tod, the practice of the Rájputs conforms so far to the original institution, that for forty days after the Vasanta Panchamí, or up to the full moon of Phálguna, the utmost licence prevails at Udaypur, both in word and action; the lower classes regale on stimulating confections and intoxicating liquors, and even respectable persons roam about the streets like bacchanals, vociferating songs in praise of the powers of nature. The chief orgies, however, take place after the beginning of Phálguna, when the people are continually patrolling the streets, throwing the common powder at each other, or ejecting a solution of it from syringes, until their clothes and countenances are all of the same dye. A characteristic mode of keeping the festival is playing the Holí on horseback, when the riders pelt each other with balls of the red powder, inclosed in thin plates of talc which break when they strike.

On the full moon, or Púrńimá, the Ráńá goes in state to an open pavilion in the centre of a spacious plain, where he is attended by his chiefs, and passes an hour listening to the Holí songs. The surrounding crowd amuse themselves with throwing the red powder on all within their reach. After this, the Ráńá feasts his chiefs, and presents them with cocoa-nuts and swords of lath, in burlesque of real swords; "in unison," Tod observes, "with the character of the day, when war is banished, and the multiplication not the destruction of man is the behest of the goddess who rules the Spring." At nightfall the forty days conclude with the burning of the Holí, when they light large fires into which various substances as well as the abíra are cast, and around which groups of children are dancing and screaming in the streets. The sports continue till three hours after sunrise, when the people bathe, change their garments, worship and return to the state of sober citizens; and princes and chiefs receive gifts from their domestics.

Amongst the Tamils, or people of Madras and the farther south, the Dolotsava, or Swing Festival, does not occur until about a month later; but on the fifteenth of Phálguna they have a celebration more analogous to the Holí of Hindustan, and which is no doubt a genuine fragment of the primitive institution, the adoration of the personified Spring as the friend and associate of the deity of Love. The festival of the full moon of Phálguna is the Káma-dahanam, the burning of Kámadeva, whose effigy is committed to the flames. This is supposed to commemorate the legend of Káma's having been consumed by the flames which flashed indignant from the eye of Śiva, when the archer god presumed to direct his shaft against the stern deity, and inflame his breast with passion for Párvatí, the daughter of the monarch of the Himálaya Mountains. Kámadeva was reduced to a heap of ashes, although he was afterwards restored to existence by the intercession of the bride of Mahádeva. The bonfires in the Dekhan are usually made in front of the temples of Śiva, or sometimes of Vishńu, at midnight, and when extinct the ashes are distributed amongst the assistants, who rub them over their persons. The scattering of the abira, the singing and abuse, and the ordinary practices of the festival in Upper India, are also in use in the South.

The prominence given to Kámadeva at this season by the Tamil races, and their preserving some remnant of the purport of the primitive festival, are the more interesting, that little or no trace of the chief object of worship is preserved in Upper India. Kámadeva and Vasanta are quite out of date, and legends of a totally different tendency have been devised to explain the purpose of the bonfire and the effigy exposed to it. The heroine of these legends is a malignant witch, or a foul female goblin, or Rákshasí, named Horí, Holí, or Holiká, a word which, although it occurs in some of the Puráńas, is not of a very obvious Sanskrit etymology[1].

---

[1] It appears from the Bhavishyottara Puráńa, as given below,

According to one account Holí is the same as the female demon Pútaná, of whom it is related in the Vishńu and Bhágavata Puráńas*, and in the popular biographies of Kŕishńa taken from them, that she attempted to destroy the baby Kŕishńa, by giving him her poisoned nipples to suck. The little god, knowing with whom he had to deal, sucked so hard and perseveringly, that he drained the Rákshasí of her life. The popular legend adds, that the dead body disappeared, and the Gopas, or cowherds of Mathurá, burnt the Rákshasí therefore in effigy. The chief authority for the institution of the Holí, however, is the Bhavishyottara Puráńa**, and as an authentic representation of the popular notion which now prevails, and which is nevertheless no doubt erroneous, I shall give a translation of the legend told in that compilation.

"Yudhishthira said, 'Tell me, Janárdana, wherefore on the full moon of Phálguna, a festival is celebrated in the world, in every village, and in every town; why are children playing and dancing in every house, why is the Holiká lighted, what words are uttered, what is the meaning of the name Atáṭajá, what of Śíloshńá, what divinity is worshipped at this

---

to be derived from Homa, burnt offering, and Loka, mankind; because the latter are made prosperous by the performance of the former on this occasion: an evidently fanciful derivation.

* [V. P. V, 5. Bhág. P. X, 4. Harivanśa, 3423 ff.]
** [c. 117.]

season, by whom was the rite instituted, what observances are to be practised? Give me, Krishńa, a full account of these things.' Krishńa replied: 'In the Krita age, Yudhishthira, there was a king named Raghu, a brave warrior, endowed with all good qualities, a kind speaker, and deeply read in the Vedas; he had subdued the whole earth, had brought all its princes under his authority, and virtuously cherished his subjects, as if they had been his own children. In his reign there was neither famine, nor sickness, nor untimely death, nor any iniquity, nor departure from the precepts of religion. Whilst he was thus governing his kingdom, agreeably to the duties of his regal caste, all his people came to him and called upon him to preserve them. They said, 'Lo, into our houses a female Rákshas named Duńdhá enters, both by day and by night, and forcibly afflicts our children, and she cannot be driven out either by charmed bracelets, or by water, or by seeds of mustard, or by holy teachers skilful in exorcismus. Such, oh king! as we have related, is the story of Duńdhá.'

"When the king heard these things, he consulted the Muni Núrada. The Muni replied: 'I will tell you by what means the fiend is to be destroyed. This day is the fifteenth of the light fortnight of Phálguna; the cold season has departed, the warm weather will commence with dawn. Chief of men! let the assurance of safety be this day given to your people, and let them, freed from terror, laugh and sport; let the children go forth rejoicing, like soldiers delighted to go to battle, equipped with wooden swords. Let also a pile of dry wood and stones be prepared, and let it be lighted according to rule, while incantations are recited destructive of wicked fiends. Then let the people, fearless, thrice circumambulate the fire, exclaiming, 'Kila, kila!' and clapping their hands; and let them sing and laugh, and let every one utter, without fear, whatever comes into his mind. In various ways, and in their own speech, let them freely indulge their tongues, and sing and sing again a thousand times, whatever songs they will. Appalled by those vociferations, by the oblation to fire, and by the loud laughter (attahása) of the children, that wicked Rákshasí shall be destroyed, and thenceforth the festival of the Holiká shall be renowned among mankind. Inasmuch as the oblation to fire (homa), offered by the Brahmans upon this day, effaces sin and confers peace upon the world (loka), therefore shall the day be called the Holiká; and inasmuch as the day of full moon comprises the essence of all lunations, so from its intrinsic excellence is Phálguna the bestower of universal happiness. On this day, upon the approach of evening, children should be detained at home; and into the court-yard of the house, smeared with cowdung, let the master of the house invite many men, mostly youths, having wooden swords in their hands: with these they shall touch the children, with songs and laughter, and thus preserving them, shall be entertained with boiled rice and sugar. Thus Dundhá is to be got rid of at the hour of sunset, and by this means the safety of children is ensured on the approach of night.'"

The same authority describes a domestic ceremony to be held on the following morning, when offerings are to be made to a water-jar, as a type of Vishńu; and presents are to be given to bards, singers, and Brahmans. The observance of this secures the enjoyment of all desires, and the continuation of life, wealth, and posterity.

Of the songs that are sung at this season, the character is generally said to be higly exceptionable. All that I have had an opportunity of seeing are characterised by little else than insipidity; they are short, seldom exceeding two or three stanzas, the first of which is repeated as a sort of refrain or burden, and the whole song is sung da capo, over and over again. They are either praises of the month or allusions to the juvenile Kŕishńa, in connexion with the festival, and are supposed to be uttered by the female companions of his boyish frolics in Vrindávana. The following are a few of them:

I.

"Oh friend! proud as you are of your youth, be careful of your garments. The month of Phálguna fills with grief those whose lovers are far away. Oh friend! proud as you are of your youth," &c.

II.

"The month of Phálguna has arrived; I shall mingle with the crowd, and partake of the sports of the Hori.

Oh friend! an hour of pleasure is worth a night of
mortification. The month of Phálguna has arrived," &c.

III.

"I met on my way the lord of Vṛindávana: how can
I go to fetch water? If I ascend the roof, he pelts me
with pellets of clay; if I go to the river, he sprinkles
me over with red powder; if I repair to Gokul, he
showers upon me tinted dust. Thus he drives me distracted. I met in the way the lord of Vṛindávana."

IV.

"My beloved has sent me a letter to summon his
bride home; I blush for my unworthiness. How can
I repair to one who knows my imperfections? I blush
for my unworthiness. The litter is prepared, but no
female friend accompanies me. I blush for my unworthiness, now that my lover summons me home."

V.

"My boddice is wet through; who has thrown the
tinted liquor upon me? It is Kanhaiyú, the son of
Nanda. It is the month of Phálguna. My boddice is
wet through," &c.

VI.

"Oh lord of Vraj! gaily you sport to the merry sound
of the tabor, and dance along with the nymphs of
Vṛindávana. Oh lord of Vraj!" &c.*

---

* [M. Garcin de Tassy gives a description of this festival,
extracted from the works of Jawán, Mír Taqi and Zamir, in his

The deviation from ancient times and practices which marks the recurrence of the Vernal Festival among the Hindus themselves, renders it far from surprising that we should fail to find an exact accordance, in all respects, between the Indian observance, as now followed, and that which has prevailed in other seasons and places, with respect to celebrations, the general purport and character of which present probable analogies. We have no right to look for a minute agreement, but it can scarcely be doubted, that there were festivals among the Romans, and that there are even yet observances in Europe which express a similar intention, and originated in the same feelings, and which are, possibly, as well as the Hindu Holi, reliques of what was once the universal method adopted by mankind to typify the genial influence of Spring upon both the inanimate and animated creation, and to express the passionate feelings inspired by the season, and the delight which the revival of nature diffused.

The season of Spring began with the Romans, as with the Hindus, as has been observed, early in the year, on the fifth of the Ides of February; between this and the middle of March different festivals occur,

---

"Notice sur les fêtes populaires des Hindous". Paris: 1834, p. 38-46, and his "Histoire de la Littérature Hindoui et Hindoustani", 1, 549 f. See also Chrestomathie Hindoustani. Paris: 1847, p. 122. Price's Hindee and Hindoostanee Selections. Calcutta: 1827, I, 250 and 276, and the articles *Dolah* and *Holdkd* in the Sabdakalpadruma, p. 1442-6, and p. 7230 f.]

which exhibit some, though not very striking points of coincidence with the Holí.

It is clear, however, that their origin and character were not very well understood by the Romans themselves. Thus of the Lupercalia, when young men ran naked through the city, and married women placed themselves in their way to be struck by them as they passed with leather thongs, under an idea that they were to become prolific thereby, little seems to have been known, except that the festival was of foreign origin and high antiquity, and that it was referable to the rustic sports of the shepherds and cowherds, the Gopas of Arcadia. Again, of the Festum Stultorum, the accounts are meagre and by no means satisfactory. The Matronalia Festa, on the Kalends of March, were more intelligible, and had for their object the increase of progeny, in harmony with the foliation of the trees, the budding of the grass, the pairing of birds, which were the effects of the season of Spring, and which are equally held in view in the celebration of the Holí, which is considered to be especially promotive of the multiplication of offspring, and preservative of the health and life of children. Another festival of the period, held on the fifteenth of March, is very imperfectly described, and still more imperfectly explained, the worship of the goddess Anna Perenna; a goddess identified with Themis, with Io, with Atlantis, with Luna, or with Anna, the sister of Dido*. This was

---

* [L. Preller, Römische Mythologie. Berlin: 1858, p. 304 ff.]

celebrated in the open air by country people with rustic sports, as drinking, singing, and dancing; and a remarkable and unaccountable part of the celebration was the use of ancient or vulgar jokes and obscene language, *joci veteres obscænaque dicta canuntur.* Finally, on the sixteenth of the Kalends of April, or the seventeenth March, occurred the Liberalia, or Festival of Bacchus, of whom, in this place, Ovid makes a singular remark, possibly embodying an ancient tradition, that burnt-offerings and oblations originated with Bacchus after his conquest of India and the East.

> Ante tuos ortus aræ sine honore fuere,
>   Liber, et in gelidis herba reperta focis.
> Te memorant Ganga, totoque oriente subacto,
>   Primitias magno seposuisse Jovi.—*Fasti* III, 727-30.

The character of these festival days in the Roman Calendar, and the period during which they took place, suggest probable analogies to the practices of the Hindus at the same season. The analogies are, it is true, very general and unprecise, but to use the words of Brand, "in joining the scattered fragments that survive the mutilation of ancient customs, we must be forgiven if all the parts are not found closely to agree. Little of the means of information have been transmitted to us, and that little can only be eked out by conjecture." Nothing can be more meagre than the Fasti of Ovid in respect to the celebrations above adverted to, and it is obvious that some of them, at least, had become obsolete, even in his day, and that he knew little concerning their origin, or their mode of observance[1]; yet little doubt can be entertained that their influence is traceable in practices which are to be found about this time of the year in several of the nations of Europe, particularly in the Carnival and in the day of All Fools.

The Carnival is derived, according to Moresin, from the times of Gentilism, and he quotes Joannes Boemus Aubanus for an account of the extravagancies and indecencies with which it was formerly observed in Germany, that identify its affinity to the Lupercal on the one hand, and, as we should say, the Holi on the other. On the three days preceding Lent he observes[2],

---

[1] That this was by no means singular is plain, from the admission of Macrobius, which he puts into the mouths of two of his interlocutors, Horus and Vettius.— I Saturn. cap. XV.

[2] Quo item modo tres præcedentes quadragesimale jejunium dies peragat, dicere opus non erit, si cognoscatur qua populari qua spontanea insania cætera Germania, a qua et Franconia minime desciscit, vivat, comedit enim et bibit, æque ludo jocoque omnimodo adeo dedit, quasi usus nunquam veniant, quasi cras moritura hodie prius omnium rerum satietatem capere velit; atque ne pudor obstet qui se ludicro illi committunt, facies larvis obducunt, sexum et ætatem mentientes, viri mulierum vestimenta, mulieres virorum induunt. Quidam Satyros aut malos demones potius repræsentare volentes, minio se aut atramento tingunt; habituque nefando deturpant; alii nudi discurrentes Lupercos agunt, a quibus ego unnuum istum delirandi morem ad nos defluxisse existimo.

Naogeorgus, in his description, has a variety of passages as applicable to the Holi as the Carnival:—

Then old and young are both as much as guests of Bacchus' feast; And four days long they tipple, square, and feede, and never rest.

"the whole of Germany eats and drinks and gives itself up to jokes and sports, as if there was not another day to live, and people wear disguises and masks, or stain their faces and vestures with red and black paint, or run about naked like the Luperci, from whom, I think, this annual exhibition of insanity has descended to us."

The practices of the Carnival, as now observed in Italy, have been trimmed of their excesses, but even in them there remain vestiges which denote their community of origin with the Holi of the Hindus. The time properly embraces the whole period from the beginning of the year[1], but as in the festival of Phálguna, the last few days are those on which the principal demonstrations take place, and in the licence which is permitted both in speech and conduct, the wearing of masks and disguises, the reciprocal pelting

—————— feare and shame away;
The tongue is set at libertie, and hath no kind of stay.
All thinges are lawfull then and done, no pleasure passed by,
That in their mindes they can devise, as if they then should die.

He also speaks of the nudity of some of the revellers, an indecency of which even the Holi players are never guilty:—

Some naked runne about the streetes, their faces hid alone
With visars close, that so disguised they may of none be knowne,

and of the insults to which decent people were subjected,—

No matrone olde, nor sober man can freely by them come.

[Brand's Pop. Ant., 1, 64 ff.]

[1] According to Spalding, the Carnival is supposed to begin from New Year's Day. Matthews says it lasts eight days, with intervals, before Lent.

with real or with mock comfits, and in some places sprinkling with water or throwing powder over each other, obvious analogies exist[1].

There is another practice which presents also a parallel, the extinguishing of the Carnival. This, in Italy, is refined into frolicsome attempts to blow out each other's lighted candles; but the notion appears to be the same as the burning of the Holī, the lighting and extinction of the bonfire, and scattering of the ashes.

There is another of the usages of the Holī which finds a parallel in modern times, although at a somewhat later period. It is mentioned by Colonel Pearce, that one subject of diversion during the Holī, is to send people on errands and expeditions that are to end in disappointment, and raise a laugh at the expense of the person sent. He adds that, Sura-ad-daula, the Nawāb of Bengal, of Black Hole celebrity, was very fond of making Holī Fools[2]. The identity of this practice with making April Fools as noticed by Colonel Pearce, is concurred in by Maurice, who remarks, "that the boundless hilarity and jocund sports, prevalent on the 1st day of April in England,

---

[1] Amongst the Portuguese the practices are these: "on the Sunday and Monday preceding Lent, as on the first of April in England, people are privileged here (Lisbon) to play the fool. It is thought very jocose to pour water on any person who passes, or throw powder in his face, but to do both is the perfection of wit."—Southey's Letters [p. 497].

[2] Asiatic Researches, Vol. II, p. 334.

and during the Holī Festival in India, have their origin in the ancient practice of celebrating, with festival rites, the period of the vernal equinox, when the new year of Persia anciently began."

There was a Festum Stultorum about this period amongst the Romans, the purport of which is not very clearly expressed, but some antiquaries have supposed that it constituted the original of the festivals of the Romish Church, the Festa Stultorum, Innocentium, and the like, the extravagances of the Abbot of Unreason, and the sleeveless errands of All Fools, or April Fool day. The periods at which these rude and boisterous manifestations of merriment took place were something different; but, as Brand observes, the crowded state of the Romish Calendar often led to the alteration of the days set apart for festivity, and in the case of the feast of Old or All Fools he quotes authority for its removal to the first of November from some other date, it being expressly stated in the calendar, Festum Stultorum veterum huc translatum est. The period, therefore, is little material — the identity of designation, and similarity of practice render it not unlikely that the day of All Fools had originally something in common with the Festum Stultorum and with the Holī*.

---

* [See Brand's Popular Antiquities (Bohn), I, 63-102. 131-41. Still more striking coincidences between the Holī and the other above-mentioned festivals and customs will be found in the following books: Fest-Kalender aus Böhmen. Wien und Prag: 1861,

BÚRWA MANGAL.—On the first Tuesday* after the Holí, a supplementary repetition of it is held at Benares, with sundry modifications of a not uninteresting description. An account of the festival has been given by the late Mr. J. Prinsep, in his valuable views of Benares, and I had also an opportunity of witnessing its observance. During the day the people go in crowds to a place called Durgá kuńda, a large tank

---

pp. 56-64. 162-8. Calendrier Belge. Bruxelles: 1861, pp. 116-32. 203-6. Nork, Fest-Kalender. Stuttgart: 1847, p. 261-6. 791-828. J. Grimm, deutsche Mythologie (2nd ed.), p. 724-34. Montanus, die deutschen Volksfeste. Iserlohn und Elberfeld: 1854, I, 20-28. Wolf, Beiträge zur deutschen Mythologie. Göttingen: 1852, p. 78. Wolf's Zeitschrift für deutsche Mythologie. Göttingen: 1853, I, 89. W. Müller, Geschichte der altdeutschen Religion. Göttingen: 1844, p. 135 f. Simrock, deutsche Mythologie. Bonn: 1856, p. 547-60. Panzer, Beitrag zur deutschen Mythologie. München: 1855, II, 246-52. Liebrecht, Gervasius von Tilbury. Hannover: 1856, p. 173-204. Wuttke, der deutsche Volksaberglaube. Hamburg: 1860, p. 21 f. 182 ff. Rochholz, Schweizersagen aus dem Aargau. Aarau: 1856, II, 190. 196. Rochholz, Allemannisches Kinderlied. Leipzig: 1857, p. 505 f. Vernaleken, Alpensagen. Wien: 1858, p. 350 ff. and Mythen und Bräuche des Volks in Oesterreich. Wien: 1859, p. 293 ff. Zingerle, Sitten und Bräuche des Tiroler Volkes. Innsbruck: 1857, p. 88-91. Kuhn und Schwartz, Norddeutsche Sagen. Leipzig: 1848, p. 369 ff. Kuhn, Märkische Sagen. Berlin: 1843, p. 307-11, and Sagen aus Westfalen. Leipzig: 1859, II, 124-31. Schmitz, Sitten und Sagen des Eifler Volkes. Trier: 1856, I, 13-22. Meier, deutsche Sagen aus Schwaben. Stuttgart: 1852, p. 371-80. 395 f. Lynker, deutsche Sagen und Sitten. Cassel: 1860, p. 236 f. von Hahn, Albanesische Studien. Jena: 1854, pp. 156. 200.]

* [Hence its name *mangal*. See also Price's Hindee and Hindoostanee Selections, I, 277, l. 4-6.]

and temple dedicated to Durgá, who is worshipped on this occasion. Although there are no regular processions, yet horses and elephants, gaily caparisoned, are plentifully scattered amongst the throng, and the garden walls along the road are crowded with spectators. Strolling actors, disguised as religious mendicants, or as individuals of inferior caste, both male and female, mingle with the crowd, and divert them with singing and dancing and absurd buffoonery. Sometimes different parties oppose each other in a contest of poetical improvisation. In the evening, the more opulent inhabitants of Benares embark on board boats fitted up for the occasion with platforms and awnings, and parade up and down the river throughout the night, having with them bands of musicians, and singers, and dancing girls. When the evening is advanced, the pinnace of the Rájá of Benares moves from his residence at Rámnagar, and slowly descends the stream, followed by other boats, lighted up, and displaying fireworks from time to time, until they take their station off one of the principal gháts. The boats on the river are also illuminated, and are rowed up and down the stream, accompanied by numerous lesser craft selling refreshments, or bearing less wealthy amateurs to catch the strains of some popular songstress. The shore is thronged with people, and discharges of fireworks, with the river pageantry, amuse them until the end of the night. At day-break they are again clustered along the magnificent gháts of Benares, and by their numbers, their order, their diversified and many-tinted costumes, in harmony with the elegant architecture of the surrounding edifices, the broad river, and the unclouded sky, present a picture of singular richness, gracefulness, animation, and beauty.

Upon the occasion on which I witnessed this festival, the Rájá, on the morning, received the visits of the Governor-General's agent, Mr. Brooke, and other European gentlemen of the station. They were entertained as usual with náching, but upon taking leave, in addition to the ordinary aspersion of rose-water, which was bestowed so copiously as to amount to a ducking, the guests were pelted with rose-leaves, immense trays of which were brought in for the purpose. The attack was retaliated by a shower of the same missiles, which have at least the character of greater refinement than the confitti di gesso, the plaster of Paris pellets of the Carnival.

According to Mr. Prinsep, the ceremony originated with Zemíndár Balwant Sing, the father of Rájá Chait Sing, who adopted the celebration of the Holí on the river, for the gratification of Mír Rustam Alí, the Mohammedan Governor of the province, who had a house on the river-side. As he observes, however, the name Búrwa, old, indicates higher antiquity.

V.

ON
HUMAN SACRIFICES
IN THE
ANCIENT RELIGION OF INDIA.

From the Journal of the R. Asiatic Society, Vol. VIII (1852), p. 96—107.

I PROPOSE to offer to the Society some illustrations of the sacrifice of human beings as an element of the ancient religion of India.

In the first book of the Rámáyaṅa[*] a curious legend is narrated of the son of the Rishi Richíka, named Sunaḥśepha, who was sold by his father for a hundred thousand cows to Ambarísha, the king of Ayodhyá, to supply the place of a sacrificial animal or victim[1]

---

[*] [c. 61 f. Schlegel, c. 63 f. Gorresio. Comp. also Muir's Sanskrit Texts, I, 104 ff.]

[1] Schlegel's reading is *yajna-paśu*, which he renders simply by *victima*. Gorresio's text is more explicit: in the first place the victim is carried off from the post whilst the king is engaged, *nara-medhena*, "intanto ch'egli offriva un sacrifixio umano;" and in the next it is said, in a rather questionable hemistich, however, that the theft was a man endowed with all lucky marks, appointed to be a victim, *naraṁ lakshaṇa-sampūrṇam paśutwe niyo-*

intended for a sacrifice, but stolen by Indra. Śunahśepha is accordingly conveyed to the place of sacrifice, and being dressed in red garments and decorated with garlands of red flowers, is bound to the stake. By the advice of Viśwámitra he prays to Indra and Agni with two sacred verses (gáthás, according to Schlegel's edition; richas, in Gorresio's) communicated to him by the Rishi, and Indra bestows upon him long life, whilst at the same time the king is not disappointed of his reward. This version of the legend leaves it doubtful whether an actual sacrifice of the victim, or one only typical, is intended.

The reference made in the Rámáyańa to the *sacred verses* by which Śunahśepha propitiated Indra, might lead us to expect some account of the transaction in the text of the Veda; and accordingly, in the first Ashtaka of the *Rig-veda* the sixth section contains a series of seven hymns, attributed to Śunahśepha, who addresses different divinities in succession. The object of his prayers is not, however, very decidedly pronounced, and in many respects they resemble those of any other worshipper soliciting food, wealth, cattle, and long life; and although liberation from bonds is asked for, yet the text itself intimates that these are only figurative, being the fetters of sin. Neither does it appear that any of the deities called upon to rescue

---

jitam. Schlegel's edition also has a passage to the same purport, that the stolen victim is to be recovered, or a man substituted in its place, and virtually, therefore, the two editions agree, although not exactly in words.

him from any situation of personal peril, and the recompense of his praises is the gift of a golden chariot by Indra, a present rather incompatible with his position as an intended victim. Hence the late Dr. Rosen was led to infer that the Vaidik hymn, except in one or two doubtful passages, bore no relation to the legend of the Rámáyaña, and offered no indication of a human victim deprecating death.—"In nullo autem horum carminum (si initium hymni quatuor-vigentesimi excipias, quod sane ita intelligi potest) ne levissimum quidem indicium hominis in vitæ discrimen vocati et mortem deprecantis*."

Whatever may be the conclusions to be drawn from the legend of Śunahśephas as it appears in the Rámáyaña or in the Ṛig-veda, there is no question of its purport as it is found in the Aitareya Bráhmaña which is considered to be the Bráhmaña portion of the Ṛigveda; and as the story as there told is characteristic of the style of that and similar works, the precise nature of which is yet but little known, none having been translated or printed, and as several curious circumstances are comprised in the tradition, it will not perhaps be uninteresting to have the story as it is there narrated**.

---

* [Rigveda, ed. Rosen. Adnotationes p. LV.]

** [Aitar. Br. VII, 13-18. Translated also by R. Roth, in A. Weber's "Indische Studien", I, 458-64 (his further remarks Ib. II, 112-23), and M. Müller, in his History of Ancient Sanskrit Literature, 408-19; the original Sanskrit text ib. p. 573-88.]

Harischandra, the son of Vedhas, was a prince of the race of Ikshwáku: he had a hundred wives, but no son. On one occasion the two sages, Nárada and Parvata were residing in his palace; and he said one day to Nárada, "Tell me, why do all creatures, whether possessed of intelligence or devoid of it, desire male progeny? What benefit is derived from a son?" Nárada thus replied: "A father who beholds the face of a living son discharges his debt [to his forefathers], and obtains immortality. Whatever benefits accrue to living beings upon earth, in fire, or in water, a father finds still more in his son. A father, by the birth of a son, traverses the great darkness [of both worlds]. He is born as it were of himself, and the son is a well freighted boat to bear him across [the ocean of misery]. What matter the impurity [of childhood], the skin [of the student], the beard [of the householder], the penance [of the hermit]. Wish, Brahmans, for a son, for he is a world without reproach. Food, vital air, vesture, dwelling, gold, beauty, cattle, wedlock, a friend, a wife, a daughter, are all contemptible: a son is the light [that elevates his father] to the highest heaven. The husband is himself conceived by his wife, who becomes as it were his mother, and by her in the tenth month he is newly born; therefore is a wife termed genitrix (jáyá), for of her is a man born again (jáyate). Gods and Rishis implant in her great lustre, and the Gods say to men, this is your parent. There is no world for one without a son. This even know the beasts of the field, and to beget offspring pair indiscriminately with their kind. [A son] is the much-commended certain path to happiness, by which all [rational] beings having male progeny travel; and birds and beasts are conscious of the same."

Having repeated verses to this effect, Nárada advised Hariśchandra to pray to Varuña for a son, promising to present him as an offering to that divinity. "So be it," said the prince; and repairing to Varuña he said: "Let a son be born unto me, and with him, I will sacrifice to you."—"So be it," said Varuña, and a son was born to the king, who was named Rohita. "A son has been born to you," said Varuña, "sacrifice with him to me."—"An animal," replied the king, "is fit for sacrifice only after ten days from birth. When the term of purification shall have passed, I will sacrifice to you."—"Very well," said Varuña. The ten days expired, and Varuña said, "Now sacrifice with him to me." The king replied, "An animal is fit for sacrifice only when the teeth are cut; let the teeth come through, and then I will sacrifice to you." Varuña consented: the teeth were cut: "and now," said Varuña, "sacrifice with him to me."—"No," replied the king, "an animal is fit for sacrifice only when the first teeth are shed: let the teeth be shed, and then I will sacrifice to you."—"So be it," said Varuña.

Well, the teeth were shed; "And now," said Varuña, "sacrifice with him to me."—"No," objected the king; "an animal is fit for sacrifice only when his [second] set of teeth are through; wait till then, and I will perform the sacrifice." Varuńa assented. The second teeth were cut. "Now," said Varuńa, "his teeth are produced; sacrifice with him to me."—"No," replied the king, "for a Kshatriya is not fit for sacrifice until he has been invested with arms: let him receive his martial investiture, then I will sacrifice to you."—"So be it," said Varuńa. The youth grew, and was invested with arms; and Varuńa said, "now sacrifice to me with him." The king replied, "Be it so." But he called his son, and said, "My child, Varuńa gave you to me, and I have also promised to sacrifice with you to him."—"By no means," said the youth; and taking his bow, he set off to the forest, where he wandered for a twelvemonth.

Upon Rohita's disappearance Varuńa afflicted the descendant of Ikshwáku with dropsy; which when Rohita heard he set off to return home. On the way he was met by Indra in the shape of a Brahman, who said to him, "We have heard, Rohita, that prosperity attends him who undergoes great labour, and that a man, although excellent, is held in disesteem if he tarries amongst his kin. Indra is the friend of the wanderer, therefore do thou wander on—wander on." Thus spake the Brahman; and Rohita passed a second year in the woods.

At the end of that period he turned towards home, but Indra, as a mortal, again met him, and said, "The feet of the traveller bear flowers, his body grows and puts forth fruit. All his sins are effaced by the fatigue he incurs in travelling a good road¹, and they fall asleep. Wander on, therefore—wander on." So said the Brahman; and Rohita spent another year in the woods.

At the end of the third year the prince resumed his journey homewards. He was met as before by Indra in a human form, who said to him, "The prosperity of a man who sits down inactive sits also still. It rises up when he rises, it slumbers when he sleeps, and moves when he moves. Wander on, therefore—persist—wander on;" and Rohita remained a fourth year in the forests.

At the end of the fourth year, Rohita was again stopped by Indra, who said, "The sleeper is the Kali age; the awaker is the Dwápara; the riser is the Tretá, but the mover is the Kŕita age*. Wander on, therefore—wander on;" and Rohita tarried a fifth year in the woods.

At the close of the fifth year he was returning home, but as before Indra encountered him, and said, "The wanderer finds honey—the wanderer finds the sweet fig-tree. Behold the glory of the Sun, who, ever-moving, never reposes. Wander on, therefore—wander on." So Rohita returned for the sixth year to the forests.

Whilst wandering thus in the woods he encountered the Ŕishi Ajígartta, the son of Suyavasa, who was

---

¹ भयद्. The commentary says, "in going to tírthas," &c.

* [Weber's Ind. Stud. I, 286.]

distressed through want of food. He had three sons, Sunaḥpuchchha, Sunaḥsepha, and Sunolángúla. Rohita said to him, "Rishi, I will give thee a hundred cows for one of these thy sons, that by him I may redeem myself." But the Rishi, taking hold of the eldest, said, "Not this one;" "No, nor this one," said the mother, securing the youngest; but they both agreed to sell the middle son Sunaḥsepha, and Rohita having paid the hundred cows, took the youth and departed from the woods. He proceeded to his father and said, "Rejoice, father, for with this youth shall I redeem myself." So Hariśchandra had recourse to the royal Varuṅa, and said, "With this youth will I sacrifice to you." And Varuṅa replied, "Be it so—a Brahman is better than a Kshatriya;" and thence directed the king to perform the sacrificial ceremony termed the Rájasúya; and he, on the day of initiation, appointed Sunaḥsepha to be the human victim.

At that sacrifice of Hariśchandra, Viśwámitra was the Hotṛi or reciter of the Rich; Jamadagni the Adhwaryu or repeater of the Yajush; Vaśishṭha the Brahmá or superintending priest, and Ayásya the Udgátṛi or chaunter of the Sáma; but they had no one who was competent to perform the office of binding the victim, when consecrated, to the stake, whereupon Ajígartta said, "If you give me another hundred cows I will perform the duty;" and they gave him the cows, and he bound the victim. But for the victim thus consecrated and bound, sanctified by the divinities of sacrifice, and thrice circumambulated by the priests bearing burning brands of sacred grass, no immolator could be found [amongst the ministrant Brahmans], when Ajígartta again offered himself, saying, "Give me another hundred cows, and I will immolate him;" accordingly they gave him the cows, and he went forth to sharpen his knife[1]. In this interval Śunahśepha reflected, "These [people] will put me to death as if I were not a man[2], but an animal; my only hope is the aid of some of the gods, to whom I will have recourse." So thinking, he prayed to Prajápati, the first of the gods, with the prayer 'Kasya núnam,' &c.[*]; but Prajápati said, "Agni is the nearest of the gods, appeal to him." He did so, saying, 'Agner vayam[**]:' on which Agni said to him, "Savitri is the lord of all the protecting powers, pray to him;" so Śunahśepha repeated 'Abhi twá deva[***].' Savitri said, "You are dedicated to the royal Varuńa, appeal to him," which Śunahśepha did in the thirty-one following stanzas, beginning 'Na hi te kshatram[†].' Varuńa said "Agni is the mouth of the gods, and most friendly [to man], praise him, and we will set you free," which Śunahśepha did in twenty-two stanzas[‡],

---

[1] Or sword, "asim nisádndy rydya."

[2] Or, "as if I were not a man;" for according to the Veda, in the case of a man, after circumambulating, they let him go, and substitute a goat.

[*] [Rig-V. 1, h. 24, 1.]　　[**] [ib. 2.]　　[***] [ib. 3.]

[†] [h. 24, 6-15 and h. 25.]

[‡] We have twenty-three in the text; the last is to be omitted, as not addressed to Agni.

beginning 'Vasishthá hi*.' Agni said, "Praise the Viśwadevas, and then we will liberate you;" so Sunahśepha praised them, saying, 'Namo mahadbhyah,' &c.**; but the Viśwadevas said, "Indra is the mightiest of the gods, the most excellent, and the most able to lead men to happiness; worship him, and we will loose you;" so Sunahśepha praised Indra with the hymn beginning 'Yach-chid-dhi satya somapá***;' and Indra, being pleased by this prayer, gave him a golden chariot[1]. He nevertheless recommended him to propitiate the Aświns; he did so, and they desired him to praise Ushas, or the personified dawn, which he did in three concluding stanzas, on repeating which his bonds fell off, and he was set free; and the king, the father of Rohita, was cured of his complaint.

Then the priests said to him, "Perform the completion of this our rite to-day;" on which he showed to them the [mode of] offering the libation of the Soma juice, accompanying it by four stanzas, beginning 'Yach-chid-dhi†;' then having brought the pitcher (droṅa kalaśa), he directed the remainder to be poured into it, with the stanza 'Uchchhishṭam chambor††;'

---

* [h. 26 and 27, 1–12.]

** [h. 27, 13. See also Muir's Sanskrit Texts II, 195 f.]

*** [h. 29.]

[1] It is said, "in his mind;" perhaps meaning that he purposed to give it to him.

† [h. 29, 1–4.] †† [h. 28, 9.]

and then with the swáhá, preceded by four stanzas*, made the oblation, concluding with an offering to fire[1].

When the rite was completed, Sunahśepha placed himself by the side of Viswámitra, to whom Ajígartta the son of Suyavasa said, "Give me my son;" but Viswámitra answered, "No, the gods have given him to me." Hence he was called Devaráta[2] (the God-given), the son of Viswámitra, from whom descended the Kápileyas and Bábhravas. Ajígartta then appealed to Sunahśepha, and said, "My son, your mother and I entreat your return;" and finding him silent, continued, "you are by birth the son of Ajígartta of the race of the Angirasas, learned and renowned; do not separate from your great grandsire's descendants, but come back to me." To which Sunahśepha answered, "All present saw you with the implement of immolation in your hand[3]: such a sight was never beheld even amongst Śúdras. Descendant of Angiras, you have preferred three hundred cows to me." Then said Ajígartta, "My child, the wicked act that I have committed afflicts me sorely. I repent me of it. Let the three hundred cows be thine." Sunahśepha an-

---

* [h. 28, 1–4.]

[1] This is obscure, being little else than the text; but it relates to a particular ceremony called the "Anjas Sava" (Sava Abhisava rijju-márgeṇa), "the rightway oblation."

[2] Theodotus, Deodatus.

[3] *Sása-hastam sarve api adriśuh*. *Sása* is explained by *ciśana-hetuś*, the cause or implement of immolating, or *khadga*, a sword.

17

swered, "He who has once done a wicked deed will be liable to repeat it. Thou canst never be free from the disposition of the vile [Śúdras]. Thou hast done what is unpardonable."—"Unpardonable!" repeated Viswámitra, and said, "Dreadful appeared the son of Suyavasa, armed with a weapon, intending to slay. Let not his son be his, but become a son of mine." But then said Śunahśepha to Viswámitra, "Son of a king, explain to me how this may be, that I, of the race of Angiras, can be in the relation of a son to thee?" Viśwámitra answered, "Thou shalt be the eldest of my own, and an excellent progeny shall be thine. Thou comest to me as the gift of the gods, and therefore I welcome thee."—"But," said Sunah-sepha, "who will assure me, best of the Bháratas, of the concurrence of these [thy sons] for my affiliation and seniority if I become thy son?" Thereupon Viswámitra called his sons together and said, "Madhu-chhandas, Rishabha, Reńu, Ashtaka, and all the rest of the brethren, listen to my commands, and dispute not the seniority of Śunahśepha." Now Viśwámitra had a hundred and one sons, fifty of whom were senior and fifty junior to Madhuchhandas. The seniors did not approve of the adoption, and Viśwámitra cursed them and said, "Your progeny shall be degraded;" and consequently their descendants were the Andhras, Puńdras, Sabaras, Pulindas, and Mútivas. Thus there are numerous degraded races sprung from Viśwámitra, forming the greater portion of the barbarous tribes [Dasyus]. On the other hand, Madhuchhandas and the fifty who were his juniors said, "We accede to whatever our father considers right. We all give thee, Śunahśepha, precedence, and acknowledge ourselves to be subordinate to thee." Viśwámitra, therefore, much pleased with them, said, "Your sons shall be affluent in cattle and possessed of offspring."

The latter circumstances told by the *Aitareya Bráhmana* of the descent of barbarous tribes from the sons of Viśwámitra, although suggestive of inquiry, are foreign to our present purpose, and need not be further noticed. The main purport of the quotation, the actual sacrifice of a human victim, is fully established, at least at the period of the compilation of the Bráhmaṅa: how far that expresses the practice of the Veda period may admit of question.

It is the received opinion of Hindu writers that the Bráhmañas are an integral part of the Veda. Thus Sáyaña, the great scholiast on the Vedas, in the introductory discussion on these writings prefixed to his explanation of the text of the Rich, observes upon the authority of Ápastamba, "Veda is the denomination of the Mantras and the Bráhmañas*." By the Mantras are meant the hymns and prayers; and the Bráhmañas, say the Mímánsakas, are intended to elucidate and, as it were, individualize the objects which are only generally adverted to in the hymns, as where it is said in the Súkta, or hymn, "give abundantly," the Bráhmaña explains it, "give or offer

---

* [Ṛig-V. ed. M. Müller, I, p. 4.]

clarified butter in abundance." The same authorities declare that the Veda consists of two parts, Mantra and Bráhmaṇa; and that the only unexceptionable definition which can be given of the latter is, that all that portion of the Veda which is not Mantra is Bráhmaṇa[*]. In exact conformity to these original authorities is the following statement of Mr. Colebrooke. "Each Veda consists of two parts, denominated the Mantras and the Bráhmaṇas, or prayers and precepts. The complete collection of the hymns, prayers, and invocations belonging to one Veda is entitled its Saṇhitá. Every other portion of Indian Scripture is included under the general head of divinity—Bráhmaṇa. This comprises precepts which inculcate religious duties, maxims which explain those precepts, and arguments which relate to theology[**]." To these may be added narratives which illustrate precepts and practices, or explain incidents connected with the origin or objects of the Mantras, such as that of Sunaḥsepha, which has been cited.

Notwithstanding the concurrence of these authorities and the generally prevalent opinion of the Hindus, it requires but a cursory inspection of such a work as the Aitareya Bráhmaṇa to deny the accuracy of the attribution. This Bráhmaṇa is not an integral part of the Ṛig-veda, and never could have been so. It is a work of a totally different era, and a totally different

---

[*] [ib. p. 22. History of Ancient Sanskrit Lit. 342 ff.]

[**] [Essays, p. 7. Weber, Ind. Stud., I, 3. 14. Mánava-kalpa-sútra, ed. Th. Goldstücker, Introduction, p. 70 ff.]

system, and if, as is likely it may be, it is to be received as a type of other similar compilations, conforming as it does accurately enough to the general description, we shall be authorized to draw the same inference with respect to all, and to separate the Bráhmaṇas from the Hindu religion as it appears in the Sanhitás, or collections of the prayers and hymns.

The Aitareya Bráhmaṇa, as will have been observed in the translation of the legend of Sunahśepha, refers to the hymns or Súktas of the Sanhitá, specifying the number of verses in which he was fabled to have addressed the gods, agreeably to their order and place in the Sanhitá. Again, in stating that he taught to the priests the manner of offering libations, it quotes the leading phrases of different Súktas which are to be found in different and distant portions of the Sanhitá. This, it may be observed, is in strict agreement with the general arrangement of the Bráhmaṇas: directions are given for the performance of various religious rites, and the hymns, or portions of the hymns which are to be repeated on such occasions, are quoted in the same manner, merely by a few initial phrases, and taken from separate and unconnected parts of the Sanhitá, very commonly having little relation to the actual ceremony.

Now the fact, and still more, the manner of quoting the texts of the Sanhitá, necessarily lead to the conclusion, that the Sanhitá must have existed in its present form before the compilation of the Bráhmaṇa was undertaken, and as it must have been widely current and familiarly known, or the citation of broken and isolated texts could neither have been adopted nor verifiable, it must have assumed its actual arrangement long anterior to the compilation of the Bráhmaṇas. But the Sanhitá itself is of a date long subsequent to its component parts. There is no doubt of the accuracy of the tradition that the hymns of the Vedas had long been current as single and unconnected compositions, preserved in families or schools by oral communication, probably for centuries; and that they were finally collected and arranged as we now have them, by a school or schools of learned Brahmans, of which Vyása (possibly an abstraction, as it means merely an arranger) was the nominal head. Allowing, therefore, a considerable period before the Sanhitás were collected into form, and another interval before they could be familiarly referred to, it follows that the Bráhmaṇas cannot be an integral part of the Veda, understanding thereby the expression of the primitive notions of the Hindus, and that they are not entitled to be classed as authorities for the oldest and most genuine system of Hindu worship.

In fact, in the Bráhmaṇas we find fully developed the whole Brahmanical system, of much of which we have but faint and questionable indications in the Mantras. We have the whole body of both religious and social institutions—a variety of practices alluded to of a more complicated texture than the apparently simple ritual of the Sanhitá; and the complete recognition both in name and practice of the different castes, the Brahman, the Kshatriya, the Vaisya, and the Sûdra: we have also the Brahmans distinguished as differing among themselves in tribe and dignity, and sometimes engaged in disputes for precedence and the exclusive performance of particular rites, all which it may be observed is incontrovertible proof that a very long interval had elapsed between the composition of the Súktas and the Bráhmanas — between the first dawn and the noon-day culmination of the Brahmanical system.

Having come to the conclusion then that the Bráhmanas are not an integral part of the primitive Veda or Hindu system, but admitting that they may be considered as an essential part of the Veda of the Brahmans, or as a scriptural authority for the Brahmanical forms of worship, and for their social institutions when fully developed, we have next to consider the period to which they may belong, and how far they may be regarded as authentic representations of an ancient (though not the most ancient) religious and social system in India. This, as usual with all Hindu chronology, is a difficult question: certainty is unattainable, but we may come to probable conclusions within reasonable limits from internal evidence. The Bráhmanas are posterior to the discontinuance of exclusively oral teaching; they could not cite miscellaneous and unconnected texts to the extent to which they cite them, unless those texts had been accessible in a written shape. They are subsequent therefore to the use of writing, to which the hymns or Mantras were in great part, if not wholly, anterior. They are prior in all probability to the heroic poems, the Rámáyana and Mahábhárata, as we have no allusions to the demigods and heroes whom they celebrate; no allusion to Kṛishṇa and Ráma, although the latter name occurs as that of a Brahman, the son or a descendant of Bhṛigu, which has nothing to do with Ráma, the son of king Daśaratha, any more than the name of Kṛishṇa, which occurs in the Sanhitá as the name of an Asura, implies any allusion to the Kṛishṇa of the Mahábhárata. There is no reference to any controversial opposition to the doctrines, or rites of Brahmanical Hinduism, although differences of opinion as to the purport of the performance of some ceremonies are adverted to, and so far therefore, we have no reference to Buddhism. Again, the Aitareya Bráhmaṇa is prior to the Sútras, or rules for conducting religious rites, ascribed to Áswaláyana, Baudháyana, and others who are undoubtedly authors of a remote period. It is, perhaps, not far from the period of the oldest passages in the laws of Manu, in some of which * we find allusions to the narratives of the Bráhmaṇa, as in the case of Śunaḥśepha, and also of a prince named Paijavana, who is not named in later works. In the etymology also of the term *jáyá*, a wife, as one in whom a man is born again in the person of a son, we have the very same words[1]. The

---

* [VII. 41 f. X, 105 ff. Mahábh. XII, 2304, quoted by Weber, Ind. Stud., II, 134.]

[1] Manu, b. IX, v. 8.

Brâhmaña may be the earlier of the two, but not by any very great interval. Finally, the style, although more modern than that of the Veda, is ancient and obscure, and contains many words and phrases of Vaidik antiquity. Upon the whole, as a mere matter of conjecture, subject to reconsideration, I should be disposed to place the Aitareya Brâhmaña about six or seven centuries before the Christian era.

So far, therefore, it may be received as authority to a qualified extent for the primitive practices of the Hindus, and for including amongst them the sacrifice, on particular occasions, of human victims. Not that the practice ever prevailed to the extent to which it spread through most of the ancient nations, or partook in general of the same character. These, it has been asserted, were entirely of an expiatory nature, performed under an impression of fear, and intended to deprecate the anger of the Gods. Such were the sacrifices of the Druids, the Scythians, and the Phœnicians; and such were the Thargelia of the Athenians, when a man and woman were annually put to death in order to expiate the sins of the public, and redeem them from any national calamity. They were not, however, restricted to this source, but were not unfrequently vindictive, as when prisoners taken in war were sacrificed, like the three hundred citizens of Perusia whom Augustus offered in one day to his deified uncle (Divo Julio); or as the Grecian navigators whom the barbarians of Tauris sacrificed to Artemis whenever cast upon their shores. They had their origin also in notions of divination, as was the case in the worship of Mithra, when auguries were taken from the entrails of human victims[*]; and they seem in some instances to have been suggested by a purely sanguinary spirit, as was the case with the perpetually recurring sacrifices to Baal and Moloch in the Phœnician Colonies, and especially in Carthage[1]. No intimations of any such purposes are traceable in the indistinct allusions to human sacrifices in the Veda. Their object seems to have been the propitiation of some divinity, by devoting to him that which was most precious to the sacrificer. This feeling seems also to have been very widely diffused throughout the East in the most ancient times, as was the practice of the individual of pledging himself to the act by a solemn promise or vow. We might infer that the practice was not unknown to the patriarchal era, from the conduct of Abraham when commanded to offer up his son; for although he would not under any circumstances have hesitated to obey the divine command, yet he might, consistently with his obedience, have expressed some surprise at the injunction, had the purport of it been wholly unfamiliar. At a later date in the Jewish history we have a similar sort of sacrifice under a solemn previous engagement in the vow of Jephtha; and it is worthy of remark that one of

---

[*] [Windischmann, Mithra. Leipzig: 1857, p. 68.]

[1] See Bryant's Chapter on Anthropothusia and Teknothusia, Vol. VI, p. 296.

the causes assigned by the Greek writers to the detention of the fleet at Aulis, and consequent sacrifice of Iphigenia, was Agamemnon's violation of the vow which he had made to offer to Diana the most lovely thing which the year in which his daughter was born should produce: Iphigenia was that thing, and the sacrifice was insisted on in satisfaction of the vow. The offering of children to Moloch, subsequently borrowed by the Jews from their idolatrous neighbours, originated probably in a similar feeling, which it is evident exercised a very extentive influence over the nations of Western Asia in remote antiquity, and, as appears from the story of Śunahśepha, was not confined to that quarter, but had reached the opposite limits of Asia at a period at least prior by ten or twelve centuries to the Christian era.

Further, we find a like community of ideas in the institution of vicarious sacrifices. In the story of Śunahśepha, one human victim is substituted for another, whilst in the parallel cases of antiquity the substitutes were animals. It is not unlikely that this was also a primitive notion of the Hindus, and at any rate it had become so by the time of the Bráhmaṇas; for Śunahśepha is made to say, "They will put me to death as if I were not a man"—that is, according to Sáyaṇa's commentary, founded upon a text of the Veda which he cites, but which is not easily verified, when the assistants had circumambulated the person bound to the stake, they set him free without any detriment, and substituted an animal (a goat) in his place. Hence Mr. Colebrooke concluded that the Purusha-medha, or sacrifice of a man, was never anything but typical; and the ceremony as enjoined in the Śatapatha Bráhmaṇa of the Yajush, on which his opinion was founded, is evidently of that character. In this, one hundred and eighty-five men of various specified tribes, characters, and professions, are bound to eleven yúpas, or posts, and after recitation of a hymn celebrating the allegorical immolation of Náráyaṇa, they are liberated unhurt, and oblations of butter are offered on the sacrificial fire[*]. Hence Mr. Colebrooke[**] concludes that human sacrifices were not authorized by the Veda itself, but were either then abrogated and an emblematical ceremony substituted in their place, or they were introduced in later times by the authors of such works as the Káliká Puráṇa, for instance, in which minute directions are given for the offering of a human victim to Kálí, whom it is said his blood satisfies for a thousand years.

That human offerings to the dark forms of Śiva[***] and Durgá were sometimes perpetrated in later times, we know from various original sources, particularly from that very effective scene in the drama of Mádhava and Málatí, in which Aghoraghaṇṭa is represented as about to sacrifice Málatí to Chámuṇḍá, when she is

---

[*] [White Yajurveda c. 30 & 31.]

[**] [Essays, p. 35.]

[***] [India three thousand years ago, by Dr. J. Wilson. Bombay: 1858, p. 68, Note.]

rescued by her lover*. No such divinities, however, neither Śiva nor Durgá, much less any of their terrific forms, are even named, so far as we know, in the Vedas, and therefore these works could not be authority for their sanguinary worship. That the practice is enjoined on particular occasions by the Tantras and some of the Puránas connected with this branch of the Hindu faith, is, no doubt, true; but these are works of a much later date, within the limits mostly of the Mohammedan government within the period of which the works were compiled, and under which their injunctions could not safely have been carried into operation; and they never amounted perhaps to more than the expression of the feeling inspired by the character of the divinities worshipped, although they may have been occasionally attempted to be realized by some fierce and fanatical enthusiasts. These practices, therefore, are of a very different character from those which there is reason to believe might have actually taken place, though rarely and under special circumstances, under the authority of the Veda, and which originated in a common feeling and faith diffused throughout the most civilized nations of the world—the nations of the East—in the remotest periods of antiquity.

* [Act V, p. 82 ff.]

VI.

ON THE SUPPOSED VAIDIK AUTHORITY
FOR
THE BURNING OF HINDU WIDOWS,
AND ON
THE FUNERAL CEREMONIES OF THE HINDUS.

From the Journal of the R. Asiatic Society, Vol. XVI (1854), p. 201-14.

In the lecture on the Vedas which I read during our last session I had occasion to notice some very remarkable passages in one of the Súktas, or Hymns of the Rich, relating to the disposal of the dead, and especially to the burning of widows, for which the hymn in question was always cited as authority. I stated then that the text quoted for that purpose had a totally different tendency, and that there was some reason to doubt if it was the ancient practice of the Hindus to burn their dead at all, quoting texts which seemed to enjoin burying, not burning. I added, however, that I had not had time to consider the passages with that care which they required, and that I communicated only the results of my first impressions. I have since examined the passages more deliberately, and propose now to offer to the Society the conclusions which I have deliberately formed; namely, that the text of the Ṛig Veda cited as authority for the burning of widows enjoins the very contrary, and directs them to remain in the world, and that, although the expressions relating to the disposal of the dead are somewhat equivocal, yet it seems most probable, upon a comparison with other texts and authorities, that the corpse was burned, although the ashes and bones were afterwards buried.

The Súkta or hymn affording the ground of these observations is a remarkable one: it is the second of the second Anuváka of the tenth Mańḍala, or the twenty-sixth to the twenty-eighth Varga of the sixth Adhyáya or section of the seventh Ashtaka. It is attributed to Śankuśuka, the son of Yama, of course a fabulous attribution, and is addressed, at least in the earlier verses, to Mṛityu, or Death, and in the last to the Pitṛis, the Manes or progenitors. To leave no doubt of its purport, I propose to give the following translation of the entire Súkta, as well as a transcript of the original Sanskrit.

1. Depart, Mṛityu, by a different path, by that which is thine own, different from the path of the Gods. I speak to thee who hast eyes, who hast ears. Injure not our female progeny, harm not our male.

2. Ye who approach the path of death, but are possessed of prolonged existence, ye who are entitled to reverence, prosperous with offspring and wealth, may ye be pure and sanctified.

3. May those who are living be kept distinct from the dead; may the offering we present this day to the gods be propitious. Let us go with our faces to the east, to dance and be merry; for we are in the enjoyment of prolonged life.

4. I place this circle [of stones] for the living, on this account, that no other may go beyond it. May they live a hundred years; keeping death at a distance by this heap.

5. As days follow days in succession, and seasons are succeeded by seasons, as one man follows another, so, Dhátŕi, do thou prolong the lives of these [my kinsmen].

6. Reaching to old age with still-ascending life, and following active in succession as many as may be, may Twáshtŕi, being propitiated, grant you prolonged life.

7. May these women, who are not widows, who have good husbands, who are mothers, enter with unguents and clarified butter: without tears, without sorrow, let them first go up into the dwelling.

8. Rise up, woman, come to the world of living beings, thou sleepest nigh unto the lifeless. Come; thou hast been associated with maternity through the husband by whom thy hand was formerly taken.

9. Taking his bow from the hand of the dead, that it may be to us for help, for strength, for fame, [I say] here verily art thou, and here are we: accompanied by our valiant descendants, may we overcome all arrogant adversaries.

10. Go to the mother earth, this wide-spread blessed earth; to the liberal man she is a maiden soft as wool; may she protect thee from the proximity of the evil being.

11. Lie up [lightly] earth, oppress him not, be bounteous to him, treat him kindly, cover him, earth, as a mother covers an infant with the skirts of her garment.

12. May earth lying lightly up, stay well; may thousands of particles [of soil] rest upon it; may these abodes be ever sprinkled with clarified butter, and may they, day by day, be to him an asylum.

13. I heap up the earth above thee, and placing this clod of clay, may I not hurt thee; may the Manes protect this thy monument, and Yama ever grant thee here an abode.

14. New days sustain me, as the feather upholds the shaft, but I restrain my voice now grown old, as the reins hold in a horse*.

The language of this hymn is, as usual, sometimes obscure; and may admit, if not in essentials, at least in some of the details, of a different version from the above. I have had the advantage, however, of comparing my translation of verses 7 to 13 inclusive with a translation of the same, as I shall presently mention,

---

* [This hymn was translated into German by R. Roth in the "Zeitschrift der deutschen morgenländischen Gesellschaft" Vol. VIII (1854), 467 ff. and by M. Müller ib. Vol. IX (1855), p. vi ff., both translations being accompanied by the Sanskrit text.]

by Dr. Max Müller, and except in one or two particulars of no very great importance, our versions agree. In verse 8, which has the most important bearing upon the question of Satí, there is no difference; and its meaning is confirmed by other circumstances which I shall presently notice.

In the first place, however, we must take the seventh verse, as it has been supposed to authorise the practice of the burning of the widow. It has been, no doubt correctly, thus translated by Mr. Colebrooke: "OM. Let these women, not to be widowed, good wives adorned with collyrium, holding clarified butter, consign themselves to the fire. Immortal, not childless nor husbandless, excellent; let them pass into fire, whose original element is water." From the Ṛig Veda.—As. Res. IV, p. 213[*].

Now this is evidently intended to be the same verse as the text before us, with the addition of the last clause, "whose element is water," for which we have no equivalent; the rest of the stanza may be readily compared and the variations accounted for.

Our verse has, "may these women not widows," *avidhavá*, a reading that at once overthrows the authority for cremation; as, if they are not widows, there is no necessity for their burning. A somewhat different version may be admitted, by interpreting the "words not to be widowed," although even in this case it implies the absence of the only condition upon

---

[*] [Essays, p. 71.]

which a woman's ascending the funeral pile depended; but *avidhavā* cannot be so rendered; it is present, not future. "Good wives" might be the rendering of *supatnī,* although as an epithet it would be preferably "those having good husbands." In either case the reason for burning is wanting. The collyrium or unguents, and the ghee, are much the same in both, but, in the next phrase, "consign themselves to the fire,"—the versions are widely at variance.

The text has, in the first place, merely *samviśantu,* —"let them enter," or as the commentator explains it,—"let them take their own place," *swastānam praviśantu;* in the second half we have, "let them go up," *ārohantu;* but it is not said, where to they are to go up; and here we have no doubt the origin of the error, if not a wilful alteration of the text,—the words are *ārohantu yonim agre,* literally, "let them go up into the dwelling first;" the reading to which it has been altered is, *ārohantu yonim agneh,* "let them go up to the place of the fire:" *agneh,* the genitive of *agni,* having been substituted for *agre,* locative of *agra* used adverbially: there is no doubt, however, that the latter is the correct reading, not only by the concurrence of the manuscripts, and the absence of the visarga, the sign of the genitive, but by the explanation given by the commentator Sáyaña, himself a Brahman of distinguished rank and learning, and who explains it *sarveshām prathamato griham āgachchhantu,*—"let them come home first of all;" the phrase having reference, therefore, to some procession, one possibly accompanying the corpse, and having nothing whatever to do with consigning themselves to the fire.

The succeeding verse of the hymn is confirmatory of the purport of the preceding one. It would be rather inconsistent with any intention of burning the woman to enjoin her to repair to the world of living beings, *jiva-lokam*, the sense of which is wholly unequivocal, as we have proof in the verse of the Hitopadeśa*: "acquirement of wealth, constant good health, a beloved mistress, a gentle wife, a dutiful son, and knowledge bringing emolument, are the six sources of happiness (*jiva-lokeshu*) in the world of living beings;" *jiva-lokam* must, therefore, imply an exhortation to the widow to return to her social duties, cherishing the recollection, but not sharing the death of her husband. Sáyaṅa explains the term precisely to this effect, when he interprets *jiva-loka*, *putra pautrádi*, "sons and grandsons," evidently understanding that the widow is to return to the bosom of her family.

The author of the Gṛihya sútra, Áśvaláyana, furnishes further proof of what is meant, as he specifies the person who is to address the stanza to the widow, placed on the north of her deceased husband's head, and who is to be her husband's brother, or a fellow-student, or an old servant, and who, having thus spoken to her, is to take her away. The authority of

---

* [Pr. 18. See the St. Petersburgh Dictionary s. v.]

the Sútras is little inferior to that of the Veda; and here, therefore, we have additional and incontestable proof, that the Ṛig Veda does not authorise the practice of the burning of the widow.

In order that there may be no room for cavil, I subjoin the whole of the hymn in the original, with Sáyaṇa's comment on the seventh and eighth verses; the passage from the Sútra also occurs subsequently[1].

[Devanagari verses 1–13 follow.]

278   THE FUNERAL CEREMONIES

The other prominent topic of the Sûkta, the disposal of the dead body, is of less importance, but is not without interest; it is treated of especially in the three verses succeeding those relating to the widow, and the phraseology is certainly more in favour of burying than of burning. The consigning of the deceased to the earth, and the anxiety expressed that

14. प्रतीचीने मामद्रमीचा: पर्वमिवा हृपु:
    प्रतीची अच्छा वाचमर्च रयथया चचा ।

The following is Sâyana's commentary on the seventh and eighth verses.

7. एमानारीरिति ॥ अविधवा: अव: पति: अविनतयतिका: जीवभर्तृका एतर्वं ॥ सुपत्नी: श्रोभनपतिका: एमा नारी: नार्यो जांवमेन सर्वतो ऽचमसाधमीन सर्पचा भूतेन चाह्मीचा: यत: संयिद्रंतु समुद्रान्यविद्रन्तु तथा चनमच: अनुवर्विता: यद्रह: चनमीवा: अनीवा रोयदुर्विता मानचतु:सर्वविता एतर्वं: । सुरदा: श्रोभनधमर्षिहुता: । अनच: अनवंतपाविमिति अनयो भार्बा: । ता चये सर्वेचां प्रवमत एव योनिम् युह चारेपतु चानक्षंतु । देवरादिष: प्रेतपत्रीमुढीर्च मारीच- मया अनुसकार्याद्रुत्यापयेत्सुचितं च ॥

8. उदीर्वोंति । हे मारि मृतक्ष पत्नि जीवलोकं जीवानाम् पुश्पी- वाहीनां लोकं खालम् मृतमभिजज उत्तीर्च वक्षात्स्यानादु- त्तिष्ठ । हर मती चातादिक: । मताचुल्ला मतमाक्षमेत पति उपस्मे तस्य समीपे स्तपांति तच्चात्स एहि चानच्च पश्चात् इत्थ्यमभच चाविणाएं कुर्वत: द्विविधो: अर्मस निधातु: तवास पातु: संवंभाह्चातम् एवं अनिलं आचालमभिजन संचभूत संभूतानि पुज्ञसरचिनयवनकार्यी: तद्वाह्यानच्च ॥

From the expression anusarana nichayam akârshih, "thou hast made the determination of following," it would appear as if Sâyana considered the burning as only delayed; but, besides that subsequent burning is not consistent with the presence of the corpse, we must recollect the commentator expresses only the notion of his own time, or the 14th century, when of course the practice existed.

it may lie lightly upon, and may defend, his remains, is clearly enjoined, but it is possible that it may refer only to the ashes and remaining bones after burning, the collection and formal burial of which is always directed. We have here also the analogy of other ancient people, by whom we know the dead were burned and the ashes entombed, over which a mound or monument was raised.

> Mœrentes altum cinerem et confusa ruebant,
> Ossa focis tepidoque ornabant aggere terræ.

And again:—

> At pius Æneas ingenti mole sepulcrum
> Imponit

And a common funeral inscription was:

> Sit tibi terra levis;

although nothing but the reliquiæ were to be pressed upon.

So far, therefore, it is possible, that the verses refer only to the burying of the ashes and the bones, and that the bodies were burned. There are other passages in favour of this view of the subject, whilst the Grihya Sútras are sufficiently explicit. The following directions for the burial of the dead are derived from the Sútras of Áswaláyana; and as they differ in many respects from the actual practice described by Mr. Colebrooke in the seventh volume of the Asiatic Researches[*], and are obviously of a much more ancient

---
[*] [Essays, p. 97.]

and primitive character, they may be thought to deserve publication. I have been favoured with the version by Professor M. Müller, but I have verified it by comparison with the original text: the commentary which he has used I have not had the means of consulting.

"The burial ceremonies, as observed by the Brahmans during the Vaidik period, are explained in Áśvaláyana's Gṛihya-sútras, in the fourth or last chapter*. The Gṛihya-sútras describe what might be called the domestic or family rites of the Hindus. They lay down general rules which are to be observed at marriages, at the birth of a child, on the day of naming the child, at the tonsure and investiture of a boy, &c. In fact, they describe all those essential and purificatory ceremonies which are known under the general name of "Sanskára"[1]. Although in the performance of these festive rites, allowance is made for local customs, still, according to the Brahmans, these should be followed only as long as they are not opposed to the general and more sacred rules of the Gṛihya-sútras. These general rules of the Gṛihya must be obeyed first, and the omission of any one of the ceremonies prescribed by them as "nityáni karmáṇi" or "obligatory rites", is sinful. Here lies the distinction between the Gṛihya and Śrauta-sútras.

---

* [Edited, with a German translation and notes, by M. Müller in the "Zeitschrift der deutschen morgenl. Gesellschaft", Vol. IX.]

[1] Cf. Wilson's Sanskrit Dict. s. v.

The Śrauta-sútras describe the great sacrifices (Havir-yajnás and Soma-yajnás) which can be performed by rich people only, and which therefore are obligatory only under certain restrictions. They require the assistance of a number of priests, and great preparations of all kinds. They are called "vaitánika", from "vitána", spreading, because the fire in which the oblations are to be burnt has to be spread or divided on three hearths (dakshiṅa, gárhapatya, áhavaníya). This is done at the Agnyádhána, "the placing of the fires", the first Śrauta sacrifice which a Brahman has to perform after his marriage. Although the Śrauta sacrifices are enjoined by the Śruti (the Bráhmaṅas), and the highest rewards on earth and in heaven are held out for their performance, still their non-performance is not sinful, as is that of the Gṛihya rites. Another characteristic of the domestic ceremonies is this, that the person for whose benefit they are performed is himself passive. It is only after his marriage that he becomes himself the Yajmána or sacrificer, though even then he may still be assisted by other priests in the performance of his sacrifices. A third class of rites, besides the Gṛihya and Śrauta ceremonies, are those laid down in the Sámayáchárika or Dharma sútras. They are rather observances based on secular authority than sacred rites. They detail the duties of a boy while living as Brahma-chárin or catechumen, in the house of his Guru. They determine the proper diet of a Brahman, what food may be eaten or not, what days should be kept for fasting, and what penance ought to be performed for neglect of duty. The duties and rights of kings and magistrates, civil rights, and even rules of social politeness, are determined by them in great detail. They are the principal source of the latter lawbooks[1], and are considered as sacred and indirectly revealed, because, according to the notions of the Brahmans, no law can derive its sanction except from a divine authority.

"All these Sûtras have come down to us, not as one single code, to be acknowledged as such by every Brahman, but in the form of various collections which are represented as the traditional property of some of the most prominent families or communities of India. The ceremonies described in these different collections of Sûtras, are almost identical in their general bearing. With regard to the Śrauta sacrifices, there are different collections of Sûtras for the different classes of priests, who have peculiar parts to perform at each sacrifice, and employ respectively the hymns as collected in the Rig-veda, Sáma-veda, or Yajur-veda-sanhitá. However, each class of priests has again not one, but several collections of Sûtras, coinciding in many places almost literally, and kept distinct only by the authority of the name of their first collectors. The Grihya ceremonies, though they are less affected by the differences of the three or four classes of priests employed at the great sacrifices, are yet described in

---

[1] See Morley's Digest of Indian Cases, Introduction, page cxcvi.

different collections of Sútras belonging to the same classes, and depending apparently on the authority of one of the three or four collections of sacred hymns (Ṛik, Sáma, Yajus, Atharvaṇa). Thus we have for the Ṛigveda or Hotṛi priests, the Gṛihya-sútras of Áśvaláyana and Śánkháyana; for the Sámaveda or Udgátṛi priests, the Gṛihya-sútras of Gobhila; for the Yajurveda or Adhvaryu priests, the Gṛihya-sútras of Páraskara, and several collections (Baudháyana, &c.) belonging to the Taittiríya branch; for the Atharvaṇa the Gṛihya-sútras of Kauśika.

"The ceremonies to be observed at a burial have been described in detail by Áśvaláyana only, and it is possible that the burial was not considered as an essential part of that class of rites which is comprehended under the name of Sanskára. However, the burial also is an obligatory rite to be performed by others for the benefit of the dead, who of course performs as passive a part in it as could be required in a Gṛihya rite. The following details are taken from the Gṛihya ascribed to Áśvaláyana.

"First comes some medical advice. If a person who keeps the sacrificial fires in his house be ailing, let him betake himself away from his home towards the east, north, or north-east, and carry his fires with him. People say that the fires love their home, and therefore they will wish to return home, and will therefore bless the sick and make him whole. After he has recovered, he should perform a Soma-sacrifice, or an animal-sacrifice, or a burnt-offering. But if he cannot afford to perform any of these sacrifices, he must go home without.

"But if he should not recover but die, then a piece of ground must be dug, south-east or south-west of the place where he lived and died. The ground should be slightly inclined toward the south or the south-east; or, according to others, to the south-west. It should be in length as long as a man with his arms raised, a fathom in width, and a span in depth. The burning and burying-ground (for both according to the Commentator are called śmaśāna) should be open on all sides, rich in shrubs, particularly of thorny and milky plants (as has been explained before, Âśv. Gṛihya, II, 7), and be elevated in such a manner that waters would run down on every side. The last requisite, however, belongs more particularly to a burning ground.

"How the body of the dead is first to be washed, how his nails, his hair, and his beard are to be cut, and similar matters, are not explained in this place, because, as our author says, they have been explained before, that is to say, in the Śrauta-sûtras (Âśv. Srauta-sûtras, VI, 10). The case under consideration there was, what should be done if a person who is performing a great sacrifice, for which all preparations have been made, and where numbers of priests are engaged, should happen to die before the whole sacrifice, which, in some cases, may last for weeks, months, and years, is finished. Different views are entertained on this point, but the leading idea seems to be that a sacrifice once commenced is to be finished although the person who offers it should happen to die before. Áśvaláyana says, that as soon as he dies his body should be carried to the place where the sacrificial utensils are cleaned, that there his nails, his hair, his beard, and the hairs on his body should be cut off, that the body should be anointed with spikenard, and a wreath of spikenard be placed on his head. He remarks, that in some places the ordure also is taken out of the body, and the body filled with melted butter and curds. The corpse is then covered with a new cloth, but so that the feet remain uncovered. The seam of the cloth is cut off, and must be kept by his sons.

"So much is to be supplied here from the Śrauta-sútras. After this the Gṛihya-sútras continue. It is enjoined that a large quantity of sacred grass and melted butter, which is to be offered to the Manes, must be of a peculiar kind, a mixture of milk and butter, called Pṛishadájya. It need not be mentioned that as the whole ceremony of burning and burying belongs to the "ancestral rites", the persons engaged in it have always to look toward the south-east, and to wear their brahmanical cord passing over the right and under the left shoulder.

"The relations of the deceased take his three sacred fires and his sacrificial implements and carry them to the place where the ground is prepared. Behind follow the old men, without their wives, carrying the corpse. Their number should not be even. In some places the corpse is carried on a wheel-cart drawn by an ox; an animal, either a cow, or a kid of one colour, or a black kid, is led behind by a rope tied to its left leg. This is called the Anustaraní, because it is afterwards to be strewed over the corpse and to be burnt with it. This, however, is optional; nay, some authors, for instance Kátyáyana, rather discountenance the custom, because after burning, it might become difficult to distinguish which were the bones of the man or the animal. Then follow his friends, the old ones first, the young ones last, their brahmanical cord hanging down, and their hair untied.

"After the procession has reached the ground, he who has to perform the sacrifice steps forth, walks three times round the place towards the left, sprinkles it with water with a branch of the Śamítree, and repeats this verse of a hymn of the Ṛig-veda (X, 14, 9, or VII, 6, 13): "Depart, disperse, fly away [ye evil spirits]! The fathers (our ancestors) made this place for him (the dead). Yama grants him this resting-place, which is day and night sprinkled with waters."

Thereupon the fires are placed on the borders of the pit, so that the Áhavaníya fire stands south-east, the Gárhapatya north-west, and the Dakshiña fire south-west, and a person skilled in these matters piles the wooden pile in the midst of these fires. All is ready now for the corpse to be burnt. But before this is done, fresh water, as the commentary says, is to be brought in a chamasa or ladle, and a piece of gold is to be placed in the pit: oily seeds also are to be sprinkled over it. Áśvaláyana mentions nothing about this, but only enjoins that grass should be strewed upon the pile; that the hide of the black antelope, the fur outside, should be spread over it; and that on this the corpse is to be placed, so that it lies north of the Gárhapatya fire, and with the head toward the Áhavaníya fire. His wife[1] is placed to the north of her husband. If he be a Kshatriya, a bow also is placed there. The wife is then to be led away as already stated, and in respect of the bow, that also is to be removed by the same persons, with the repetition of the following řik:

[1] As this is a critical passage, I subjoin the *ipsissima verba* of Áśvaláyana and his commentator.

उत्तरतः पत्नीं ॥ Com. ततःप्रेतस्योत्तरतःपत्नीं संवेशयति । त्राचर्यंतीतिलर्षः । चितायांव उपवेश इति लिंगात् ॥ एतावद्वर्षवचनादपि समार्थं ॥

धनुष सविषाच ॥ Com. प्रेतः सविषचैवमुरत्तरतः वेशि-यंति ॥

तामुत्थापयेद्देवरः पतिस्थानीयोऽन्तेवासी जरद्दासी वेदीर्व ज्ञायंभि श्रीवस्त्रोक्षमिति ॥ Com. अथ पत्नीमुत्थापयेत् कः । देवरः पतिस्थानीयः । स पतिस्थानीव उच्यते । येन ज्ञायते पतिकर्म कर्म पुंशवनादि पार्श्वंभवि देवरः कुर्यादिति ॥ पतिस्थानी शिष्यः । स वा । यो वज्र ज्ञानं दास्यै जरा मुखो अभूत् स वा ॥

कर्ता मृषले जपेत् ॥ Com. अदृशासं उत्थापयितरि कर्ता मंत्र मृयात् । धनुदोत्थापयितेव मंत्रं मृयात् ॥

धनुराददानो मृतकर्तीति धनुः ॥ Com. धनुरित्यूह्या धनु-रुत्पयेत् । अपनयेदित्यर्थः ॥

The last word, "apanayet" (he may lead away), as an explanation of "utthápayet" (he may lift up), which is applied to the bow and the wife, leaves no doubt that, according to the intention of the sútras, the wife is to be removed from the pile, and not to be burned with the dead.

"I take the bow from the hand of the dead, to be to us help, glory and strength. Thou art there: we are still here with our brave sons; may we conquer all enemies that attack us."—Rv. X, 18.

Hereupon he fixes the bow-string, walks round the pile, and after having broken the bow he throws it on the pile. If this act is performed by an old servant, somebody else must recite the verses for him (because as a Śúdra he would not be allowed to recite sacred verses).

After this, according to the Commentary on the Sútras, pieces of gold are to be placed on the seven apertures of the head, and oily seeds with butter are to be sprinkled over the dead. Áśvaláyana himself proceeds to give rules as to how the different sacrificial implements, which are to be burnt with the dead, are to be attached to different parts of the corpse.

After this is done, the animal which was led behind is brought, the fat is cut out, and put like a cover over the face and head of the dead. The following verse is used at this occasion:

"Put on this armour [taken] from the cows [to protect thee] against Agni, and cover thyself with fat! that he, the wild one, who delights in flames, the hero, may not embrace thee, wishing to consume thee!"—Rv. VIII, 16, 17.

The kidneys also are taken out and put into the hands of the dead with the following words:

"Escape on the right path the two dogs, the four-eyed, tawny breed of Saramá; then approach the wise fathers who, happy with Yama, enjoy happiness."—Ṙv. X, 14, 10.

The heart of the animal is put on his heart and, according to some, two cakes of ground rice. Others recommend these cakes only if the kidneys are wanting; nay, according to some accounts, all these parts of the animal may be shaped of ground rice and be burnt instead of the real animal. However, where a real animal is burnt with the dead, it is first to be cut up, and the limbs so thrown on the dead that every limb of the animal lies upon a corresponding part of the corpse; the hide is to be thrown over the whole, and a libation to be made with the following words:

"Agni, do not destroy this vessel, which is dear to the gods and our exalted fathers; this is the vessel from which the gods drink; in it the immortals rejoice."—Ṙv. X, 16, 8.

The chief performer of the sacrifice then kneels down on his left knee, and throws the oblations of Ajya into the Dakshiṅa fire, saying "Sváhá to Agni, the lover of Sváhá, Sváhá to the world, Sváhá to Anumati, Sváhá!

The fifth oblation is to be offered on the breast of the dead, with the following (not-vaidik) words: Thou (fire) hast been produced by him; may he be reproduced from thee, that he may obtain the region of eternal bliss!

Thereupon the word is given, "Light the fire at once!"

As the fires are burning round him, and consuming him, twenty-four verses of the Ṛig-veda, the same as specified in the Śrauta-sútras, are to be recited.

Then the dead body is left burning; all turn to the left and go away without looking back. A verse is recited from the Ṛv. X, 31, 3:—

"These men are still alive and separated from the dead. There was to-day amongst us a holy invocation of the gods. Let us go forward now to dance and mirth; for we are leading a longer life!"

When they arrive at a place where there is flowing water[1], they stop, immerse themselves, and on rising throw a handful of water into the air, while they pronounce the name of the deceased and that of his family. They then get out of the water, put on dry clothes, and after once wringing those they had on before, they spread them out toward the north and sit down there themselves till the stars are seen. According to others, they do not go home before sunrise. Then the young ones walk first, the old ones last. And when they arrive at their home, they touch (by way of purifying themselves) the stone, the fire, cow-dung, grain, oil, and water, before they step in. They must not cook food that night, but according to

---

[1] This portion of the ceremonial is called the udakakarma, and described in other Gṛihya-sútras also [e. g. in that of Páraskara, III, 10. See Zeitschrift der deutschen morgenländ. Ges., VII, 540 f.]. Yājnavalkya explains it in the beginning of the third book of his Dharma-śāstra; Manu in the fifth book, verse 68 seq.

some, food may be bought. Again, for those nights, they have to abstain from salt and spices.

After the death of a parent or spiritual father (Guru), reading of the Veda and alms-giving must be omitted for twelve days.

After the death of a near relative, the same abstinence must be observed for ten days. If they are females, the mourning lasts for ten days, if they had not been given away in marriage. The same number of days must be observed, if a spiritual teacher (Guru) die, though he was not a near relative. For other teachers (Ácháryas), the mourning lasts three nights. The same for more distant relations; but if females, only if they had not been given away in marriage. Children also who die before breathing, or those still-born, are mourned for three nights only. If a school-fellow dies, and if a Śrotriya-brahman dies who lived in the same village, mourning is to be observed for one day.

It is to be remembered, however, that the corpse is still left smothering on the pile. Therefore Áśvaláyana, in the fifth Section, proceeds to direct that after the tenth of the dark half (i. e., of the waning moon) on odd days (i. e., on the 11th, 13th, or 15th), under any Nakshatra except Asháḍhá, Phalguní and Proshṭhapadá, the bones must be collected. The general rules as to how people are to walk, &c., are the same as before. Milk and water are sprinkled on the spot with a śamí-branch, and he who is doing this, walks thrice round the pile, always towards the left, saying: "Pale earth with pale leaves, propitious earth with blessed fruits! go and be well embraced by a frog (a shower of rain), and make this fire cheerful "—Ṙv. X, 16, 14.

The bones are to be taken up carefully with the thumb and the little finger, without cracking them. They are to be placed in a vessel, the feet first, the head last. For a man the vessel is to be a simple kumbhá or water pot (without a spout); for a woman a simple kumbhí (with a spout). After the bones have been well put together, the place is to be swept with a broom (pavana), and the vessel or coffin is placed in a hole in a place over which the water cannot flow, except perhaps in the rainy season. It is now that the concluding verses of the hymn are recited: "Go to the mother earth," &c. (Ṙv. X, 31, 10), as the earth is thrown upon the coffin and heaped up over the spot in which it is deposited.

Thereupon all walk home without looking back, and after they have performed an ablution, they offer the first Sráddha to the deceased (ekoddishta), who thenceforth is enrolled amongst the Pitris or Manes, and receives oblations with them on their appointed days.

VII.

REMARKS

BY

RÁJÁ RÁDHÁKÁNTA DEVA,

ON ART. XI, JOURNAL ROYAL ASIATIC SOCIETY, VOL. XVI, PAG. 201;

WITH OBSERVATIONS.

From the Journal of the R. Asiatic Society, Vol. XVII (1859), p. 209—20.

THE sixteenth volume of the Journal of our Society[*] has given insertion to a communication made by me on the supposed authority of the Vedas for the burning of Hindu widows, in which I have shown that the passage quoted as enjoining the practice, and as published by Mr. Colebrooke, in his Paper in the Asiatic Researches[**], upon the "Duties of a Satí or Faithful Widow," had been either purposely or accidentally wrongly read, and that so far from authorizing the rite, its real purport was the reverse; and that it expected the widow to repress her affliction and return to her worldly duties. This view was entirely

---

[*] [See the preceding Article.]   [**] [Essays, p. 70-75.]

confirmed by the explanation of the passage given by the celebrated commentator, Sáyaṅa Áchárya, and by the precepts of Áśwaláyana, cited by Professor Maximilian Müller, published in continuation of my remarks on the same occasion. The revised reading has not proved acceptable to the Paṅdits of Calcutta, and the following letter is the expression of their sentiments. The writer, a friend of many years, Rájá Rádhákánt Deb is well known as a leading member of the Native Society of Calcutta, who adds to the distinction of rank and station that of a foremost place amongst Sanskrit scholars, as evinced by his great Lexicon or Literary Encyclopædia of the Sanskrit language, in seven quarto volumes, the Śabdakalpadruma, which enjoys a European as well as Indian celebrity. Any opinion coming from him on subjects connected with the ancient literature of his country is entitled to the greatest deference. The question of the authority for the Satí cremation is now, as he rightly observes, a matter merely for literary discussion, but as it is not without interest for the historian and antiquarian, his remarks will, I doubt not, be highly acceptable to those scholars who are engaged in the investigation of the ancient religion and history of the Hindus; and as he has no objection to their being laid before the public, I have thought it advisable to request a place for them in the Journal, although, as I shall subsequently explain, they have not induced me to modify in the least my opinions on the subject, as my esteemed correspondent seems to anticipate.

My dear Dr. Wilson,

Although the abolition of the practice of Sahamaraṇa in the British Indian territories has legally set the question at rest, and deprived it of all interest in the public eye, yet its discussion will always afford pleasure to the historian and antiquarian, and has its peculiar value in a literary point of view.

The perusal of your very interesting article "On the supposed Vaidic authority for the burning of Hindu Widows, and on the Funeral Ceremonies of the Hindus", which appeared in the Journal of the Royal Asiatic Society of Great Britain and Ireland, Vol. XVI, Part I, having induced me to inquire whether any trace of this custom can be found in the Vedas, I have made certain discoveries and come to a conclusion, which I believe would lead you to modify considerably the opinion you have formed on the subject.

The most explicit authority for the burning of a widow with her deceased husband is to be found in the two verses of the Aukhya Śākhā of the Taittirīya Sanhitā, quoted in the eighty-fourth Anuvāka of the Nārāyaṇīya Upanishad, of which I give the following literal translation, and subjoin[1] the original text with the commentary of Sāyaṇāchārya:—

---

[1] Text. इमे जीवानां जनपतिरसि पत्नानुजवमन्त परिधानि तस्मै देवं तवे राजसाम ॥ १ ॥ Com. ये जीवे कर्मसाचिवः । यतः स्व जनानां प्राजापत्यार्जिजनतानां जनपतिरसि । पुनर्जन्मयद्व तदेव जनानामधिपतिर्भव इति नियमबोधनाय ॥ तस्मादावाचर्यमाण वत्स्यामितिके बने तववाये कमी खदेव तवाराजता किनतानिजर्व: ।

1. "Oh Agni, of all Vratas[1], thou art the Vratapati[2], I will observe the vow (Vrata) of following the husband. Do thou enable me to accomplish it!"

2. "Here (in this rite), to thee, oh Agni, I offer salutation; to gain the heavenly mansion I enter into thee; (wherefore) oh Játavedah[3], this day, satisfied with the clarified butter (offered by me), inspire me with courage (for Sahagamana) and take me to my lord."

Agreeably to this general Vaidic injunction, the Sútrakáras direct that the widow, like the sacrificial utensils of a Bráhmaṅa, should be made to lie upon the funeral pile of her husband, and accordingly as he was a Bráhmaṅa, Kshatriya, or Vaiśya, a piece of gold, a bow, or a jewel is to be respectively placed thereupon.

भातूजानमेकार्यत्तात् । किं सर्वार्चमानं तटुतनिमिति पत्नानुकमेति यत्ता मर्षा तद् बहुवृत्तनमनमत परिखामि परिखामीतर्षः ।

Text. एत ता चये नमसा विधेम सुवर्णकं लोकका समेति । सुयावक्रो यव हविवा जातवेदो विशानि ता कवनसौ नव मा पत्युर्द्ये ॥ Com. हे चये एत वान्तिन्यकर्माणि । ता ल्वार्थातृक्ष । हविषा हविर्भोजेन । नमसा नमस्कारेच च । विधेम नमो विदधामीतर्षः । किमर्षमितुता तपाह । सुवर्णकेति सुवर्णकं पतिसंप्राप्तलोकल । समेति यम्बद्मधार्यं । ता लघीतर्षः । सहस्त्रचें विलीया कुसरी । विशानि प्रविशानि यत एव चव चक्षिख्विने । हे जातवेदो हविषा मत्पीय हविर्भोजेन । सुयाहः घनुङः सन् । सन्नत सन्नमार्गमहर्षं महारा सहवमनविषयक्वावसुखप्रहाखहरदीति यायन । मा मां पतिसाषिकटेवतां पतुर्मनं भर्तुरन्त्ये सर्व नव प्रापयेतर्षः ।

---

[1] Vowed or voluntary observances.

[2] Lord of Vratas.

[3] Source of the Vedas.

To the widow so placed beside the lifeless body of her husband, the Mantras beginning with "... Udírshwa, &c.," and "Suvarṅa goong hastát, &c., Dhanurhastát, &c.," or "Maṅigoong hastát, &c.," are to be addressed[1] to her by her husband's brother or fellow-student, accordingly as he belonged to the priestly, military, or mercantile class.

If the widow thus addressed has not made up her mind for her immolation, she obeys the call; but should she be firm in her resolve, she consoles her friends and relatives, and enters the fire.

Extracts[2] from Bháradwája and Aśwaláyana, and

---

[1] The first part of the address beginning with "Udírshwa," &c., is the same in respect of the funeral of the first three classes: by this Mantra the widow is requested to leave the corpse and to return to her abode. The remaining three Mantras are to be addressed to the widow of a Bráhmaṅa, Kshatriya, and Vaiśya respectively, whereby she is required to lift up from the funeral pile the respective symbols of the deceased, and therewith to rub his hands. This call forms an important part of the ceremony.

[2] चयनं चितानुपर्वम्‌तत्वेवेन वा वन्त्या: संवेष्टना चिवत एति ॥
Bháradwája's Sútra, Praśna I.

चयिलानि पाचाचि सोचयेत्‌विषे इहे जुष्ठं जब उपभृत हविषे
पार्षे सक्तं सर्वे ४ चिधीषदमयीमुरसि धुवां चिररिष कयानानीलारि्‌ः॥
Aśwaláyana's Grihya Sútra, Adhyáya IV, 8. [M. Müller in "Zeitschrift der d. morgenl. Ges.", IX, p. VI.]

उत्तारत: पत्नीं ॥ Com. तत: प्रेतऔतारत: पत्नीं संवेष्टदर्मिति ।
ज्ञावयतीसर्प: । चितायेव उपदेय एति चिद्वत्‌ एतावदर्वयज्ञादपि
बमानं ॥ Ibid. Adh. II, 8.

चतीर्धनार्धमिक्षीयकोर्थ मतायुमेतसुयद्येव एति । इक्षयामच हि-
विषीठयेदं पत्‌नुर्वमिसलमभिर्वमयूख ॥

from the Sahamaraṇavidhi, a work of much repute in Drávida, are quoted below in elucidation of these practices. From these Vaidic and Sautric injunctions have been derived the rules and directions for the immolation of the Satí, in the Smṛitis and Puránas.

After having thus shown the Vaidic authority for the Sahamaraṇa, I shall offer some observations upon the conclusions you have drawn, on perusing the seventh and eighth Verses[1] of the second Sūkta of the second Anuvāka of the tenth Maṇḍala of the Ṛigveda.

In the first place, on referring to Raghunandana's Śuddhitattwa, whence Colebrooke derives his mate-

इती सम्मार्ति युर्वेन ग्राह्यवस युनर्थ इसादिति । प्रशुमा राव-
वस भगुर्षार्दिति । सविसा पैथस मर्षि इसादिति ॥ Bhāra-
dwāja's Sūtra.

तालुस्वापर्यदेवरः पतिज्ञानीवी ऽलोमावी चरहाजो गोदीर्घं
गार्य्यमिवसोऽभिति ॥ Áswalāy. II, 2.

उत्तरतः पत्नीं । मां प्रेतम्रोत्तरतः यूयां वनरत्रिनां देवरः
शिष्यो वा चरे भूला नमकृता उदीर्व्वेति व्याख्यातुत्पादेत् । तस्मा-
द्विचायु क्रयमेव युद्धः सर्व्वाष्यन् पुत्रांव समामंत्र्य भर्त्तारं विष्णु-
रूप भूला इत्ताय्ं प्राविषेहिलुते ॥ Sahamaraṇavedhi.

[1] एषा नारीरविधवाः सपत्नीराज्जनेन सर्पिषा सं विषन्तु चम्य-
वो ऽनमीवाः सुरत्ना चारोहन्तु अग्नयो योनिसये ॥ ७ ॥
उदीर्व्वं गार्य्यभि जीवलोकं गतासुमेतं उप छेष एहि इदयागम
हिरयीकर्त्यद्यं पत्युर्व्वनिलवमभि वं वभूव ॥ ८ ॥

* Her (the widow) lying on the north of the deceased, if she want courage, her husband's brother, or fellow-student, or old servant shall, by reciting the two Mantras Udīrshwa, &c., raise, holding her by the hand and saluting her; but if she have sufficient courage, she bidding adieu to her friends, relatives, and children, and contemplating the Vishṇu-like form of her husband, enters the fire.

rials for his "Essay on the Duties of a faithful Widow", published in the fourth volume of the Asiatic Researches, we find the author citing a verse[1] from the Rigveda and a passage[2] from the Brahma Puráńa, in order to show that the Veda authorizes Sahamarańa. You suppose this verse to be an incorrect reading of the seventh Rich above alluded to, and support your reasoning by the Commentary of Sáyańa and the directions of Aświaláyana.

Now, the shortest way in which our pandits would dispute this opinion, would be to assert that for aught that we moderns know, Raghunandana's citation may be altogether a different verse from the seventh Rich, and may be found somewhere, in any of the Sákhás[3] of the Rigveda; inasmuch as the same verse, with slight variations of reading, and hence with different import and application, often occurs in the different Vedas, in various Sákhás of the same Veda, and sometimes in different places of the same Sákhá of a Veda. The objection to the use of the epithets "Avidhavá" and "Supatní", whereby you suppose the reason for burning to be wanting, can be easily answered by supposing the Satí (whose soul is, as it

---

[1] इमा नारीरविधवाः सपत्नीराग्नेन सर्पिषा संविशन्तु । अन-स्रवो ऽनमीवाः सुरत्ना आरोहन्तु जनयो योनिमग्रे ॥

[2] ॰्मृतेब्रार्तसाध्वी स्त्री न भवेदात्मघातिनी ॥[*]

[3] चाकलायनी, शांखायनी, बाक्कला, वाक्कला, माण्डूकेयी.

[*] "The loyal wife (who burns herself) shall not be deemed a suicide."

were, wedded to that of her husband), not to be widowed; actual practice, when it prevailed in India, may be considered as confirmatory of this opinion. The Satí, in making preparations for ascending the funeral pile, used to mark her forehead with Sindúra, and to deck herself sumptuously with all the symbols of a Sadhavá.

But so long as the proper place of the verse quoted by Raghunandana is not pointed out, the occidental pandits, who are making wonderful progress in Vaidic learning, may regard it an idle assertion. I shall therefore, for argument's sake, grant Raghunandana's citation to be a false reading of the seventh verse in question.

On this supposition you may be justified in coming to the conclusion, that the genuine reading of the passage rather discountenances than enjoins Sahamaraña; but by referring to the subjoined Sútras¹ of

---

¹ नवस्यां कुहायां यज्ञोपवीतीक्षकराणां समग्रानं वापिमुपस्पाथाय संपरिकीर्यापरिकार्यपि नीहितं चर्मानमुखं प्राचीनयीवमुसरेजोमाक्षीर्यं वेतसमाविनो ज्ञातीगारोहतारोहतेलेर्धानमु पूर्वाम्यवनि नवाधानीनि मतिलोमहतया वारक्षा चूषा हे चतुर्मृनीति नुहोनि न हि ते वचे तमुव हनि दग्रा च सुवाक्षतीरवपनक्षौ गुष्टार्विनि ज्ञलापाञ्जां सम्पातयत्वभोभयं प्रहरति चेन गुहोलपरिकार्यपि नीहितो ऽनुग्राहसूत्रौ ऽवक्षितौ भवनि नं ज्ञातयो ऽन्वारभ्ये ऽनुग्रामन्वारभामहं इति मात्री ऽहमीमे जीवा इति अवचो वेनतथाजचा चचकाभिव पदानिगछलौभवते ग्रुवो: पदनिलद्वेभी ऽआर्युर्दीपिजलो ऽदमानं परिधिं हधानि एवं वेविभ: परिधिं तथानीति क्षीवानञ्जिनु संपाक्तानवमवतीमा नारीरिति मैर्मुकानि नुमती सदाज्ञानं वेकुदहिति वेकुदेनांचमेनाहि यदि वेकुदं नावस्येजैव केनचिद्द्वाक्षनीमागीरन्। ॥ Bháradwája's Sútra, Praśna I, Khaṇḍa II.

Bháradwája and Áswaláyana, wherein they specify the rites in which many of the verses of the tenth Mańdala quoted by you are to be respectively cited as Mantras, you will at once see what you rightly guess—that the verse in question has nothing to do with the concremation of a Satí; it is directed to be chaunted on the tenth day after the burning of the dead, when the relatives of the deceased assemble on the Smaśána to perform certain ceremonies, on the conclusion of which, the Adhwaryu takes butter with a new blade of kuśa grass, or clarified butter between the thumb and ring finger, and applying it, as collyrium, to the eyes of Sadhavás, recites the seventh hymn in question, the moment they are directed to depart towards the east.

Now, as the text, which has been supposed to authorize Sahamaraṅa, clearly appears to be appropriated to quite a different occasion, the argument based upon its interpretation proving it to discountenance concremation, necessarily falls to the ground.

The succeeding verses (to wit, the eighth and ninth),

उत्तरआद्वार्विमुपसमाधाय पश्चादखान्तुवं वर्मास्तीर्य माञ्जी-
वनुत्तरलोम तस्मिन्नमात्तारोहयेदारोहनायुर्भरसंवृणाना एति
एवं दीचेश्व: परिधिं दधामीति परिधिं दधादकर्मृतु दधतां पर्वत-
निवक्षानमुनरतो ६पे: ज्ञला परे सुक्तो बनुपरीहि पन्नामितादि
पतधूमि: मस्तुषं ज्रत्वा यशान्वमुपूर्वे अवनीक्ष्मात्तादोमीचेत ।
युवमद: पुनक्यार्विभां दर्भतरक्षेमवर्नीनिलांमुद्रोपक्षिहिकाभामा-
वेगाविक्षो चाच्च पराक्षो विसुक्षेयुरिमा नारीरविश्वा: सुपत्नी-
रिति चक्रमा दृषेत । करमन्तीरविते सरभच्वमिति ॥ Áswaláyana's Gṛihya Sútra, Adhyáya III.

as I observed before, are enjoined to be addressed to the widow, lying on the funeral pile of her husband, and therefore have no relation with the seventh.

Had there been no explicit Vaidic injunction for Sahamaraṅa, these passages, taken by themselves, would certainly have justified the conclusion that the Rigveda prohibits or ignores, by these texts, the self-immolation of a Satí, but when we find in the Ankhya Sákhá of the Taittiríya Sanhitá, the Satí's address to Agni while throwing herself into it, and thus discover the Vaidic sanction for concremation, we must pause before we regard the eighth verse as an authority against this tragic act.

The Mímánsákára would argue thus,—"Where there are two authorities of a contradictory character, but of equal cogency, an alternative must be supposed to have been allowed[1]." The Sútrakáras, upon the Vaidic authorities above set forth, direct that the widow as well as the sacrificial utensils of the deceased Bráhmaṅa should be placed upon his funeral pile; but, as the widow has a will of her own, she cannot be disposed of like the inert utensils. The Rigveda therefore gives her the option of sacrificing herself or not, according as she may or may not have her courage "screwed up to the sticking place."

When the Satí lies on the funeral pile, it is presumed[2]

---

[1] गुरुवविरोधे विकल्पः ।
Gotama quoted by Kullúkabhaṭṭa in his Com. on Manu, v. 14, B. 2, which see.

[2] Sáyaṅa, when he says, in his Commentary on the 8th Rich:

she is inclined to immolate herself, and the eighth verse is addressed to her, as the author of the Sahamaraṇavidhi explains, only to test her resolution, and to induce her to retire, if she be not sufficiently firm in her purpose. The necessity of giving her this option and trying her fortitude beforehand, appears the more strong, when we find it declared[1] that the Satí who becomes Chitábhrashtá, who retires from the funeral pile after the conclusion of the rites, commits a highly sinful act, although it admits of expiation by the performance of the Prájápatya.

Our personal observation of the actual practice when it prevailed in British India confirms this view; from the moment a Satí expressed her desire to follow her lord, up to the time she ascended the funeral pile, every persuasive language was used to induce her to continue in the family, and to discharge her proper duties there, and it was not until she was found inflexible that she was allowed to sacrifice herself; this was perfectly in keeping with the Udírshwa, &c., Mantra.

Thus the 8th verse of the Rigveda, above alluded to, appears to be, in fact, a Sahamarańa Mantra,

---

"Yasmád anusaraṅa nischayam ákárabis tasmád ágachchha," be takes the same view; he does not consider the burning as delayed, as may be supposed from a technical interpretation of the word "anusaraṅa", because, as you say, subsequent burning is inconsistent with the presence of the corpse.

[1] चिताभ्रष्टा तु या नारी मौद्गादिविवर्जिता भवेत् । प्राजापत्येन शुद्धेतु तस्यादिपापकर्मणः ॥

though its interpretation, apart from other considerations, may, on a first view, seem to discountenance the practice.

A very strong presumption in support of the opinion, that Sahamaraṅa rests upon Vaidic authority, arises from the circumstance of its having prevailed in India in very remote times, when Vaidic rites only were in vogue. On referring to the Mahábhárata, for instance, we find the widows of the heroes slain in the battle of Kurukshetra consuming themselves in the funeral fires of their husbands, when there lived great kings and sages imbued with Vaidic learning, and devoted to the observance of Vaidic rituals.

Nearly two thousand years ago Propertius describes the prevalence of this custom in India, in a passage of which the following is a translation by Boyses (see Brit. Poets, Chalmer's Ed., Vol. XIV, p. 563):—

> "Happy the laws that in those climes obtain,
> Where the bright morning reddens all the main,
> There, whenso'er the happy husband dies,
> And on the funeral couch extended lies,
> His faithful wives around the scene appear,
> With pompous dress and a triumphant air;
> For partnership in death, ambitious strive,
> And dread the shameful fortune to survive!
> Adorned with flowers the lovely victims stand,
> With smiles ascend the pile, and light the brand!
> Grasp their dear partners with unaltered faith,
> And yield exulting to the fragrant death."

Cicero, also, who lived about the same time, mentions this fact in his Tusculum Questions. Herodotus speaks of a race of Thracians, whose women sacrificed themselves on the tombs of their husbands: these people, as well as the Getæ by whom this custom was also observed, were perhaps some tribe of degraded Kshatriyas.

You may, if you think it worth while, read this paper at the next meeting of the Royal Asiatic Society.

I remain,
My dear Dr. Wilson,
Yours sincerely,
RADHAKANT DEB.

CALCUTTA, 30th June, 1858.

Observations.

In disproving the genuineness of the citation of the passage which had been quoted as authority for the Satí, I confined my objections to the particular passage in question, and in this respect the Rájá is obliged to admit, that I may be justified in coming to the conclusion, that the genuine reading rather discountenances than enjoins Satí. This was all I maintained. Of course I never intended to deny, that there were numerous texts in the Sútras and law-books, by which it was enjoined. I restricted my argument to the individual text quoted from the Rigveda, and with Rájá Rádhákánt Deb's own concurrence, I have no occasion to modify the view I have taken, as limited to this object: the text of the Rigveda, that has been quoted as authority for the burning of the widow, is no such thing, "it rather discountenances than enjoined the practice." I have not expressed any opinion, whether any such injunction is to be found in any other part of the Sanhitá of the Rigveda, or of the Sanhitás of the White or Black Yajush, or the Sámaveda. That is quite a different question, although, as the topic is started by the Rájá, I may venture to intimate an opinion, that the burning of a widow will not be found even alluded to in the genuine text, the Sanhitá, of either of the three principal Vedas. Whatever may be the antiquity of the rite, and that it is of long standing is not to be disputed, I suspect its origin is later than the Sanhitá, or primary Vedic period. I have now translated, although not yet published, nearly the whole of the Súktas, or hymns, the primitive portions of the Rigveda, and have yet found no notice of any such ceremony: the prohibition which would imply the existence of the rite, is matter of inference only; the direction, that the widow is to be led away from the proximity of her deceased husband, does not necessarily imply that she was to depart from his funeral pile, and there is no term, in the text, that indicates such a position.

In the course of my translation of the Rigveda, I have had a great number of occasions to refer to the printed texts of the Vájasaneyí Sanhitá, of the Yajurveda, published by Professor Weber, of the Sámaveda printed by the late Mr. Stevenson and Professor Benfey, and I do not remember to have met with any allusion whatever in either of those works to the Satí ceremonial. There remains therefore only the Taittiríya Sanhitá of the Black Yajush to be examined: a part only of this has been printed by the Asiatic Society of Bengal, in their Bibliotheca Indica, and, as far as it goes, the same absence of allusion to the Satí occurs: so far, therefore, I have reason to believe, that the burning of widows was unknown to the Vedic period of Hindu ritual or belief.

That the Sútras of Áswaláyana, Bháradwája, and other Sútrakáras contain Sútras, or rules, for the cremation, is indisputable, but all Vedic scholars agree in considering these works as of much more recent date than the Sanhitá, or text period; they, therefore, prove nothing, and of still less weight are the Sahamaraña-vidhi or the Tattwas of Raghunandana, or other equally modern writings: the question is not whether there be any authorities at all for the practice, but whether such authority be discoverable in the original Vedic texts; there is no lack whatever of the former—I cannot yet positively deny, but I question the existence of the latter. To this Rádhákánt replies, "the most explicit (Vedic) authority is to be found in the two verses of the Aukhya Śákhá of the Taittiríya Sanhitá, quoted in the 84th anuváka of the Náráyañíya Upanishad," of which he gives the literal translation as well as of the comment; unfavourably for his argument, the authority is liable to obvious exceptions.

In the first place, the two verses are not cited direct from the text of the Taittiríya Sanhitá itself; they are a quotation of a quotation, and, as in the case of the passage of the Ṛigveda, which has given rise to this discussion, we know that quotations cannot always be trusted. The Paṅḍits should have made a reference to the Taittiríya Sanhitá itself, and have given us chapter and verse for the passages; we should then be able to test their accuracy by collation with the printed text when complete. In the next place, the quotation occurs in an Upanishad, the Yájniki, or Náráyańíya: the Upanishad period is of doubtful determination, because the Upanishads, which are numerous, one list enumerating above a hundred, are evidently of widely different dates, and not unfrequently of equivocal character. The Náráyańíya Upanishad is not altogether unexceptionable, for it constitutes the tenth Prapáthaka, or section, of what is usually considered a Bráhmańa, the Taittiríya Áraṅyaka; Sáyańa calls it even khilarúpá, or of the nature of an additional or supplementary section, so that it is scarcely acknowledged to be a part of the original Áraṅyaka[*].

Upon referring to the manuscripts of the library of the India House, another difficulty arises; neither text nor comment consists of more than 64 anuvákas, whilst the verses quoted by Rádhákánt are said to be taken from the 84th anuváka; consequently no such verses could be expected to be found in our copy,

---

[*] [See A. Weber, Ind. Stud., I, 75 ff.]

and accordingly they do not occur. Sáyaña, however, observes, that different recensions do exist, of which the Drávira has 64 anuvákas, the Ándhra 80, the Karnáta 74, others 89. There may be a copy belonging to a different Śákhá, Aukhya for instance, of which we have no copy, with 84 anuvákas. Sáyaña, however, avowedly follows the Drávira recension, containing only 64 anuvákas, the actual number of two copies consulted, and in which no such passages are met with; whence then do the Pańdits derive their scholia of the 84th? it is for them to give a satisfactory explanation. Therefore, as the matter stands, the verses cited, together with their commentary, wear a somewhat suspicious appearance, not less observable that the different recensions specified are all named after the divisions of *Southern India*, where the Vedas did not penetrate probably till long after their compilation. Although, however, their authenticity be admitted, their occurring in an Upanishad, or even in a Bráhmańa, is no proof that the Sanhitá of the Taittiríya Yajush contains them, or sanctions the burning of widows, or that the rite was cotemporary with the ritual of the Vedic period.

VIII.

ON

BUDDHA AND BUDDHISM.

From the Journal of the R. Asiatic Society, Vol. XVI (1856), p. 229–65.

[Read as a Lecture, April 8, 1854.]

MUCH has been written, much has been said in various places, and amongst them in this Society, about Buddha, and the religious system which bears his name, yet it may be suspected that the notions which have been entertained and propagated, in many particulars relating to both the history and the doctrines, have been adopted upon insufficient information and somewhat prematurely disseminated. Very copious additions, and those of a highly authentic character, have been, but very recently, made to the stock of materials which we heretofore possessed, and there has scarcely yet been sufficient time for their deliberate examination. Copious also and authentic as they are, they are still incomplete, and much remains for Oriental scholars to accomplish before it can be said that the materials for such a history of Buddha as shall command the assent of all who study the subject, have been conclusively provided. I have, therefore, no purpose of proposing to you in the views I am about to take, that you should consider them as final; my only intention is to bring the subject before you as it stands at present, with some of that additional elucidation which is derivable from the many valuable publications that have recently appeared, and particularly from the learned and authentic investigations of the late Eugène Burnouf, the only scholar as yet who has combined a knowledge of Sanskrit with that of Páli and Tibetan, and has been equally familiar with the Buddhist authorities of the north and south of India: unfortunately he has been lost to us before he had gone through the wide circuit of research which he had contemplated, and which he only was competent to have traversed; and although he has accomplished more than any other scholar, more than it would seem possible for any human ability and industry to have achieved, it is to be deeply and for ever regretted that his life was not spared to have effected all he had intended, and for which he was collecting, and had collected, many valuable and abundant materials. Still he has left us, in his "Introduction à l'Histoire du Bouddhisme", and in his posthumous work "Le Lotus de la Bonne Loi", an immense mass of authentic information which was not formerly within our reach, and which must contribute effectually to rationalize the speculations that may be hazarded in future on Buddha and his faith. Some of those which have been started by the erudition and ingenuity of the learned in past ages will best introduce us to the opportunity we now have of ascertaining what is probable, if we cannot positively affirm that it is all true.

It is sometimes supposed that the classical authors supply us with evidence of the Buddhist religion in India three centuries before the era of Christianity, drawing this inference especially from the fragments which remain of the writings of Megasthenes, the ambassador of Seleucus to Chaudragupta, about the year B.C. 295, according to his latest editor, Schwanbeck[*], and to whose descriptions of various particulars respecting India the other ancient writers are almost wholly indebted. It is well known that he divides the Indian philosophers into two classes, the Brachmanai and the Sarmanai; and the latter it has been concluded intend the Sŕamańas, one of the titles of the Buddhist ascetics. This is not impossible. If we trust to the traditions of the Buddhists, their founder lived at least two centuries before the mission of Megasthenes, and in that case we might expect to meet with his disciples in the descriptions of the ambassador. At the same time Śramańa is not exclusively the designation of a Buddhist, it is equally that of a Brahmanical ascetic, and its use does not positively determine to which class it is to be applied[1]. In truth, it is clear

---

[*] [Megasth. Indica, p. 20. Lassen, Ind. Alt., II. 209. 663.]

[1] When Arjuna goes to the forest he is attended amongst others by *Sramańá Vanaukasáh*, forest-dwelling Śramańas: these could not have been Buddhists,—*Mahábhárat*, Ádi Parva, v. 7742.

from what follows that the Brahman was intended, for Megasthenes proceeds to say: "of the Sarmanai, the most highly venerated among them are the Hylobii," that is, as he goes on to explain the term, "those who pass their lives in the woods (ζῶντας ἐν ταῖς ὕλαις), and who live upon wild fruits and seeds, and are clothed in the barks of trees," in other words the Vánaprastha of the Brahmanical system; literally, the dweller in the woods, the man of the third order, who, having fulfilled his course of householder, is enjoined by Manu to repair to the lonely wood to subsist upon green roots and fruit, and to wear a vesture of bark. Major Cunningham[*], indeed, who is a courageous etymologist, derives Hylobii from the Sanskrit *Alobhiya*, "one who is without desire", that is, the Bodhisattwa, who has suppressed all human passions; but *Alobhiya* is not a genuine Sanskrit word, nor is there any authority for its application to a *Bodhisattwa*, and Megasthenes may be presumed to have understood his own language. His interpretation of Hylobii, the dwellers in the woods, is in such perfect conformity with the meaning of Vánaprastha, that we cannot doubt the identity of the two designations.

Nothing of any value, upon this subject at least, is derivable from classical writers in addition to the information furnished by Megasthenes; but when we come later down, or to the early ages of Christianity, various curious notices of Buddhism occur in the

---

[*] [The Bhilsa Topes, 1854, p. 64. See Lassen, II, 700 ff.]

writings of the Fathers of the Church, which though meagre are in the main correct. We need not be surprised at this: there is no doubt that Buddhism was in a highly flourishing state in India in the first centuries of Christianity, and it is not extraordinary that some indications of its diffusion should have found their way to Syria and Egypt.

Clemens of Alexandria, who lived towards the close of the second century, had evidently heard of the monastic practices, and of the peculiar monuments or Topes of the Buddhists. When he speaks of the Brachmanai and the Sarmanai as two distinct classes of Indian philosophers, he uses the very words of Megasthenes, and merely, therefore, repeats his statement; but that he does not understand Buddhists by Sarmanes is clear enough, for he proceeds to add, "there are of the Indians some who worship Buddha, or Boutta, whom they honour as a god"; and in another passage he observes: "those of the Indians who are called Semnoi cultivate truth, foretell events, and reverence certain pyramids in which they imagine the bones of some divinity are deposited, they observe perpetual continence; there are also maidens termed Semnai." Semnoi and Semnai might be thought to have some relation to Śramañas, but the words, perhaps, bear only their original purport, "venerable or sacred".

About the middle of the following century, Porphyry repeats information gathered from Bardesanes, who obtained it from the Indian envoys sent to Antoninus; and although the account is somewhat confused, there is an evident allusion to Buddhist practices. "There are," he says, "two divisions of the Gymnosophists, Brachmans, and Samanai,"—not Sarmanai, but Samanai,—"the former are so by birth, the latter by election, consisting of all those who give themselves up to the cultivation of sacred learning: they live in colleges, in dwellings, and temples constructed by the princes, abandoning their families and property: they are summoned to prayer by the ringing of a bell, and live upon rice and fruits." Cyril of Alexandria also mentions that the Samanæans were the philosophers of the Bactrians, showing the extension of Buddhism beyond the confines of India; and St. Jerome, who, like Cyril, lived at the end of the fourth and beginning of the fifth century, was evidently acquainted with Buddhistical legends, for he says that Buddha was believed to have been born of a virgin, and to have come forth from his mother's side. From Cyril of Jerusalem and Ephraim, writers of the middle of the fourth century, we learn that Buddhism tainted some of the heresies of the early Christian Church, especially the Manichæan, which the latter terms the Indian heresy; the former states that Terebinthus, the preceptor of Manes, the Persian Mani, took the name of Baudas. Hyde and Beausobre explain this to mean no more than that the word Terebinthus in Greek was the same as Butam in Chaldaic, a kind of tree; but the word in Cyril is Baudas, not Butem, and it is more likely that Terebinthus styled himself a Bauddha, or a Buddha, especially as an Indian origin was assigned to the doctrines he introduced. Epiphanius, indeed, explains how this happened by going a step further. According to him Scythianus, *quasi* Śákya, the master and instructor of Terebinthus, was an Arabian or Egyptian merchant, who had grown rich by trading with India, whence he imported not only valuable merchandise, but heretical doctrines and books. Suidas calls Manes himself a Brahman, a pupil of Bauddha, formerly called Terebinthus, who, coming into Persia, falsely pretended that he was born of a virgin. These accounts are no doubt scanty and in some respects inaccurate, but they demonstrate clearly that the Buddhism of India was not wholly unknown to the Christian writers between the second and fifth centuries of our era.

Without at present referring more particularly to the information furnished us by Chinese travellers in India between the third and sixth centuries, we may next advert to the strange theories which were gravely advanced, by men of the highest repute in Europe for erudition and sagacity, from the middle to the end of the last century, respecting the origin and character of Buddha. Deeply interested by the accounts which were transmitted to Europe by the missionaries of the Romish Church, who penetrated to Tibet, Japan, and China, as well as by other travellers to those countries, the members of the French Academy especially set to work to establish coincidences the most improbable, and identified Buddha with a variety of personages, imaginary or real, with whom no possible congruity existed; thus it was attempted to show that Buddha was the same as the Toth or Hermes of the Egyptians,—the Turm of the Etruscans; that he was Mercury, Zoroaster, Pythagoras; the Woden or Odin of the Scandinavians:—Manes, the author of the Manichæan heresy; and even the divine author of Christianity. These were the dreams of no ordinary men; and, besides Giorgi and Paolino, we find amongst the speculators the names of Huet, Vossius, Fourmont, Leibnitz, and De Guignes.

The influence and example of great names pervaded the inquiry, even after access to more authentic information had been obtained, and shews itself in some of the early volumes of the researches of our venerable parent the Asiatic Society of Bengal. Thus Chambers is divided between Mercury and Woden. Buchanan looks out for an Egyptian or Abyssinian prototype, and even Sir William Jones fluctuates between Woden and Sisac. In the first instance he observes: "nor can we doubt that Wod or Odin was the same with Budh;" but in a subsequent paper he remarks: "we may safely conclude that Sacya or Sisak, about 200 years after Vyasa, either in person, or by a colony from Egypt, imported into this country [India] the mild heresy of the ancient Bauddhas." This spirit of impossible analogies is, even yet, not wholly extinct; and writers are found to identify Buddha with the prophet Daniel, and to ascribe the appearance of Buddhism in India, to the captivity and dispersion of the Jews. When, however, a more profound acquaintance with the literature of the principal Buddhist nations began to shed genuine light upon the subject, it soon scattered the shadows which the darkness of ignorance had begotten. The language of the Chinese and of the Mongols were assiduously studied in the early part of the present century, especially by Klaproth, Remusat, and Schmidt; and the application of their acquirements to the illustration of Buddhism was evinced in numerous interesting and authentic contributions to the early volumes of the Journal Asiatique, and the transactions of the Imperial Academy of St. Petersburgh, and more particularly in the copious annotations which accompany the French translation, by Remusat, Klaproth, and Landresse, of the travels of the Chinese priest, Fa Hian, in the end of the fourth and beginning of the fifth centuries. Valuable as this work undoubtedly is as a Buddhist picture of the condition of India at that period, it would have been in many respects almost unintelligible without the amplification of its brief notices into the extensive views of the sytem and its authors, which are to be found in the notes attached to the text; the details contained in which are mainly derived from the Buddhist literature of China, with some accessions from that of the Mongols.

In the mean time, however, the interest, which had languished in India, subsequently to the first vain conceits of the Bengal Asiatic Society, revived; and a whole flood of contributions of a character equally novel and important was poured upon the public, both from the north and from the south. The former took the lead, and Buddhism as still prevalent in Nepal and the adjacent Himalayan regions was zealously investigated by Mr. Hodgson, the results of whose inquiries were communicated to the Asiatic Society of Bengal, and subsequently to the Royal Asiatic Society. Besides the information which he himself collected, he contributed still more importantly to the progress of the investigation by first bringing to our knowledge the existence of a number of Buddhist writings in Sanskrit, as well as that of a most voluminous body of works, chiefly if not exclusively Buddhist, in the language of Tibet. He did more; he procured the the books, and in the exercise of a sound judgment, as well as generous liberality, sent them where they were likely to be turned to good account, to the several Asiatic Societies of Calcutta, London, and Paris. To the former, between 1824 and 1830, he presented nearly 50 volumes in Sanskrit, and 200 in Tibetan: to this Society he presented above 100 volumes in Sanskrit and Tibetan, and at various dates he forwarded to the Société Asiatique 88 volumes of Sanskrit, besides the whole of the great Tibetan collections, the Kah-gyur and Stan-gyur, in more than 300 volumes. He finally presented to the East India Company a copy of the two Tibetan collections, which are now at the India House. Mr. Hodgson sent these books to Europe, not, as M. Burnouf observes, that they might slumber in undisturbed repose upon the shelves of a library, but that they might be made to yield the information they might contain. That these expectations have not been wholly disappointed is due, I am sorry to say, to no zeal or acquirement native to the soil; and the books in the Society's possession have done little more than repose in dust and oblivion upon the shelves where they were originally deposited.

The accumulations of Mr. Hodgson have, however, not been made in vain. The Tibetan volumes especially were fortunate in finding an expounder in Alexander Csoma Körösi, whose ardent aspirations after knowledge led him, penniless and friendless, from Transylvania to Ladakh, where, with the aid of our equally adventurous countryman Moorcroft, he was enabled to study and to master the language of Tibet. Placed subsequently in communication with the Asiatic Society of Calcutta, he devoted much of his time to the examination of the volumes of the Kah-gyur, and has given the results of his labour to the public in the Journals of the Asiatic Society of Bengal, and in the 20th Vol. of the Researches; he has also afforded, by a grammar and dictionary of Tibetan, the means of prosecuting the cultivation of the language in Europe; and the Transactions of the Imperial Academy of St. Petersburgh, as well as other publications, evince the scholarship of Mr. Schmidt in Tibetan as well as in the literature of the Mongols. We have also a very valuable contribution to the History of Buddhism in a life of Buddha, translated originally from Sanskrit into Tibetan, and from that language into French, and published two or three years since by M. Foucaux M. Burnouf also qualified himself to make use of the Tibetan books supplied by Mr. Hodgson, but found abundant occupation for his time in translating from the Sanskrit originals. His Introduction to the History of Buddhism contains copious translations from many of the principal Buddhist works, whilst the work published after his death, the "Lotus de la bonne Loi", is a translation of a Sanskrit Buddhist work which has been known to be highly estimated for centuries wherever Buddhism is professed.

At the same time that Hodgson and Csoma were illustrating the literature of Buddhism, as it existed in the north of India, a like spirit of research animated the regions of the south, and the Páli scholars of Ceylon began to draw from the stores within their reach new and valuable sources of information. Besides various contributions to the Ceylon periodicals, and to the Journal of the Bengal Society[**], the late Mr. Turnour has in his edition and translation of the Maháwanso furnished us with an authentic record of the notions which are current not only amongst the

---

[*] [Soon after the appearance of Foucaux's translation and edition of the "Rgya tch'er rol pa", A. Schiefner gave from the Tibetan a full analysis, with copious notes, of a more modern life of Buddha. See his article "Eine tibetische Lebensbeschreibung Śákyamuni's" in Vol. VI of the St. Petersb. "Mémoires des Savants Étrangers".]

[**] [Ceylon Almanacs for 1833 and 1834. Journ. As. Soc. Beng., Vols. V–VII.]

people of Ceylon, but those of Ava and Siam, who belong to the same school, and whose authorities are identical. The course commenced by Mr. Turnour has been followed up with great ability by the Rev. Mr. Gogerly* in the Friend of Ceylon, and the proceedings of the branch Asiatic Society instituted on the island, whilst Mr. Hardy in his Eastern Monachism, and Manual of Buddhism, has brought together all that is at present known of the Buddhism of the South.

We are not, therefore, in want now of genuine means of forming correct opinions of the outline of Buddhism, as to its doctrines and practices, but there are still questions of vital importance to its history for the solution of which our materials are defective. Disregarding all the fancies of speculation which are based upon imperfect knowledge, and receiving with caution the accounts given us by the Chinese missionaries, the most rational course to be adopted in seeking for information on which dependence may be placed, is, to consult the works which the Buddhists themselves regard as their scriptures, and from which their own history and doctrines are derived: but then, who will answer for the authorities? what is the history, what is the date, of the numerous works that are available, and which consist of two great divisions, the Sanskrit and the Páli? and what is the comparative value of the respective classes? Are they to be

---

* [Ceylon Friend, Vols. I-IV. Journ. Ceylon Br. R. A. Soc. I, No. 1-4. II, 1. 3. IV, 1.]

regarded as synchronous and independent? and if not, which is the senior, which is the original? These are questions which M. Burnouf himself declares cannot yet be answered with confidence: an exact comparison between the two series of works, he declares to be impossible in the present state of our knowledge. We are not yet in possession of all the works that may exist in either class, but even if they were all collected in any European library, they must be read and studied, translated and commented upon, and the translations and comments must be published. This task, more tedious than difficult, would require the cooperation of many laborious and patient scholars, and upon its completion in a satisfactory manner could critical investigation alone commence.

Although, however, it is perfectly true that conclusions on which implicit reliance is to be placed must be preceded by such a series of operations as M. Burnouf indicates, yet, as that preliminary process is indefinitely deferred and may never be perfected, we must be content in the meanwhile to make use of such means as we possess, and from them to form a conjectural approximation, if not a positive propinquity, to the solution of the question upon which the whole depends—the antiquity and authenticity of the writings in which the Buddhists themselves record the history of their founder and the doctrines which they maintain, and from which alone we can derive information that is of any real value. The great body of the Buddhist writings consists avowedly of translations; the Tibetan, Mongolian, Chinese, Cingalese, Burman, and Siamese books, are all declaredly translations of works written in the language of India—that which is commonly called *Fan*, or more correctly *Fan-lan-mo*, or "the language of the Brahmans"; and then comes the question, to what language does that term apply? does it mean Sanskrit or does it mean Páli? involving also the question of the priority and originality of the works written in those languages respectively; the Sanskrit works as they have come into our hands being found almost exclusively in Nepal, those in Páli being obtained chiefly from Ceylon and Ava.

Until very lately, the language designated by the Chinese *Fan* was enveloped in some uncertainty. Fa Hian in the fourth century takes with him *Fan* books not only from India but from Ceylon, and the latter it has been concluded were Páli. No Sanskrit Buddhist works, as far as we yet know, have been met with in the south any more than Páli works in the north, although Sanskrit works are not unfrequent in Ceylon in the present day. The mystery, however, is now cleared up. In the life and travels of Hiuan Tsang, written by two of his scholars and translated from the Chinese by M. Julien, the matter is placed beyond all dispute by the description and by the examples which the Chinese traveller gives of the construction of the *Fan* language, in which he was himself a proficient, having been engaged many years in the study whilst in India, and in translating from it after his return to China. We learn then from him, that the words of the *Fan* language are distinguished under two classes, *Ting-anta* and *Sup-anta*, the Sanskrit grammatical designations of *verbs* and *nouns*; that the former have eighteen modifications or persons, in two divisions, nine in each, one called *Pan-to-sa-mi*, or, in Sanskrit, *Parasmai*; the other *O-ta-mo-ni*, or, in Sanskrit, *Âtmane*. All verbs and nouns have three numbers, singular, dual, and plural, of which he gives us examples both in conjugation and declension. All this is Sanskrit; and what is more to the point, it is not Mágadhi, the proper designation of the dialect termed in the south Páli. No form of Prákrit, Páli included, *has a dual number*, and the terminations of the cases of the noun are, in several respects, entirely distinct[1]. Hiuan Tsang also cor-

---

[1] The following examples are given by Hiuan Tsang of the inflexions of a verb and noun [Hist. de la vie de Hiouen Thsang, 168-71]:

VERB.

	CHINESE.	SANSKRIT.	ENGLISH.
Third Person.			
Sing.	P'o-po-ti	Bhavati	He is
Du.	P'o-po-pa	Bhavapa (for Bhavatah')	They two are
Pl.	P'o-fan-ti	Bhavanti	They are
Second Person.			
Sing.	P'o-po-sse	Bhavasi	Thou art
Du.	P'o-po-po	Bhavapa (for Bhavathah')	You two are
Pl.	P'o-pu-t'a	Bharatha	You are
First Person.			
Sing.	P'o-po-mi	Bhavāmi	I am
Du.	P'o-po-boa	Bhavāvat'	We two are
Pl.	P'o-po-mo	Bhavámah'	We are
V.	P'o-po-mo-sse		

rectly adds that the grammar in use in India, in his time, was the work of a Brahman of the north, a native of Tula or Sálátura, named Po-ni-ni, or Pánini, the well known Sanskrit grammarian; and he notices

NOUN.

	CHINESE.	SANSKRIT.	ENGLISH.
Nominative.			
Sing.	Po-lo-sha	Purusha	Man
Du.	Pu-lu-shao	Purushau	Two men
Pl.	Pu-lu-sha-so	Purushás	Men
Accusative.			
Sing.	Pu-lo-shan	Purusham	Man
Du.	Pu-lu-shao	Purushau	Two men
Pl.	Pu-lu-shoang	Purushán	Men
Instrumental.			
Sing.	Pu-lu-shai-ua	Purushena	By a man
Du.	Pu-lu-sha-pien	Purushábhyám	By two men
Pl.	Po-lu-sha-pi / Po-lu-sha-sae	Purushábhih / Purushais	By men
Dative.			
Sing.	Po-lu-hia-ye	Purusháya	To man
Du.	Pu-lu-sha-pien	Purushábhyám	To two men
Pl.	Pu-lu-shai-sho	Purushesha (for Purushebhyah)	To men
Ablative.			
Sing.	Pa-lo-sha-to	Purushát	From a man
Du.	Pu-lu-sha-pien	Purushábhyám	From two men
Pl.	Pu-lu-she-sho	Purusheshu (for Purushebhyah)	From men
Genitive.			
Sing.	Pu-lo-sha-taio	Purushasya	Of a man
Du.	Pu-lu-sha-pien	Purushábhyám(forPurushayoh)	Of two men
Pl.	Pu-lu-sha-nan	Purushánám	Of men
Locative.			
Sing.	Pu-lu-ch'ai	Purushe	In a man
Du.	Pu-lu-sha-yu	Purushayoh	In two men
Pl.	Pu-lu-shai-tseu	Purusheshu	In men

a form of the verb peculiar to the Grammar of the Vedas (Fei-to).

The evidence of Hiuan Tsang, therefore, is conclusive as to the language of the books which were sought for and studied by the Chinese Buddhists in India, and carried with them to China, and there translated into the form and under the appellation in which they still exist. Whether the books they took from Ceylon were Sanskrit or Páli, we have no further indication than the name *Fan*, which it seems most probable that Fa Hian employed in the same sense as Hiuan Tsang, or that of Sanskrit; and it is also to be observed that the principal works of Ceylon are subsequent to his time, which makes it further almost certain that the *Fan* books of Ceylon were also in Sanskrit.

The Buddhist authorities of India Proper, then, were undeniably Sanskrit; those of Ceylon might have been Páli or Mágadhi: were they synchronous with the Sanskrit books, or were they older, or were they younger, more ancient or more modern? To answer these questions we must endeavour to determine their

	CHINESE.	SANSKRIT.	ENGLISH.
Vocative.			
Sing.	Hi (He) Pa-lo-sha	Purasha	O man
Du.	Hi (He) Pa-lu-shao	Purushau	O two men
Pl.	Hi (He) Pa-lu-sha	Purusháh	O men

The verb does not differ materially from the Páli verb; but the inflexional terminations of the cases of the noun differ very widely: some of them are misstated, but this is probably from errors of transcription.

relative chronology, from the imperfect means which are within our reach. Both sets of authorities undoubtedly, Sanskrit and Páli, were in existence in the fifth and sixth centuries of our era. The Sanskrit works, according to the testimony of Chinese travellers, were carried from India to China in very considerable numbers from a much earlier date; in one instance it is said two years before Christ, but it was not till after A.D. 76, the date of the introduction of Buddhism into China, that they were imported in any number, and not till the third and fourth centuries that they had become very numerous. In a Chinese history of celebrated Buddhist teachers, published between 502 and 556, and from which M. Julien has given us extracts, a Buddhist priest named Dharma, is said to have brought to China one hundred and sixty-five works, amongst which were several that may be readily identified with the Sanskrit works procured by Mr. Hodgson: we cannot hesitate, for example, to recognise in the Ching-fa-hua, meaning "The Flower of the right Law", the Sad Dharma Puńdarîka, "Le Lotus de la bonne Loi", which, as has been mentioned, was the last labour of M. Burnouf. Of this work repeated translations have been made into Chinese[*], the first of which dates A.D. 280, whilst of the Lalita Vistara, or life of Sákya Muni, the earliest Chinese version was made between A.D. 70-76. We may be satisfied, therefore, that the

---

[*] [W. Wassiljew, der Buddhismus. 1860, I, 163. Burnouf, ntroduction, I, 8 f.]

principal Sanskrit authorities which we still possess were composed by the beginning of the Christian era at least; how much earlier is less easily determined.

According to the Buddhists themselves, the doctrines of Śákya Muni were not committed to writing by him, but were orally communicated to his disciples, and transmitted in like manner by them to succeeding generations. When they were first written is not clearly made out from the traditions of the north; but they agree with those of the south in describing the occurrence of different public councils or convocations at which the senior Buddhist priests corrected the errors that had crept into the teaching of heterodox disciples and agreed upon the chief points of discipline and doctrine that were to be promulgated. The first of these councils was held, it is said, immediately after Śákya Muni's death; the second 110, and the third 218 years afterwards, or about 246 B.C. The northern Buddhists confound apparently the second and third councils, or take no notice of the latter in the time of Aśoka, but place the third in Kashmir under the patronage of Kanishka or Kanerka, one of the Hindo-Scythic kings, 400 years after Buddha's Nirváńa, or B.C. 153. Both accounts agree that the propagation of Buddhism, by missions dispatched for that purpose, took place after the third council.

According to the traditions which are current in the south as well as the north, the classification of the Buddhist authorities as the Tripitaka (the three collections) took place at the first council; the portion termed Sútra, the doctrinal precepts, being compiled by Ánanda; the Vinaya, or discipline of the priesthood, by Upáli; and the Abhidharma, or philosophical portion, by Kásyapa—all three Buddha's disciples. Their compilations were revised at the second council, and were finally established as canonical at the last. Their being compiled, however, does not necessarily imply their being written; and, according to the northern Buddhists, they were not committed to writing until after the convocation in Kashmir, or 153 B.C.; whilst the southern authorities state, that they were preserved by memory for 450 years, and were then first reduced to writing in Ceylon.

It is to the former of these periods that M. Burnouf would ascribe the composition of the principal Sanskrit works which are still extant. That they continued to be written for four or five centuries afterwards is obvious from internal evidence, and even from their number and extent. In the sixth century Hiuan Tsang and his assistants translated 740 works, forming 1,335 volumes. Of these he himself took to China 657, and they had been brought thither in great numbers before his time. There is also a considerable body of works of a still more recent date, forming the basis upon which many adulterations have crept into Buddhism, evidently borrowed from the Tantras of the Brahmans: 700 works, however, all undoubtedly prior to the sixth century, must have been the work of many years, and have furnished full occupation to the Buddhist scholars of several centuries preceding.

We may consider it then established upon the most probable evidence, that the chief Sanskrit authorities of the Buddhists still in our possession were written, at the latest, from a century and a half before, to as much after, the era of Christianity.

Now what is the case with the Páli authorities of the South? We have it most explicitly stated in the great Singhalese authority, the Maháwanso*, that the doctrines of Buddha were handed down orally, for more than four centuries after his death; and that they were not reduced to writing till the reign of Wattagámini, between B.C. 104 and 76. And that then the Pitakam was first written in Páli, and the commentary upon it (the Atthakathá) in Singhalese. The latter did not exist in *Páli* until the *fifth century* of the Christian era, or between A.D. 410, 432, when Buddhaghosa, originally a Brahman of Magadha, arrived in Ceylon, and gave the first impulse to the cultivation of his own dialect, the Mágadhí, to which the people of the south have applied the term Páli; meaning, according to M. Turnour, "perfect, regular".

---

* [c. XXXIII, 106 ff. with which the following verses of the Dipawansa, c. 20, almost literally agree:

Wattagámani abhayo panchamásesu ádito
Evam dvádasa vassáni rájá rajjam akárayi ||
Pitakattayapálincha tassá atthakatháni cha
Mukhapáthena ánesum pubbe bhikkhú mahámatá ||
Hánim disvána sattánam tadá bhikkhú samágatá
Thiraṭṭhitattham dhammassa potthakesu likhápayum ||

See also N. L. Westergaard, Om de ældste Tiderum i den indiske Historie. Kjöbenhavn: 1860, p. 39.]

The word is not known in India: it is not an Indian term. Buddhaghosa, it is said, repaired with his books to Pegu, and thence also dates the introduction of Páli as the sacred language of the Buddhists of Ava and Siam. Shortly after his time, or between A.D. 459 and 477, the other great Páli work of the Singhalese (the Maháwanso) was composed. Of the Dípawanso, another of their authorities, the date is not specified; but as it brings down the history of Ceylon to the beginning of the fourth century* when it was left unfinished, and as Buddhaghosa was the main instrument of introducing the use of Páli into Ceylon, it must be of the same period, or the fifth century. The principal Páli works of the South are, therefore, of a period considerably subsequent to the Sanskrit Buddhistical writings of India Proper, and date only from the fifth century after Christ. Their subsequent date might also be inferred from internal evidence; for, although they are in all essential respects the very same as the Buddhist works of India — laying down the same laws and precepts and narrating the same marvellous legends — they bear the characteristics of a later and less intellectual cultivation, in their greater diffuseness, and the extravagant and puerile additions they frequently make to the legendary matter. They seem also to be very scantily supplied with the Abhidharma or metaphysical portion of the Tripiṭaka, as compared with the Sútra and Vinaya. Such portions

---

* [Journal As. Soc. Bengal, VII, 922.]

of the Pitaka as have been translated are, however, essentially the same as the Sanskrit Sútras, whilst the Atthakathás, or the commentaries, take a more discursive range, and are of a less authentic character; being in fact the compositions of Buddhaghosa, *taken*, as he himself states, *not translated*, from the Singhalese Atthakathá, which are no longer extant. How much therefore is his own, cannot be now determinated.

Of the three classes of works constituting the Tripitaka, that of the Sútras is historically the most important. A Sútra is properly a brief aphorism or precept, conveying a position or dogma in a few concise, and not unfrequently obscure, terms. The Buddhist Sútras are not exactly of this nature. They are supposed to be the *ipsissima verba* of Sákya himself, the Buddha-vachana, repeated by Ánanda as he had heard them; and they all begin, whether in Sanskrit or in Páli, with the expression: "This has been heard by me.—Etan-mayá śrutam, Evam mayá suttam." They are in the form of a dialogue, in which the disciple asks questions and Sákya explains; illustrating his explanation by parables and legendary tales of various extent. M. Burnouf has shewn, however, that the Sútras are of two different descriptions. In one class, no doubt the oldest, the style is much more simple, and is wholly prose; and the legends are less extravagant. They are called by M. Burnouf the simple Sútras. In the other, which the Buddhists themselves term Vaipulya Sútras, "expanded or developed Sútras", the style is more diffuse, and is mixed prose and verse; and the latter is very remarkable, as containing many ungrammatical forms; the narratives are prolix and marvellous; and new persons are introduced who, although unknown to the simple Sútras, evidently performed a conspicuous part in the subsequent dissemination and corruption of the Buddhist religion; such are Nágárjuna or Nágasena, Manjusrí, and Padmapáni, to the latter of whom the invocation that is now so conspicuous in the temples of Nepal and Tibet is addressed under a modified name in ungrammatical Sanskrit, and with additions palpably borrowed from the Tantras of the Brahmans—Om! Mańipadme! Hûm!—Glory to Mańipadma—Hûm! Another personage is also, for the first time, introduced,—Avalokiteswara, who is regarded by the Tibetans as their particular patron, and who is an object of especial worship to the Mongols and Chinese, amongst whom he is sometimes represented as having eleven heads and eight arms; or sometimes a thousand eyes and a thousand hands, as expressed by his Chinese name Kwan-shi-in[*]. Many absurd legends respecting this Bodhisattwa are current amongst the Buddhists of the north, but they, and the multiplied limbs of Avalokiteswara, are, no doubt, unauthorized additions, even to the texts of the Vaipulya Sútras. The introduction of such legendary and mythological personages is, however, sufficient evidence that these works are later than the

---

[*] [See Wassiljew, l. l., I, 135.]

simple Sútras, although most of them were current in India when visited by the Chinese in the fifth and sixth centuries.

It is, therefore, to the simple Sútras that we are to look for the earliest and least corrupt form in which, according to Buddhist notions, the doctrines of their founder are delivered. M. Burnouf has given us specimens in the Mándhátrí and Kanakavarńa Sútras[*], portions of a larger work, the Divya-avadána; they record severally the names of Buddha when he was the king Mándhátrí, a name well known in Pauráńik fiction, and when, as king Kanakavarńa, he gave away to a Bodhisattwa the last morsel of food which a long drought and famine had left for his sole sustenance. Of course this act of charity was followed by an immediate fall of rain and the return of plenty. To judge from these specimens, the simple Sútras, although the earlier, are not the most interesting of the Buddhist writings, and details which are of more value to the history, if not to the doctrine only, are to be found in the Vaipulya Sútras—constituting the authorities of the Mahayána, the great vehicle, which were the particular objects of Hiuan Tsang's studies and collections. Amongst these we may particularize the Lalita Vistara—the expansion of the sports [of Buddha]; being his life—and in Buddhist belief, his autobiography—having been repeated by himself. The Sanskrit original is not very rare in India, and

---

[*] [Introduction à l'histoire du Bouddhisme Indien, p. 74 ff. 90 ff.]

the Asiatic Society of Bengal has undertaken the publication of the text and translation by Rájendra lál Mitra. The entire work has been published at Paris, translated from the Tibetan, as I have mentioned, by M. Foucaux*, who has compared it carefully with the Sanskrit, and bears testimony to the closeness of the Tibetan translation. He ascribes its composition to a period subsequent to the third convocation, or about 150 years B.C. It was translated, as I have stated, into Chinese in the first century after, which is compatible enough with the date assigned to its first composition, and there is internal evidence in favour of the same date**.

It is, undoubtedly, subsequent to the Mahábhárata, which I have elsewhere conjectured to be about two centuries prior to Christianity; for it is said, that when the choice of the family in which the Buddha should be born was under consideration in the Tushita heaven, that of the Páńdavas of Hastinapura was objected to, because they had filled their genealogy with confusion, terming Yudhishthira the son of Dharma, Bhímasena the son of Váyu, Arjuna of Indra, Nakula and Sahadeva of the Aswins; all very correct citations***. In the proofs also of his skill in archery

---

* [See A. Schiefner in "Mélanges Asiatiques". St. Pétersbourg: 1852. I, 217 ff.]

** [Wassiljew, l. l., 1, 192. St. Julien in Foucaux's Lalitavistara, II, p. xvi.]

*** [Lalitavistara, Calcutta edit., p. 24.]

which Śákya displays in his youth he pierces with his arrow an iron effigy of a boar, the very feat which Arjuna performs, only that the Pándu prince achieves it within the reasonable compass of a meadow, whilst, in the usual strain of Buddhist exaggeration, Śákya hits the mark at the distance of ten *kos*, or twenty miles off[*]: these circumstances clearly refer to the Hindu poem, and concur in placing the age of the Lalita Vistara about a century and a half before the Christian era. It embodies, however, no doubt, the traditions of an earlier date, traditions not long subsequent to the first dissemination of the principles of Buddhism.

The circumstances of Buddha's life, as told in the Lalita Vistara, have furnished all the Buddhist nations with their traditions. The life and acts of Buddha are always related to the same purport, and very nearly in the same words, in Chinese, Tibetan, Mongolian, Páli, Burman, Siamese, and Singhalese. After an infinitude of births in various characters, during ten millions of millions and one hundred thousand millions of kalpas, the shortest of which consists of sixteen millions of years, and the longest of thirty-two millions, he attained the rank of Bodhisattwa, that which is inferior only to a Buddha, in the Tushita heaven, where he taught his doctrine to innumerable millions of Bodhisattwas, or future Buddhas, and gods and spirits; and was glorified by Śakra, Brahmá, Maheśwara, Nágas, Gandharbas, Yakshas, Asuras,

---

[*] [l. l., p. 175 f.]

and other creations of the Brahmanical mythology. To rise to the elevation of a perfect Buddha one existence more on earth was necessary, and he, therefore, becomes incarnate as the son of the Śákya prince Śuddhodana, king of Kapilavastu, and Máyá his wife: he is born miraculously from his mother's side, who died seven days after his birth: as soon as born he took seven steps to each of the four quarters, announcing aloud his supremacy in language, which the Lalita Vistara and the Buddhist writings of Ava and Ceylon similarly repeat, at least substantially. The Lalita Vistara, for instance, makes him say in the east, "I shall proceed, the first of all existences, springing from the root of virtue:" in the south, "I shall be worthy of the offerings of gods and men:" In the west, "This is my last birth; I shall put an end to birth, old age, disease, and death:" in the north, "I shall have no superior amongst beings[*]." So Mr. Hardy[**], translating from various Buddhist works in Páli, says: "at his birth he was received by Mahá Brahmá in a golden net, from which he was transferred to the guardians of the four quarters, who received him on a tiger's skin, from the dewas he was received by the nobles, who wrapped him in folds of the finest and softest cloth, but at once Bodhisat

---

[*] [l. l., p. 96 f.]

[**] [Manual of Buddhism, p. 145 f. See also Bigandet's "Legend of the Burmese Budha", in the Journal of the Indian Archipelago, Vol. VI (1852), p. 500; and Bennett's "Life of Gaudama", in the Journal of the American Oriental Society, Vol. III (1853), p. 11.]

descended from their hands to the ground, and looked to the four points, and to the four half points, and above and below; when he looked towards the north he proceeded seven steps in that direction and exclaimed: 'I am the most exalted in the world. I am chief in the world. I am the most excellent in the world. Hereafter there is to me no other birth.'" The legend is evidently the same although slightly varied.

Siddhártha, his name as a prince, was educated as a prince, married to different wives, and led a life of pleasure and enjoyment, until the vanity of worldly existence was impressed upon his conviction by his meeting, on three several occasions, with a sick man, a corpse, and a mendicant, on which he resolved to abandon his royalty and devote himself to solitary meditation. His father disapproves of his intention, and places him under restraint; but he makes his escape miraculously by night, with one attendant, and having reached a convenient distance from the city changes his dress with a hunter,—a demigod in disguise,—and with his sword cuts off his own hair. According to a Páli authority quoted by M. Burnouf[*], this was the origin of the curly hair of the figures of Sákya, which induced early European writers to consider him as of Abyssinian origin, for the hair, shortened to the length of two fingers, turning upwards, remained in that position the rest of his life. He then engages in sacred study under different Brah-

---

[*] [Lotus de la bonne Loi, p. 660 ff. 864. Bigandet, l. l., p. 519. Bennett, l. l., p. 23.]

mans, but, dissatisfied with their teaching, retires into solitude, followed by five of his fellow-disciples, and for six years practises rigorous austerities: finding their effects upon the body unfavourable to intellectual energy, he desists and adopts a more genial course of life, on which his five disciples quit him and he is left alone. He is then assailed by the demon of wickedness, Mára, "the killer", who is identical with Kámadeva, or the God of Love; but terrors and temptations fail to disturb his serenity, and the Tempter is compelled to acknowledge his defeat, and to withdraw. Buddha, resuming his meditations, contemplates the causes of things, which is the key to the well-known formula of the Buddhists found upon so many of their images, and of which the various readings, as given in a communication by Colonel Sykes, in the forthcoming number of our Journal*, are evidently nothing more than the blunders of ignorant transcribers, or defects in cutting the letters on clay or stone. In the Lalita Vistara, Buddha's meditations are thus recapitulated:—

"Thus thought the Bodhisattwa: 'from what existing thing come disease and death? age and death being the consequences of birth, birth is the cause of disease and death.'" He then proceeds to analyse in the same strain the causes of birth, of conception, of desire, of sensation, of contact, of the senses, of name and form, of comprehension, of ideas; and concludes that igno-

* [Journ. R. As. Soc., Vol. XVI, p. 87 ff.]

rance, Avidyá, is the cause of ideas, and is the remote cause of existence*.

The next subject of his meditations is the means by which this chain of causes is to be counteracted, and he concludes: "Birth being no more, old age and death are annihilated; and as ignorance is the ultimate cause of existence, then by the removal of ignorance all its consequences are arrested, and existence ceases, by which means old age, death, wretchedness, sorrow, pain, anxiety, and trouble, the whole mass of suffering, becomes for ever extinct**." This is the summary of Buddhistic wisdom set forth in the popular stanza,

"Ye dharmá hetu-prabhavá,"

with which we have long been familiar***.

The Lalita Vistara is somewhat silent on the subject of Sákya's peregrinations, and represents him as chiefly engaged in discourses to his Bhikshus, or mendicant followers, or in intercourse with the Nágas and the Devas. He attains to the perfection of a Buddha at Bodhimańda †, which is apparently ancient Gayá, and resides there until he thinks it necessary to look out for some person who may succeed him as teacher of the law; he then proceeds to Benares, and on his way, having no money to pay for being ferried across the Ganges, he transports himself over it in the air.

---

* [l. l., p. 144.] ** [l. l., p. 145.]
*** [Burnouf, Lotus, p. 521 ff. Journal R. A. Soc., Vol. XVI. 38—44. Koeppen, Religion des Buddha, I, 223.]
† [Rgya tch'er rol pa, II, p. 47. Hiuen thsang, Mémoires, II, 456. Wassiljew, I, 46.]

At Benares he recovers his five original disciples, but it does not appear that they are appointed to succeed him: on the contrary, Buddha addressed these words, it is said, to Mahá Kásyapa, Ánanda, and the Bodhisattwa Maitreya: "Friends! the Supreme Intelligence, perfect and full, which I have acquired in a hundred thousand millions of kalpas, I deposit in your hands. Do you yourselves receive this part of the Law, teach it fully in detail to others." He then praises the Sútra, the Lalita Vistara, after which, "the sons of the gods, the Máheśwaras, and the rest of the gods, the Śuddha-káváśakáyikas, Maitreya, and all the other Bodhisattwas, Mahásattwas, Mahá Káśyapa, and the rest of the Mahá Srávakas, Ánanda, and the worlds of the gods, of men, of Asuras, of Gandharbas, rejoiced, and praised aloud the instructions of Bhagaván *."

As the Lalita Vistara is attributed to Śakya himself, it cannot contain any account of his death. For this we must have recourse to the Mahá Parinirváńa Sútras, of which we have only the Tibetan translation, in the eighth and two following volumes of the Nya division of the Do Class of the Kahgyur, and of which Csoma has given us an abridged translation; we have it also in the life of Śakya in the Mongol, as translated by Klaproth in the Asia Polyglotta, and we have what is no doubt the same work in Páli, the Parinibbáńa Suttam, a section of the Dígha nikáyo, of which Mr. Turnour has given us an analysis (J. A.

---

* [Rgya tch'er rol pa, II, p. 406 f.]

S. B., VII, 991)*. The accounts, as far as they go, are substantially the same, but the proximate cause of Sákya's death, illness brought on by eating pork, seems to be an addition of the compiler of the Singhalese narrative; no such incident is alluded to by either Csoma or Klaproth, and it seems very inconsistent with Sákya's recommendation of abstinence: as also Sákya had attained the age of eighty he might have been allowed to die of natural decay. The Páli legend adds that the pork was provided for him, and for him alone, by his host, at his particular desire, because he knew it would cause his death**. According to both narratives he directed his disciples to dispose of his remains after the fashion of that of the Chakravarttís, or universal monarchs, the ashes of whose bodies, after burning, were collected and deposited in stately pyramidal monuments. Accordingly his ashes were at first placed in a monument erected where he died, in Kusinagara, or Kusia in Gorakhpur, but portions were claimed by various persons; and the warriors of Kusa, although they at first refused to give up any of the precious deposit, were at last induced by the mediation of a Brahman, who is not named in Csoma's analysis, but is termed Doño, that is, Droña, by Turnour, to assent to a division. The distribution is in some respects not very intelligible; one part is for the champions of Kusa, one for those of Digpachan or

---

* [Burnouf, Introduction à l'histoire, p. 74.]
** [Koeppen, L. L. I, 114 f.]

Tibet, one for the royal tribe of Baluka, one for the royal tribe of Krodtya, one for a Brahman of Vishńúdwípa, one for the Śákyas, one for the Lichhavis of Allahábád, and one for Ajátaśatru, king of Magadha: they all built chaityas over them and paid them worship. The urn in which the reliques had first been placed was given to the Brahman who had mediated, and another Brahman received the cinders: they also erected chaityas. Of the four eye-teeth, two were distributed to the deities called Trayastrinsats, and the Nágas; one was placed in "The Delicious City", and one in the country of the king of Kalinga, whence in time it found its way to Ceylon, where it is still preserved. Hence originated the practice of constructing the monuments called Sthúpas, or Topes, which have excited so much interest of late years, and of which a subsequent sovereign of Magadha, Aśoka, is said to have constructed 84,000. In many parts of Tibet, where they are more usually termed Chaityas, or Chaits, they are numerous but small, containing, it is supposed the ashes of distinguished Lamas. Chaitya, which is a Sanskrit term, is in fact equally applicable to any sacred object, a temple, or a tomb; every Sthúpa may be a Chaitya, but a Chaitya may be also something else of a religious character*.

These accounts of Śákya's birth and proceedings, laying aside the miraculous portions, have nothing very impossible, and it does not seem improbable that

---

* [Koeppen, I. l. I, 533 ff. Lassen, Ind. Alt., II, 266.]

an individual of a speculative turn of mind, and not a Brahman by birth, should have set up a school of his own in opposition to the Brahmanical monopoly of religious instruction, about six centuries before Christ; at the same time there are various considerations which throw suspicion upon the narrative, and render it very problematical whether any such person as Śákya Sinha, or Śákya Muni, or Sramaña Gautama, ever actually existed. In the first place, the Buddhists widely disagree with regard to the date of his existence. In a paper I published many years ago in the Calcutta Quarterly Magazine, I gave a list of thirteen different dates, collected by a Tibetan author, and a dozen others might be easily added, the whole varying from 2420 to 453 B.C. They may, however, be distinguished under two heads, that of the northern Buddhists, 1030 B.C. for the birth of Buddha, and that of the southern Buddhists, for his death B.C. 543. It is difficult, however, to understand why there should be such a difference as five centuries, if Śákya had lived at either the one or the other date.

The name of his tribe, the Śákya, and their existence as a distinct people and principality, find no warrant from any of the Hindu writers, poetical, traditional, or mythological; and the legends that are given to explain their origin and appellation are, beyond measure, absurd. The most probable affinity of the name is to that of the Śakas, or Scythians, or Indo-Scythians, as if they were an offshoot from the race that dislodged the Indo-Bactrian Greeks, but this is not countenanced by any of the traditions, Brahmanical or Buddhist.

The name of Sákya's father, Suddhodana, "he whose food is pure,"—suggests an allegorical signification, and in that of his mother, Máyá, or Máyádeví, "illusion, divine delusion,"—we have a manifest allegorical fiction: his secular appellation as a prince, Siddhártha, "he by whom the end is accomplished,"—and his religious name, Buddha, "he by whom all is known," are very much in the style of the Pilgrim's Progress, and the city of his birth, Kapila Vastu, which has no place in the geography of the Hindus[*], is of the same description. It is explained, "the tawny site," but it may also be rendered, "the substance of Kapila," intimating, in fact, the Sánkhya philosophy, the doctrine of Kapila Muni, upon which the fundamental elements of Buddhism, the eternity of matter, the principles of things, and final extinction, are evidently based. It seems not impossible, after all, that Sákya Muni is an unreal being, and that all that is related of him is as much a fiction as is that of his preceding migrations, and the miracles that attended his birth, his life, and his departure.

At the same time, although we may discredit the actuality of the teacher, we cannot dispute the introduction of the doctrine, and there may have been, about the time attributed to Sákya's death by the southern Buddhists, a person, or what is more likely,

---

[*] [But compare L. Vivien de St.-Martin in "Mémoires sur les contrées occidentales", II, 356 ff.]

persons of various castes, comprising even Brahmans, who introduced a new system of hierarchical organisation, for that seems to have been the chief, if not the sole innovation intended by the first propagators of Buddhism. The doctrine of transmigration was common to the Buddhists and to every division of the Brahmanical Hindus: the eternity of matter and the periodical dissolution and renovation of the world were also familiar to all the schools; the Buddhists did not abolish caste, they acknowledged it fully as a social institution, but they maintained that it was merged in the religious character, and that all those who adopted a religious life were thereby emancipated from its restrictions, and were of one community: the moral precepts which they inculcated, with at least one exception—the prohibition of taking away animal life, were common to them and to the Brahmans; and the latter seem to have adopted from the Buddhists, very possibly, the merit of *Ahinsá*: the Buddhists recognised the existence of all the gods of the Brahmanical pantheon, with perhaps one or two exceptions which may have been of later date, such as Krishńu for instance: the notion of final extinction or Nirváńa, although more unqualified, was not exclusively confined to the Buddhists. In short, the philosophy of Buddhism, as is observed by Mr. Gogerly, was essentially eclectic, and the main point of disagreement was the political institution of a religious society which should comprise all classes, all castes, women as well as men, and should throw off the authority of the Brahmans as the sole teachers of religious faith. It seems likely also that the same innovators discarded the ritual of the Vedas, and discontinued the adoration of the Hindu divinities, placing the observance of moral duties and the practice of a life of self-denial and restraint above the burthensome and expensive charges of formal worship. Their departure from the Brahmanical system started about the time ascribed to Śákya's teaching, became gradually developed as the organization of those by whom they were professed became more perfect, and by the middle of the third century before Christ, they may have enjoyed the patronage of Aśoka, the Rájá of Central India, as the Buddhist traditions maintain, and under his encouragement a convocation may have been held, at which the associated Buddhists commenced that course of propagation which spread their religion throughout India and beyond its confines to the north and to the south. I do not think that the difficulties which attend the identification of Aśoka with Piyadasi have yet been cleared up, but we may admit that the edicts on the columns and the rocks were inscribed about the time of Aśoka's reign, or in the third century before Christ. We may admit also that they are intended to recommend Buddhism, but their tone is not that of a triumphant or exclusive form of belief, and the spirit of toleration which they breathe is an unequivocal proof of a nascent faith, a system that courts compromise rather than provokes and defies hostility. At this period we may conceive the marvels of Śákya's life and the more detailed expansion of the doctrines ascribed to him to have been devised, as calculated to excite the admiration and win the belief of the natives of India, ever ready to give credit to the supernatural, and to pay superstitious homage to the assumption of divinity. Besides the inscriptions attributed to Aśoka, he is said to have been a profuse constructor of Vihāras, Buddhist monasteries, and of Sthúpas or monuments over Buddhist reliquiæ. Vihāras were probably multiplied about this time or even earlier: we have not yet met with any Sthúpas to which so high an antiquity can be confidently assigned. It seems little likely that Śákya, or the first propagators of the system, would have enjoined the construction of monuments to preserve the frail relics of humanity, when their first dogma was the worthlessness of bodily existence, and it could not have been until Śákya was elevated by his followers to the rank of something more than a god that his relics, or those of his early disciples, should have been held entitled to such veneration; at any rate we have no evidence of the erection of any Sthúpa as early as the middle of the third century before Christ, whilst we have several proofs of their construction after the era of Christianity, down as late as the sixth century afterwards. These are afforded by the discovery, in the solid body of the monuments, of the coins of the consular families of Rome, and of the first Cæsars; of the coins of the emperors of Constantinople, Theodosius, Marcian, and Leo, who reigned from A.D. 407 to A.D. 474; and of great quantities of the coins of the Sassanian princes of Persia, down to Kobad, who died A.D. 531. These coins are found in the Topes of the Punjáb and Afghánistán, and establish beyond dispute that the practice of constructing monuments of this class prevailed in the north-west of India from some time after the beginning of the Christian era until the sixth century. The most remarkable monument of this class in Central India is that of Bhilsa or Sánchi, in its neighbourhood. This was first brought to notice by Captain Fell, who published a description of it in the Calcutta Journal in 1819; this description, with additions, was reprinted by Mr. J. Prinsep*, in the third volume of the J. B. Asiatic Society, and at his suggestion sketches of the most remarkable objects and facsimiles of inscriptions abounding on the spot, were sent him by Captains Smith and Murray, and published by him, with translations and important comments, in the sixth volume of the Journal. More recently, Lieutenant Maisey has been employed by the government of Bengal to make careful drawings of these remains; and some of his sketches which have been sent home evince his great merit as an artist as well as an antiquarian. The publication of these documents has been anticipated by Major Cunningham, who had associated himself with Lieutenant Maisey in the investigation, and who has published the results of his own labours in a work entitled The Bhilsa Topes, in which he has

---

* [See also J. Prinsep's Essays on Indian Antiquities, ed. E. Thomas. 1, 171 ff.]

given not only sketches of various interesting objects, but copies and translations of more than 200 inscriptions. They are mostly short, merely specifying the liberality of some devout Buddhist in a gift which is not specified; as, Dhamma rakhitasa bhichhuno dánam, "the gift of the mendicant Dharma Rakshita*." Major Cunningham conjectures the gifts to have been stones or sculptured contributions to the structure. From one of them he infers the date of the inclosure to have been the early part of the reign of Asoka — "Subahitasa Gotiputasa Rája-lipikúrasu dánam — the gift of the king's scribe, Subahita, son of Goti**;" Gotiputra being the teacher of the celebrated Moggaliputra. From an inscription in one of the gateways in which the name of Sri Sát Karńi occurs, Major Cunningham concludes the gateways were erected about the beginning of the Christian era, in which Lieutenant Maisey concurs***. These, however, he considers long posterior to the body of the building, which he would carry as far back as 250 B.C., or even 500 B.C., on somewhat insufficient evidence; its being as old as Asoka depending upon the identification of Gotiputra the teacher of Mogguli-putra, who presided, it is said, at the third council in A.D. 241, a statement altogether erroneous, as Mogguli-putra, Maudgala, or Maudgalyáyana, was one of Sákya's first disciples, three centuries earlier. In the second and third of the topes of Sánchi, Major Cunningham found relic boxes,

* [Bhilsa Topes, p. 238, No. 19.]
** [l. l., p. 251, No. 110.]   *** [l. l., p. 264 ff.]

inscribed with the names of Káśyapa, Moggaliputra, and Śáriputra, from which he would seem to infer that the topes must have been erected soon after their deaths, or some time between 550 B.C. and 250 B.C.; but, as he himself remarks, the reliques of Buddha and his principal disciples were very widely scattered, being found in different places; and once the notion of their sanctity was adopted, they were no doubt multiplied, as so many pious frauds, in order to give a reputation to the building in which they were said to be enshrined; similar vases were also found at Satdhara and Andher, furnishing examples of this multiplication of relics in the same immediate neighbourhood. Their asserted presence, in any monument, is no more a proof of its antiquity than would the hairs of Buddha, if ever dug up, prove the Shwedagon of Rangoon to have been built in his day. No legitimate conclusion can be drawn, therefore, from inscriptions of this class, as to the date of the Sánchi monuments, whilst the name of a Sát Karńi prince is a palpable indication of their being erected subsequent to the Christian era. The topes of Ceylon, however, appear to be of an earlier date, if we may credit the tradition which ascribes the erection of the Ruanvelli mound at Anurádhapura to king Dutthagámani, who reigned, 161 B.C. to 137 B.C.*

A somewhat earlier period than that of the Indian Sthúpas may be assigned to another important class

---

* [Lassen, Ind. Alt., II, 428 f. Journ. As. Society Bengal, XVI, 291.]

of Buddhist monuments—the Cave Temples belonging
to that persuasion—but they also, as far as has been
yet ascertained, are subsequent to Christianity. The
Rev. Mr. Stevenson has lately furnished important
illustrations of this subject to the Journal of the Branch
Asiatic Society of Bombay, in his translations of the
inscriptions in the Cave Temples of Kanheri, Karlen,
Junir, Nasik, and other places in the Sahyádri range
of hills, from facsimiles taken under the authority of
the government by Mr. Brett. They, like the inscriptions on the Sthúpas, are usually brief records of
gifts not specified, by persons, for the most part, of
no mark or likelihood, but there are a few names of
historical value, as well as a few dates. In one case,
the excavation at Nána Ghát, Mr. Stevenson conjectures for it an antiquity of 200 B.C., but there do
not seem to be sufficient grounds for such a conjecture*. In another case he proposes**, for a column
at Karlen, the date 70 B.C., as it was set up by Agnimitra, son of Mahárája Bhoti, whom he would identify
with the last of the Sunga dynasty, Devabhúti; but
this, to say the least, is problematical, and in this, as
well as in the preceding, Mr. Stevenson himself que-
ries the chronology: the dates which he proposes
without hesitation begin with A.D. 189, but we tread
upon tolerably safe ground when we come to various
dates from 20 B.C. to A.D. 410, because the inscrip-

---

* [Journ. Bombay Br. R. A. Soc., V, 174 f. 428.]
** [ib. 3 f. 152 f. 426 f. (where he corrects *bhoti* into *goti*).]

tions give us several of the names of the Ándhrabhŕitya, or, in the dialect of the inscriptions, Ádhábhati princes; such as Bálin, Kŕipa Karńa, Gautamiputra, and Yajna Srí Sát Karńi, members of a dynasty who were the powerful princes of the "Andhra gens", noticed by Pliny, and who, we learn from the Puránas, confirmed by the accounts of the Chinese travellers, extended their authority to Central India, and reigned at Pútaliputra from the commencement of the Christian era to the fifth century after it, which period we may consider as the date of the principal Buddhist excavations in the west of India.

The evidence thus afforded by the Sthúpas, and the caves, of the time in which the principal monuments of Buddhism were multiplied, harmonises with that which we have derived from the more lasting literary monuments of the same faith, and leaves no doubt that the first four or five centuries after Christ, were the period during which the doctrine was most successfully propagated, and was patronized by many of the Rájás of India, particularly in the north and in the west. Ever ready as the Chinese traveller, Fa-Hian, at the end of the fourth century, is to see Buddhism everywhere dominant, he furnishes evidence that in the east, and particularly in the place of its reputed origin, the birth place of Śákya, which had become a wilderness, it had fallen into neglect. In the seventh century, Hiuan Tsang abounds with notices of deserted monasteries, ruined temples, diminished number of mendicants, and augmented proportion of heretics. It has been already conjectured that this was the term of its vitality, and that the seventh century witnessed its disappearance from the continent of India. Traces of Buddhism lingered, no doubt, till a much later period, as is shewn by the inscription found at Sárnáth as late as the eleventh century[*]; but it was then limited to a few localities, and had shifted its scene to the regions bordering on its birth-place, being shortly afterwards so utterly obliterated in India Proper, that by the sixteenth century the highest authority in the country, the intelligent minister of an inquiring king, the minister of Akbar, Abulfazl, could not find an individual to give him an account of its doctrines.

It would be impossible, in the limited time at our disposal, to enter upon a detail of what those doctrines are; but I may briefly advert to one or two of those which may be regarded as most characteristic. Some of those which are common to Buddhists and Brahmans have been noticed, and of those which are peculiar, the difference is rather in degree than in substance.

Thus the attribution to a Buddha of power and sanctity, infinitely superior to that of the Gods, is only a development of the notion that the gods could be made subject to the will of a mortal, by his performance of superhuman austerities; only the Buddhists ascribed it to the perfection of the internal

---

[*] [Lassen, Ind. Alt., III, 741 ff.]

purity acquired during a succession of births. The notion of Buddha's supremacy once established, the worship of the gods became superfluous; but as the mass of mankind are in need of sensible objects to which their devotions are to be addressed, Buddha came to be substituted for the gods, and his statues to usurp their altars. In the course of time, in some of the Buddhist countries, at least other idols, several of them very uncongenial with the spirit of Buddhism, and evidently borrowed from Hinduism, came to be associated with him, particularly in Tibet and China, in which latter country the temples commonly present three principal colossal images, which are the representatives of Buddha and two of his chief disciples, Sákya, Sáriputra, and Maudgalyáyana; or, according to some authorities, of Buddha, Dharma, and Sangha, or Buddha, the Law and the Community. They are sometimes also said to be the Buddhas of the past, present, and future ages. The temples, however, present many other idols, such as a goddess of mercy, a queen of heaven, a god of war, a god of wealth, a tutelary divinity of sailors, tutelary divinities of cities, and various other fanciful and not unfrequently grotesque beings, amongst whom we have Ganeśa with his elephant head. In Japan, if we may trust to Kæmpfer, we have representations of the avatárs of Vishńu; and in Nepal and western Tibet, as already remarked, we have the Dhyáni Buddhas, and Bodhisattwas, Mańipadma, Manjuśrí, and Avalokiteśwara, and a host of inferior spirits and divinities, of whom pictures or statues fill the courts, or cover the walls of the temples. The representation and worship of these idols, although not prohibited by anything in the religion of Buddha, is obviously incompatible with its spirit, and must be regarded as exotic corruptions; no such auxiliaries seem to be admitted in those countries where the system exists in its greatest purity, as in Ava, Siam, and Ceylon, as, although the images in the temples are often exceedingly numerous, they are, with exception of subsidiary figures which are not worshipped, such as dragons and lions, all of the same character, representing Gautama or his disciples generally in a sitting posture, with the legs crossed, and the hands in the act of prayer or benediction; the indefinite multiplication of the images arising from its being considered an act of merit to set up a statue of a Buddha or of a Buddhist priest of reputed sanctity.

The organization of a regular priesthood from all classes, and their assemblage in Vihâras or monasteries under a superior, is also one of the distinguishing features of Buddhism, as opposed to Brahmanism, although not wholly unknown to the institutes of the latter. The monastic system, however, does not seem to have originated with Sákya himself, for he and his immediate followers were migratory, passing from one part of central India to another, except during the rainy season, when they dispersed to their respective homes, reassembling after the rains; the organization commenced probably with the first convocation, and was brought to perfection by the third. In the first instance, the heads of the communities were elected by the associates, on account of their superior age and learning; but other motives, no doubt, soon came to influence the choice, and in time new principles were introduced, which were not originally recognized, although not wholly foreign to the spirit of the system, particularly the notion that guides the election of a successor to a deceased Dalai Lama of Lhassa, or a Tashi Lama of Tashilumbo, the selection of a child in whose person the soul of the deceased is supposed to have become regenerate, being in fact that of a Buddha on his way to perfection. This notion is now, at least, no longer confined to Tashilumbo, or to Lhassa; but is spread very generally through Tartary, according to the French missionaries; and every monastery of note seeks, upon the demise of its Superior, for a child to succeed him, sending usually to western Tibet to discover him, and detecting him by placing before the boy a variety of articles, from which he picks out such as had belonged to the deceased, and which he is supposed to recognize as having been his property in a prior existence. This, if true, may no doubt be easily managed by a little dexterity, but Messrs. Huc and Gabet suspect that Satan is at the child's elbow, and prompts the verification of the articles. The notion however is admitted to be of comparatively modern introduction, as late as the thirteenth or fourteenth century [*].

---

[*] [Koeppen, l. l., II, 120-31.]

Another essential difference between Brahmanism and Buddhism, was the proselyting spirit of the latter. Although Brahmanism has spread into countries where it could not have been indigenous, yet a Brahman, like a poet, "nascitur non fit;" and, consistent with the spirit of the code, a man must be born a Hindu, he cannot become a Hindu by conversion. The Buddhist adopted the opposite course, and hence, no doubt, their early success. The public teaching of Buddha or of the founders of the faith must have been so novel and attractive, that we can easily believe the Buddhist narratives, that vast multitudes of all classes and of both sexes attended the public preaching of the Buddhist missionaries, an encouraging precedent we may observe, by the way, for those of pure religion. There are, however, some peculiar features in the teaching of Sákya and his disciples, which render it more surprising that it should ever have been successful than that its success should have been of temporary duration. Its object is not the good of the people in their social condition: it no doubt enjoins the observance of moral duties, and reverence to parents and teachers, and the general practice of compassion and benevolence, but to whom are these injunctions addressed? according to the authorities of the religion, whether Sanskrit or Páli, to Bhikshus and Bhikshunís, persons who have separated themselves from the world, and who, besides professing faith in Buddha, engage to lead a life of self-denial, celibacy, and mendicancy, and to estrange themselves from all domestic and social obligations: with all its boasted benevolence it enjoins positive inhumanity where women are concerned, and in its anxiety for the purity of the mendicant, prescribes not only that he should not look at or converse with a female, but that, if she be his own mother and have fallen into a river, and be drowning, he shall not give her his hand to help her out; if there be a pole at hand he may reach that to her, but if not, she must drown. An interesting illustration of this barbarity occurs in the drama called Mrichchhakati*, which represents Buddhist institutions with singular fidelity. In this spirit is the whole of the Vinaya or Buddhist discipline conceived: it is a set of rules for individuals separated from society, in whom all natural feeling is to be suppressed, all passions and desires extinguished, consistently enough with the doctrine that life is the source of all evil, and that one means of counteracting it is by the checking the increase of living beings. Rigid compliance with the restraints imposed, has, however, been found impracticable, and considerable latitude has been allowed in practice. The rules of abstinence and celibacy must be strictly observed whilst the individual continues in the order of the priesthood, but he may withdraw from that order, either for ever or for a season, and may marry and lead a secular life; he may, after an interval, be readmitted, and his second admission is considered as

---

* [End of Act VIII.]

final, but even this does not seem to be very rigorously enforced.

Belief in a Supreme Being, the Creator and Ruler of the universe, is unquestionably a modern graft upon the unqualified atheism of Sákya Muni: it is still of very limited recognition. In none of the standard authorities translated by M. Burnouf, or Mr. Gogerly, is there the slightest allusion to such a First Cause, the existence of whom is incompatible with the fundamental Buddhist dogma, of the eternity of all existence. The doctrine of an Ádi Buddha, a first Buddha, in the character of a Supreme Creator, which has found its way into Nepal, and perhaps into Western Tibet, is entirely local, as is that of the Dhyáni Buddhas and the Bodhisattwas, their sons and agents in creation, as described by Mr. Hodgson. They are not recognised in the Buddhist mythology of any other people, and have no doubt been borrowed from the Hindus. There can be *no first* Buddha, for it is of the essence of the system that Buddhas are of progressive development: any one may become a Buddha by passing through a series of existences in the practice of virtue and benevolence, and there have been accordingly an infinitude of Buddhas in all ages and in all regions. One of the Páli authorities records the actions of twenty-four[*]; Schmidt, from a Mongol work, has given us the names of a thousand Buddhas. (Trans. Soc. St. Petersburg, 2, 68.) There are Sans-

---

[*] [Mahawanso, Introd. xxxii ff.]

krit authorities for seven in the present age of the world, whose praises I have translated (Asiatic Researches, Vol. XVII)* and who are represented in the Ajunta paintings. An eighth, Maitreya, is to come; but these are only a few, confined to certain periods: the number during all the extravagant intervals of Buddhist chronology has no limitation, and there can no more be a *first* than there can be a *last*, each passing on his turn to the end and aim of his existence,— extinction — nirváňa.

Utter extinction, as the great end and object of life, is also a fundamental, and in some respects a peculiar, feature of Buddhism. Nirváňa is literally a blowing-out, as if of a candle,—annihilation: it has been objected to this that Buddhism recognises a system of rewards and punishments after death, and no doubt its cosmology is copiously furnished with heavens and hells; but this it has in common with Brahmanism: it is a part of the scheme of transmigration; the wicked are punished and the good rewarded, but the punishment and reward are only in proportion to their bad or good deeds, and when they have been balanced the individual returns to earth to run up a fresh score, to incur in fact, according to Buddhism, a fresh infliction of suffering, life being the cause of evil from which there is no escape, but by finally ceasing to be. Brahmanical speculation contemplates, equally with Buddhism, exemption from being born

---

* [Art. I of this volume.]

again as the summum bonum, but proposes to effect
this by spiritual absorption either into universal spirit,
or into an all-comprehending divine spirit; but the
Buddhists recognize no such recipient for the liberated
soul. No doubt, amongst the Buddhists, as amongst
the Brahmans, differences of opinion occasionally prevailed, giving rise to various schools; four of these
were known to the Brahmanical controversial writers
before the sixth century; but, besides them, who are
styled Sautrántika, Vaibháshika, Mádhyamika, and
Yogáchára*, there was an Aiswarya, or theistical
school, with which the notions admitted into Nepal
may have originated: the more ancient and genuine
school, however, was that of the Swábhávikas, whose
doctrine is thus summarily indicated in a Buddhist
Páli book: "Whence come existing things? from their
own nature, — *swabhávát*. Were do they go to after
life? into other forms, through the same inherent
tendency. How do they escape from that tendency?
where do they go finally? into vacuity, — *śúnyatá*,"
such being the sum and substance of the wisdom of
Buddha**. That this was the meaning of Nirváňa is
shown in numerous passages both in Sanskrit and in
Páli. In the Saddharma Laṅkávatára***, Śákya is
represented as confuting all the Brahmanical notions
of Nirváňa, and concludes by expounding it to be the
complete annihilation of the thinking principle, illus-

---

* [Wassiljew, l. l., 1, 285-367. Koeppen, l. l., 1, 151 ff.
St. Julien in Journal Asiatique, Vol. XIV (1859), p. 327 ff.]
** [Burnouf, Introd., 441 ff.] *** [ibid., 514 ff.]

trating his doctrine by the comparison generally employed of the exhaustion of the light of a lamp which goes out of itself. In the Brahma-jála*, a Páli Sútra, where again Sákya is made to confute sixty-two Brahmanical heresies, he winds up by saying: "Existence is a tree; the merit or demerit of the actions of men is the fruit of that tree and the seed of future trees; death is the withering away of the old tree from which the others have sprung; wisdom and virtue take away the germinating faculty, so that when the tree dies there is no reproduction. This is Nirvána."

The segregation of the Buddhist priesthood from the people, although, in the first instance, probably popular, from the priestly character being thrown open to all castes alike, must have been unpropitious to the continued popularity of the system, and its success can only be attributed to the activity of its propagators, and the indolent acquiescence of the Brahmans. When the influence acquired by the Buddhists with the princes of India gave them consideration, and diverted the stream of donations as well as of honours, the Brahmans began to be aroused from their apathy, and set to work to arrest the progress of the schism. The success that attended their efforts could have been, for a long time, but partial; but that they were ultimately successful, and that Buddhism in India gave way before Brahmanism, is a historical fact: to what cause this was owing is by no means

* [Burnouf, Lotus, p. 850 ff. Journal Ceylon Br. R. A. Soc., I, 2, p. 18 – 62.]

established, but it was more probably the result of internal decay, than of external violence. There are traditions of persecution, and it is very possible that local and occasional acts of aggression were perpetrated by the Brahmanical party: the Buddhist writings intimate this when they represent the Bodhisattwas as saying to Buddha: "When you have entered into Nirvána, and the end of time has arrived, we shall expound this excellent Sútra, in doing which we will endure, we will suffer patiently, injuries, violence, menaces of beating us with sticks, and the spitting upon us, with which ignorant men will assail us. The Tírthakas, composing Sútras of their own, will speak in the assembly to insult us. In the presence of kings, of the sons of kings, of the Brahmans, of Householders, and other religious persons, they will censure us in their discourses, and will cause the language of the Tírthakas to be heard; but we will endure all this through respect for the great Rishis. We must endure threatening looks, and repeated instances of contumely, and suffer expulsion from our Viháras, and submit to be imprisoned and punished in a variety of ways; but recalling at the end of this period the commands of the chief of the world, we will preach courageously this Sútra in the midst of the assembly, and we will traverse towns, villages, the whole world, to give to those who will ask for it, the deposit which thou hast entrusted to us[*]." This is the language of

---

[*] [Burnouf, Lotus, p. 165 f.]

the Sad-dharma Puṇḍarîka, which, as I have mentioned, had been translated into Chinese before the end of the third century, and shows that the career of the Buddhists had not been one of uninterrupted success, even at so early a date, although the opposition had not been such as to arrest their progress: this, if it at all occurred, was the work of a later period, but we have no very positive information on the subject. According to Mádhava Áchárya, a celebrated writer of the fourteenth century, the Buddhists of the south of India were exposed to a sanguinary persecution at the instigation of Kumárila Bhaṭṭa*, the great authority of the Mímánsakas, who, as he preceded Śankara Áchárya, may have lived in the sixth or seventh century, or earlier. Mádhava asserts that, at his recommendation, a prince named Sudhanwan issued orders to put the Buddhists to death throughout the whole of India:

"Á-setor-á-tushádre tu Bauddhánám vriddabálakán
 na hanti yaḥ sa hantavyo bhrityán ityanwaśád nṛipaḥ."

"The king commanded his servants to put to death
 the old men and the children of the Bauddhas,
 from the bridge of Ráma to the snowy mountain;
 let him who slays not be slain."

We do not know who Sudhanwan was, but his commands were not likely to be obeyed from Cape Comorin to the Himálaya, and whatever truth there

---

* [Colebrooke, Essays, p. 190. Lassen, Ind. Alt., IV, 708 ff.]

may be in his making Buddhism a capital crime, his authority must have been of restricted extent, and the persecution limited to his own principality. The dissemination of Buddhism, however, in the countries beyond the Bay of Bengal does seem to have received a fresh impulse about the sixth or seventh centuries, and this may have been connected with some partial acts of persecution in India, and consequent emigration of the Buddhists; we have no record, however, of its having been universal, and its having been of any great extent may be reasonably doubted: it seems more likely that Buddhism died a natural death. With the discontinuance of the activity of its professors, who, yielding to the indolence which prosperity is apt to engender, ceased to traverse towns and villages in seeking to make proselytes, the Buddhist priest in India sunk into the sloth and ignorance which now characterise the bulk of the priests of the same religion in other countries, especially China, and seem there to be productive of the same result, working the decay and dissolution of the Buddhist religion.

Although expelled from India, and apparently in a state of decline in some of the regions in which it took refuge, Buddhism still numbers amongst its followers a large proportion of the human race. According to Berghaus, as quoted by Lassen, there are four hundred and fifty-five millions of Buddhists, whilst the population of the Christian states is reckoned at four hundred and seventy-four millions: Mohammedans and Hindoos are very much fewer. The enumeration of the Buddhists, however, includes the whole of the population of China, without adverting to their distribution as the followers of Confucius or Taō-sse, or, as we have lately learned, as the professors of a composite Christianity.

Numerous, however, as the Buddhists still are, the system seems to be on the decline, where it is not upheld by the policy of the local governments, or where the priesthood does not constitute a very large share of the population. The people in general do not seem to take much interest in the worship of the temples, nor to entertain any particular veneration for their priests. The temples are always open, and service is regularly performed, usually three times a day, like the Sandhyá of the Brahmans: on these occasions the priests assemble, usually seated in two divisions or semi-choirs, who chaunt passages from the sacred books, Tibetan, Páli, or Sanskrit, the two latter being utterly unintelligible to the people, and understood by very few of the priests. The chaunting is relieved by the accompaniment of bells, and cymbals, and drums, and the blowing of the conch shells, or brass trumpets, or, in the eastern Himálaya, of trumpets made of human thigh bones; incense is burnt before the images of the Buddhas, and fruit and flowers, and dishes of food placed before them. The people take no part in this performance, and come in small numbers, at their own convenience, and make their offering and prostration, and then depart. The priests, again, are said to enjoy little personal consideration:

not that they forfeit it by any conduct inconsistent with their profession, for, although there may be occasional exceptions, they seem in general to lead inoffensive, if useless, lives. In Ceylon, according to Sir Emerson Tennent, the people pay more respect to the garb than to the wearer, and take every opportunity of making it known that the yellow robe, and not the individual, is the object of their veneration. According to Mr. Hardy*, the whole number of priests in Ceylon, although many of the communities possess extensive landed estates, the gifts of the piety of former princes, does not exceed 2,500, dispersed in monasteries, the largest of which has seldom more than twenty resident members. In Fa Hian's time there were, according to him, from 50,000 to 60,000 priests in Ceylon, and in one of the monasteries at Anurádhapura, there were 5,000. Mr. Hardy adds: "in no part of the island that I have visited, do the priests as a body appear to be respected by the people: although occasionally an individual may recommend himself by agreeable manners:" they are sometimes treated unceremoniously; and he mentions an instance in which a priest was driven out of a village by the women armed with their brooms, and threatening him with personal castigation. In the Burma country the priests are more numerous, but there also they are said to have but little influence over the minds of the people, who sometimes say, not without some reason in excuse of impropriety of conduct, that the precepts of

---

* [Eastern Monachism, p. 309.]

the law are not for them but for the priests. The system, however, is supported by the Government, and a high priest resides at the capital, by whom all the Punghis, or heads of establishments, are appointed. Although tolerant of the practice of other religions by those who profess them, secession from the national belief is rigidly prohibited, and a convert to any other form of faith incurs the penalty of death. The condition of Buddhism is said to be prosperous; from 2,000 to 3,000 lay worshippers make daily offerings at the great temple of the Shwe-dagon, near Rangoon; and new temples and Kyums are daily springing up, even in the districts under British authority. One great source of influence in Ava is the monopoly of education by the priesthood, and which, such as it is, is very general. Almost every Burman can write and read, for which he has to thank the Kyum or monastery of his village. Buddhism is also flourishing in Siam, where, as in Ava, it is connected with the political institutions of the state, and with the mass of the population: every male must enter the order of the priesthood at some period of his life, for however short a time; even the king must become a priest for two or three days, wearing the mendicant dress and soliciting alms of his courtiers. The high officers of the state sometimes take up their abode in a monastery, and conform to all the rules of the fraternity for two or three months together. The priests, or Talapoins as they are termed, from carrying a Tála or palm-leaf as a fan, are consequently numerous, but the permanent inhabitants of the monasteries are either persons disgusted with life, or the old and infirm; the younger and more active members continually falling back into society. The share taken by the sovereign in the organisation of the system seems to be the chief source of its prosperity.

We have no very recent accounts of the condition of Buddhism in Japan, although, to judge from the drawings of Col. Siebold in his "Nippon", the ordinary objects of Buddhist worship are numerous, and comprehend many of the later saints of the system as well as personages apparently of peculiar and local sanctity. Buddhism also is broken up into various sectarial divisions. In China, as far as there has been any opportunity of ascertaining, which however is almost confined to the maritime districts, it is evidently on the wane: although a few monasteries are respectably tenanted, the residents are much less numerous than they have been, and many are altogether deserted; many of the temples also are in a state of decay. The majority of the priests are illiterate, and seem to hold their offices and their idols in little veneration; the people regard the priests with little respect, or in some instances with contempt, and attach no great sanctity to the objects of their worship,—a curious instance of this indifference in both is mentioned by the Right Rev. Dr. Smith, the present Bishop of Victoria. In a temple belonging to a monastery, where he was allowed to occupy a residence, he first inadvertently and then designedly, overthrew several idols, which, being of clay, were broken by the fall, amidst, he says, the laughter of the bystanders. He resided several weeks in the monastery of Teen-tsung near Ningpo, where he constantly distributed Christian tracts in Chinese, without any hindrance or molestation.

The late Mr. Gützlaff, in a paper in our Journal now in course of printing[1], agrees entirely in the description given by Bishop Smith of the ignorance of the Buddhist priesthood, of the low estimation in which the priests are held, and the absence of all really religious feeling in the people.

It is in the north and north-west of China, extending thence through Mongolia and Eastern Tibet to Lhassa, that the chief seats of Buddhism are to be found, as we learn from the travels of the French missionaries, Messieurs Huc and Gabet, who traversed the whole interval. Throughout their entire route they met with, or heard of, what they term Lamaserais, that is, Vihâras, or monasteries connected with temples, inhabited by numerous resident Lamas, as well as having attached to them a number of itinerant mendicant brethren. At a monastery, at a place called Chor-chi, there were two thousand resident Lamas. At a city, which they translate Blue-town, there were twenty establishments, large and small, inhabited by at least twenty thousand Lamas. At the monastery of Kun-lun, where they were allowed to take up their residence for several months, there were four thousand resident Lamas. At the chief monastery of Tartary, that of

[1] Vol. XVI, p. 73.

the Khalkas and in its vicinity, there were, it is said, thirty thousand Lamas, the head of whom exercised the temporal as well as spiritual authority of the whole country, and was an object of uneasiness to the court of Pekin. In the province of which Lhassa, the acknowledged high seat of Lamaism, is the capital, there were said to be three thousand monastic establishments, in three of which, Khaldan, Prebung, and Sera, there were in each fifteen thousand Lamas. The missionaries estimate the Lamas at one-third of the whole population; all the males of a family, except the eldest, being expected to enter the order, at least for a term; it being allowable in Tartary, as well as in other Buddhist countries, for a member of a monastery to return to active life. Every monastery has its Superior, who is very commonly originally a boy brought from Tibet, being supposed to be the late principal regenerated; he being, in fact, as before observed, a Buddha on his way to perfection.

The vast number of the Lamas of Tartary and Tibet naturally suggests the inquiry, how countries so poor, upon the whole, and thinly peopled, can support so large a proportion of unproductive members. Some of their subsistence is derived from grants and endowments made by the Emperors of China, whose policy it has been to encourage Lamaism, as tending to keep down the population, and repress the martial spirit of the nomadic tribes: further means are supplied by the people, who are a simple and credulous race, and who, although not animated by any devotional fervour, are liberal contributors to the temples at public festivals, and to the itinerant mendicant brethren, giving largely from their stores of sheep, and wool, and butter, and various articles of consumption. The chief maintenance of the Lamas is, however, their own industry. In the Buddhist countries of the south, as Ceylon, Siam, and Ava, and apparently in China, a priest is strictly prohibited from exercising any mechanical art, or following any secular occupation; but in Tartary, the Lamas are permitted to support themselves by their own industry, even whilst living in the monastery: the monastery being, in fact, a small town of a priestly population, dwelling in houses, in streets collected round a principal temple or temples, and the main buildings occupied by the Pontiff with his staff and servants. The other Lamas are the sculptors, painters, decorators, and printers of the establishment; those who are qualified are the schoolmasters of the children of the neighbourhood, who have no other teachers; and those who are not engaged in the service of the monastery may employ their time for their own profit. There are amongst them, consequently, handicraftsmen, as tailors, shoemakers, hatters; some keep cattle and sell the milk and butter to the brethren, and some even keep shops; the consequence is great inequality of condition; those who are active and enterprising become opulent, whilst the inert and idle, who trust solely to the pittance which is doled out periodically to every member, from the common fund, may be almost in a state of starvation.

The general organization of the monasteries in Tartary and Tibet, the costume of the Lamas, and many particulars of the manner in which religious service is celebrated in the temples, have often struck travellers as presenting close analogies to the conventual system and the religious offices of the Roman Catholic Church. In this latter respect, we have the admission of the French missionaries, whose enumeration we may safely follow, and who specify the use of the cross, the mitre, the dalmatic, the hood, the office of two choirs, the psalmody, the exorcisms, the censer of five chains, the benediction of the lamas by placing the right hand on the head of the faithful, the rosary, celibacy of the clergy, spiritual retirement, the worship of saints, fasts, processions, litanies, and holy water, as so many coincidences with the Romish ritual, the origin of which cannot be accidental. The present costume and ceremonial are said to have originated with a celebrated reformer, who was born in the latter half of the fourteenth century, named Tsong Kaba, who founded the monastery of Khaldan, near Lhassa, in 1409, and died in 1419[*]. The chief pontiff of Lhassa at first opposed the innovations of Tsong Kaba, and having in vain invited him to a conference, paid a visit to the reformer, and expatiated at great length upon the sacredness of the ancient practices and his own preeminence; he was interrupted in his harangue by Tsong Kaba, who had pre-

---

[*] [Koeppen, l. l., II, 108-120. Comp. also "Arbeiten der K. Russischen Gesandtschaft zu Peking". Berlin: 1858, I, p. 315-17.]

viously taken no notice of him, and who suddenly exclaimed: "Wretch, let go the flea that you are torturing between your thumb and forefinger! I hear his groans, they penetrate to my heart." Fleas, it seems, are very abundant in Tibet, and the Grand Lama, in violation of the precept that says, Thou shalt not kill, was privily in the act of committing murder, when thus rebuked by Tsong Kaba. Struck by this proof of Tsong Kaba's divine perception, the Grand Lama acknowledged his supremacy, prostrated himself before him, and adopted his reforms. Tradition speaks of a stranger Lama from the west, who was Tsong Kaba's preceptor, and who was remarkable amongst other things for a long nose; noses in Tartary are somewhat of the shortest; from which circumstance, as well as from the palpable resemblances adverted to, Messieurs Huc and Gabet infer[*], not without some plausibility, that Tsong Kaba derived his innovations from the instructions of a European missionary, several of whom at this early period had penetrated into Tibet, Tartary, and China.

The peculiarities of the costume are certainly foreign to the original institutes of the Vinaya, which is much more faithfully followed in the south. The shaven head and yellow robes of the priests of Ceylon, Ava, and Siam, are much more orthodox than the red robes and yellow hats or mitres of the Lamas of Tartary and Tibet.

Notwithstanding the liberality shewn by the people

---

[*] [Souvenirs d'un voyage, &c., II, 104 ff.]

of Tibet, especially at particular festivals, to their
monasteries and temples, they take no part in the
celebration of the religious services, nor do they
evince any stronger devotional interest than prevails
in other Buddhist countries. In all of them, however,
there are powerful means by which the priests work
upon their feelings, and secure their adherence, and
extort their bounty. Everywhere, except in China,
learning, such as it is, is confined to the priesthood,
and they are the sole instructors of youth; they are
also the collectors and vendors of drugs, and the
practisers of medicine. They still, as in the days of
Clement, foretell events, determine lucky and unlucky
times, and pretend to regulate the future destiny of
the dying, threatening the niggard with hell, and promising heaven, or even, eventually, the glory of a
Buddha, to the liberal. Their great hold upon the
people is thus derived from their gross ignorance,
their superstition, and their fears; they are fully imbued with a belief in the efficacy of enchantments, in
the existence of malevolent spirits, and in the superhuman sanctity of the Lamas, as their only protection
against them; the Lamas in Tartary are, therefore,
constantly exorcists and magicians, sharing, no doubt,
very often the credulity of the people, but frequently
assisting faith in their superhuman faculties by jug-
glery and fraud. In the most northern provinces of
Russia, Buddhism, degraded to Shamanism, is nothing
more than a miserable display of juggling tricks and
deceptions, and even in the Lamaserais of Tibet, ex-

hibitions of the same kind are permitted, whatever may be the belief and practice of those of the community who are better instructed, and take no part in them themselves. Ignorance is at the root of the whole system, and it must fall to pieces with the extension of knowledge and civilisation. A striking conformity in this conclusion is expressed by the missionaries of different Christian communities. Messieurs Huc and Gabet observe: "After all we have seen in our long journey, and especially during our sojourn in the monarchy of Kun Lun, we are persuaded that it is by education, not by controversy, that the conversion of these people is to be most efficaciously promoted;" and we learn from Erman, in his late travels in Siberia, that both the Russian and English missionaries at Irkutsk, and on the Selinga, had abandoned all attempts at direct conversion, and had confined themselves to the cultivation of the Mongol and Manchu languages, in order to qualify themselves to give education to the people. The process is inavoidably slow, especially in Central Asia, which is almost beyond the reach of European activity and zeal, but there is no occasion to despair of ultimate success. Various agencies are at work, both in the north and the south, before whose salutary influence civilisation is extending; and the ignorance and superstition, which are the main props of Buddhism, must be overturned by its advance.

IX.

ACCOUNT

OF THE

RELIGIOUS INNOVATIONS ATTEMPTED BY AKBAR.

From the Quarterly Oriental Magazine. Calcutta: 1824, Vol. I, P. 1, p. 49—62.

The Áyíni Akbarí contains many allusions to the peculiar notions, introduced or countenanced by the illustrious patron of the author, but forbears to enter into any particular details of them. The work of Abulfazl is therefore calculated to excite, rather than to gratify curiosity, and instigates the reader to examine other authorities, in order to supply the deficiency.

It could not be expected that the Muhammedan historians should dwell with any complacency upon a deviation from the doctrines of Islam, and accordingly no mention of the new tenets of Akbar occurs in the works of Ferishta, or of the annalists of Akbar's reign. The Dabistán* gives us an account of the religious disputations, which were held in Akbar's presence, and in the character of a philosopher may be sup-

---

* [Engl. transl., III, 49—138.]

posed to personify the opinions of the king. This work does not, however, state the particular dogmas of the sect instituted by the monarch, and the sentiments of the sage are more of a negative than affirmative description, subversive of all existing systems rather than the foundations of a new code of belief.

From this uncertainty, however, we have a very satisfactory appeal, and find in a work written towards the close of Akbar's reign, a most minute recapitulation of progress of the Emperor's deflections from the faith of Mohammed, and the new institutes and observances which he laboured to introduce. The work is the Muntakhab at Tawáríkh compiled by Ábd ul káder Malik Sháh Bedáoní*.

Ábd ul káder was a man of great learning; he was the fellow student of Abúlfazl and Feizí, and shared with them the countenance of the Emperor; he executed, at least in part, the translations from the Mahábhárat and Rámáyańa into Persian, and had completed that of the Sanskrit History of Cashmir, when in the 36th year of Akbar's reign he received the monarch's instructions to compile an historical account of Mohammed, the sovereigns of India, and the annals of his own reign.

Ábd ul káder accordingly began his work in the 36th year of Akbar's accession; in the manuscript we have consulted his history comes down to the 40th; but then stops rather abruptly, and seems to be in-

---

* [H. M. Elliot's Bibliogr. Index. Vol. I. Calcutta 1849, p. 219 ff.]

complete. The author intimates his having incurred the Emperor's displeasure by remitting his personal attendance at court, and it is not impossible, that his perseverance in a sullen adherence to Mohammedanism may have cut short the Emperor's patronage, and the history together. His acquirements, however, his attachment to the Moslem faith, and his reasonable regard for his own security, if not his own interest, render him a very valuable testimony; and we may credit the aggressions on the Mohammedan system made by Akbar and his followers, as he details them, and may also conclude, that he would not venture to pervert or misstate the laws and enactments of the reformer king. We shall therefore extract from his work the substance of those passages, which relate to the new religion of Akbar, in the order in which they occur.

The bias, which Akbar felt in favour of innovation, is said to have commenced in the twenty-fourth year of his reign, and is with great probability ascribed to the discredit brought upon religion altogether by the acrimony of the polemical disputes, which took place amongst the expounders of the Law and the Prophets. In the year mentioned Akbar resided at his new palace at Fatehpur Sikri[1], and in the spirit of orthodox

---

[1] Sikri was the name of the village where Akbar built a palace, and the town that was formed about it was named Fatehpur. The two names form the modern collective denomination of the place. It is about 24 miles from Agra. Extensive remains of the palace built of sandstone still exist, and the Mosque there dedicated to Sheikh Selim Chishti, which is kept in good repair,

Mohammedanism he appropriated the Friday evenings to religious conversaziones, assembling all the most celebrated Mullás and Sheikhs. The discussions that occurred, and in which the king, who was undoubtedly a prince of liberal feeling and enlightened curiosity, evinced a warm interest, were often protracted till day-break. The disputes, from being earnest and serious, became violent and angry, and the pious controversialists, when they had in vain interchanged argument, had recourse to abuse, and liberally bestowed upon each other the epithets of infidels and schismatics.

In this manner much scandal was occasioned, and the controversies between the Shí'áh and the Sunní[1], the Hanifíah and the Sháfí'ah, the advocate of authority and the assertor of independent reason, inflicted serious injuries on the first principles of the Mohammedan faith. Concurrent circumstances con-

---

is one of the most stately specimens of Mohammedan architecture to be met with in Gangetic Hindustan.

[1] The two first distinctions are well known, as the respective sectaries who rank Alí superior or inferior to the earliest successors of Mohammed. The Hanifí is the follower of Abú Hanifah, one of the great law authorities of the Sunni sect. The Sháfeí'ah is the follower of Abú 'Abdallah Sháfí', a lawyer of the same sect; but opposed to Abú Hanifah in many of his doctrines. Abú Hanifah was also much disposed to admit the exercise of reason, sometimes even in opposition to tradition; but Ikrám Daoud rejected it altogether, and other eminent authorities seldom admitted it, where a positive rule or a tradition could be applied. See Harington's account of the Authorities of Mussulman Law. As. Res. X, 482.

spired to extend the mischief, and amongst other effects to unsettle the orthodoxy of the Emperor.

A learned and pious writer, Makhdúm al Mulk, published about this time a tract injurious to Sheikh Abd un Nabí[*]. He accused that teacher of having been wrongfully instrumental to the deaths of Khizr Khán Shirwání, who had been condemned for reviling the Prophet, and Alí Habsh, who had been charged with heresy. He added also, that the Sheikh was unworthy to mount the pulpit, both because he was subject to a bodily infirmity, and because he had been disavowed by his own father for his perverse and undutiful conduct when a youth. To these attacks Sheikh un Nabí replied by calling Makhdúm al Mulk a heretic and a fool. Opinions were divided, some of the religious men sided with one, and some with another; the dispute ran high, and a complete schism ensued. The enemies of Islam took this opportunity to augment the king's disgust and dissatisfaction, and those impressions becoming progressively more intense, he lost in the course of five or six years every particle of his original belief.

One of the first effects of this secession was the assemblage of the professors of various religions from all countries, who were not only admitted to the royal presence, but there allowed openly to assert and advocate their peculiar tenets. From the confliction of notions, with which the Emperor thus be-

---

[*] [H. M. Elliot, l. l., p. 245 and p. 253.]

came familiar, all his ideas were confounded, and he
proceeded to select and compose a religion for himself, out of such dogmas as struck his fancy, amidst
the multitude of those new opinions amongst which
he fluctuated. As his chief principles for his rule of
action, he adopted these conclusions:—That every
system of religious belief could adduce learned advocates; that saints, revelations, and miracles, were
recorded by every people; that the principle of doing
no wrong was recognised by every sect; that truth
was equally common to all; that there was consequently no sufficient reason to accept one creed, and
reject another; and that still less was it necessary to
set aside all ancient ideas, in favour of the new-fangled opinions, which could boast no higher date
than a thousand years[1].

The Brahmans had some time before these occurrences been growing into great favour with the Emperor, who with the utmost secrecy had admitted
some of them to private and nocturnal conferences.
One Purushottama was employed by him to teach
him the denominations of all things peculiar to the
Hindu faith; and Deví, a reader of the Mahábhárat,
was introduced after dark into the palace, and hoisted
up on a seat into the Emperor's bed-chamber, where
he remained throughout the night, relating to Akbar
the mythological fables of the Hindus. He also explained the adoration of material substances, of fire,

---

[1] That is to say, the religion of Mohammed. Akbar, according to Dow, ascended the throne Hij. 963, and died 1014.

of the planets and the sun, and of Brahmá, Vishńu, Kŕishńa, Mahámáyá, and others, who in the estimation of some were gods, and of others angels; but who, if they ever existed at all, were probably the children of men. These teachers influenced Akbar to form a favourable opinion of the Hindu code, and especially of the doctrine of the metempsychosis, traces of which, he maintained, could be detected in every form of belief. This last assertion was echoed by the Emperor's flatterers, and many tracts were published in its vindication.

The mystical unitarianism of the Súfís was also at this period brought to the particular notice of the Emperor. Sheikh Mán of Pánipat, who was considered as second to Sheikh Mahí ad dín Ibn Arabí alone, and who was the author of a commentary on the Lowáia[1], and other celebrated Súfí works, had amongst his chief disciples Sheikh Zechariah of Delhi, surnamed by many Táj ul Árafín[2]. This teacher was succeeded by his son Táj nd Dín, who at this time published a copious elucidation of the Nezhet al Ma'árij. The celebrity thus acquired introducing him to the knowledge of Akbar, he was summoned to the presence of the Emperor, and in many private interviews contributed to lead the monarch still farther into the paths of impiety and irreligion.

---

[1] A work on Súfyism, by Maullána Jámi.

[2] The diadem of the wise, using the term wise to imply an adept in Súfí mysticism.

One of the errors to which Táj ud Dín was chiefly instrumental was this: he maintained that the epithets "pure and perfect" might be properly applied to a temporal prince; that being then invested with the character of the most holy, he was to be reverenced by prostrations, to be considered as the source of merit, and to be regarded as the Ka'ba of all desire, and the Kibleh of all pilgrimage. A number of teachers concurred in these sentiments, and it was agreed that *Insán kámil*[1] meant a just and pious king. Sheikh Yákúb of Kashmir was one of them, and he also asserted that Mohammed implied merely a guide, and Eblis, a misleader. Another authority of this school, and a personal friend of the emperor, Muhammed Yezdí of Tebrez, added vehement invectives against the three khalifs, the companions of the prophet, and their descendants, and all past and to come of the Sunní persuasion. Such absurdities, and the contradictory tenets of the 'Ulemás, impressing Akbar with a conviction of the imbecility of all those, who were reputed learned men about his court, he was led to infer that their predecessors were no wiser, and to contemn the Ghazális and Rázís of antecedent times[2].

---

[1] In the proper import of this term, it is necessary, no doubt, that we should look to Súfi interpretation; and that it implies one exempt from human infirmities: its application in this place accords with Abúlfazl's definitions of a just king, in the introduction, and several other parts of the Áyíni Akbari.

[2] Ghazáli, or Gazáli, named also Abú Ahmed Mohammed Zein addin at Túsi, a celebrated writer on religion and jurisprudence,

Amongst the religious characters who appeared at court were certain learned men of the Franks, named Padres, the head of whom is styled Pápá, and exercises authority over all their princes and kings. They introduced the Injil, the doctrine of the Trinity, (Sáles us Siláseh,) ثلث ذات and the religion of Christ. The emperor ordered the Prince *Murád*[1] to read the gospel with them, and Abúlfazl was commanded to translate it. In place of the inceptive bismilláh, he adopted the formula, ای نامی یی زیزو کرستو "Ai námi we Jezu Kristo"[2]. And, Oh that, which as thy name, is beneficent and bountiful, ای آن له نمی تو مهربان بیسیار بخشش است Sheikh Feizi added to this, سجفند لاسراك بتو Praise to thee, who art without thy like, O God.

Again, Bírbal[3], that profligate, corrupted the em-

---

in the end of the fifth century of the Hijra. Ar Rázi was another learned teacher of a similar class, born at Rey. Hijra 543. His appellation at length is Imám Fakhr addin Mohammed Ben Omar Ben Khátib Rey attemimi al Bekri.

[1] The second son of Akbar, who died in his father's life time, Hijra 1005.   [2] [Elliot's Bibliogr. Index, I, 248.]

[3] Rájá Bírbal is the supposed utterer and hero of an endless list of facetiæ, which are familiar to both Hindus and Mohammedans in the western provinces. He was a Brahman of the Bhát tribe, or order of Bards, and was a man of ready wit, and considerable acquirements. He was the constant companion of Akbar, and the whetstone of the monarch's wit, not scrupling, however, to retort freely, if traditions are genuine. His original name was *Mahi Dás*, or, according to some, Śiva Dás. But Akbar gave him the title of Kabirai, or Malk ash Shu'ará, King of the Poets. Afterwards he gave him, in Jagbir, the fort of

peror by arguing, that the sun, as the type of all perfection, and the source of light and life, was entitled to human veneration, and that it was much more rational to address the face in prayer to the rising than to the setting of his brilliant orb. He persuaded Akbar to extend this reverence to the elements, and all nature, to fire and water, stones and trees, cows, and even cow-dung; and the frontal mark and brahmanical cord became the current fashion. The learned men of the court acknowledged, that the sun is the great fire, the benefactor of mankind, and protector of princes; and the festival of the new year, Nauroz Jelàli, was henceforth celebrated throughout the rest of Akbar's reign[1]. On these occasions the following solemnities were observed. For seven days the emperor wore every day a new dress, of the colour sacred to one of the seven planets. Prayers borrowed from the Hindus were formally addressed to the sun, at sunrise and at midnight. Cows were ordered to be held sacred, and cow-dung pure. Beef was prohibited, and pork made lawful; and an opinion was obtained

---

Nagarakoï, which was commuted for an assignment of money with the old possessor, and on this occasion he entitled him Birbal, or Birber, or Vira vara, the eminent hero. Apparently the wit indifferently merited the title, although it cost him his life. He was sent with reinforcements to Zein Khan Khota, who commanded an army against the Afghans. The generals disagreed, and their dissension or incapacity brought on their ruin. They were surprised in a narrow pass amongst the mountains, and lost most of their army. Birhal was amongst the slain.

[1] See also Ay. Ak., Vol. I, 268.

from the physicians, that the flesh of kine is difficult of digestion, and the cause of many disorders.

A number of fire worshippers, who arrived from Nausárí in Guzerat, gained many converts to the religion of Zerdusht. The emperor was, to a certain extent, amongst them; and he committed the charge of maintaining a sacred fire in the palace night and day to Abulfazl. He also assisted at the Homa, a species of fire worship, which was performed daily in the inner apartments by those ladies of the haram, who were of Hindu descent.

On the new year's day of the 25th year, the emperor worshipped fire in public, and in the evening, when the candles and lamps were lighted, all the court stood up in reverence. On the eighth day after the sun's entering Virgo in this year, the king came into the audience chamber with the *Tiká*, or mark, on his forehead, and the Brahmans present tied a string of pearls round his wrist, a ceremony which they suppose secures good fortune[1]. The omrás then presented the monarch with gifts suited to their station, and having gone through the same ceremonial of tying bracelets round their wrists, took their leave.

In all these innovations Abúlfazl conformed to the emperor's fancies, and was affected with a similar malady. He used to revile the faith of Mohammed, and hold disputations with the head Kází and other

---

[1] This is called the Rákhi bandhana, and is still observed by the Hindus of the Upper Provinces of the full moon of *Srávaña*. [See Glossary of Indian Terms, p. 436, and Elliot, l. l., p. 250.]

eminent professors, with the success his great powers ensured, much to Akbar's amusement and satisfaction. The consequence was, that almost all the chief men of the court were tempted or awed into conformity with the doctrines of Akbar and his minister, except Hakím Abúl fateh and Mullá Mohammed Yezdí. Abdul Káder states, of himself, that he withdrew as much as possible from these iniquities, and thereby lost the favour of the monarch.

In consequence of this compliance, the learned authors of many books omitted the usual prefatory forms, and, after glorifying the unity of God, proceeded to the praise of Akbar. The head Kází, the Muftí, and principal lawyers, set their seals to a decree, that the decisions of a truly just king were of equal authority with the law and tradition; that just monarchs were highly esteemed of God; that Akbar was a most just and wise king; and that in all cases where any difference of opinion existed amongst the doctors and teachers, the fiat of the emperor should be held decisive.

In the following year, Hij. 988, the conduct of Akbar exposed him to much derision, even amongst his professed adherents. He performed a pilgrimage to Ajmír, and walked five cos on foot to the shrine of Sheikh Mohin ad Dín[1]. On this occasion, it was said, he puts

---

[1] Ferishta notices one of these pilgrimages; but if he is correct in his dates, he refers to one considerably anterior to this.— Dow, II, 859. [G. de Tassy, sur des particularités de la religion Mosulmane dans l'Inde. Paris: 1831, p. 62-68.]

faith in the Khájah of Ajmír, and rejects the prophets. At this time the Mohammedan creed was very widely disused, and the current formula was لا اله الا الله , الاكبر خليفة الله Lá Iláh illá Alláh, wa al Akbar Khalífat Alláh. There is no God but God, and the Mighty (or Akbar), is his vicegerent. An insurrection in Jainpur was one consequence of these innovations.

It is asserted in the Koran, that "all children are born in the faith," and Akbar determined to put this to the test of experiment. He procured twenty infants, and ordered them to be brought up in a retired place, and separate apartments, without being allowed any communication with society. At the expiration of a few years, such as survived were liberated, when it was found that they could not talk at all. The place where they had been reared was thence called Gúng Mahal, the Dumb Asylum.

A number of new edicts were now promulgated. Wine was allowed to be drunk, with the caution, that any excesses consequent upon the use of it would be rigorously punished. Places were established for the sale of it, under the authority of the court, and the names of all purchasers were registered. It is said, that pieces of swine's flesh were put into the barrels. Singers and dancers, and persons of loose character, were confined to a particular quarter, thence called Sheitánpur, and placed under the charge of a special police. Games of chance were also sanctioned under proper superintendence, and money was advanced from the royal treasury to those who played, at usurious interest. It was enacted, that the contact of hogs and dogs entailed no impurity; and both were kept in the palace, and led forth every morning. The flesh of dogs, cats, and tigers, was declared lawful food. The distribution of viands and alms at funerals was prohibited, as was marriage between first cousins: such affinity, it was said, inducing the degradation of the breed. And on the same plea it was enacted, that boys should not marry under 16, nor girls under 14 years of age[1].

A covenant was now proposed, and signed by many persons of rank, to this effect: 'I such a one, the son of such a one, with entire consent and cheerfulness of mind, declare myself liberated from the lying traditions of Islam, which I had heard and witnessed from my forefathers, and I hereby profess my adhesion to the Iláhí religion of Akbar the king; in testimony of which, I am willing to abandon wealth, life, fame, and faith[2].'

It was one of Akbar's notions, that the prescribed duration of Mohammedanism was one thousand years, and he considered this period to have expired. Accordingly he abolished the era of Hijra, and substituted that of his accession, which was called the Taríkh

[1] Akbar's sentiments on these subjects are repeated precisely to the same purpose by Abúlfazl. Áy. Ak., I. 290.

[2] The ceremony of initiation is rather differently described in the Áy. Ak., I, 219. [See also the Dabistán, III, 97 f.]

Iláhí[1]: the names of the months also were changed to those known to the ancient Persians, and their festivals were adopted in place of those of the Mohammedan faith. These latterly were formally abolished, except the Friday's prayer. This service was allowed to continue; but it was rarely attended, except by the aged and the poor.

The study of the language and literature of the Arabs was next discountenanced, and that of its law and theology prohibited. A provision was subsequently made in favour of arithmetic, astronomy, natural history, and philosophy. In the mean time, it became fashionable to avoid the use of the Arabic alphabet as much as possible; and Abdullah was softened to Abdullah (or *ain* was changed to *alif*). The name of Mohammed was particularly obnoxious, and several persons changed it: thus Mohammed Khán adopted the appellation of Rahmán Khán.

In the year of Hijra 991, fresh regulations were published. No animals were to be killed on a Sunday, nor on any days held sacred to the solar fire. The emperor was desirous, indeed, of abolishing the use of animal food altogether, and abstained from it himself, at least six months in the year[2]. Prayers were

---

[1] This account concurs also with that given in the Áyíní Akbarí, I, 346 [and the Dabistán, III, 99].

[2] So Abúlfazl: "His majesty has a great disinclination for flesh, and he frequently says, Providence has prepared variety of food for man; but through ignorance and gluttony, he destroys living creatures, and makes his body a tomb for beasts. If I

now addressed to the sun four times a day, at his rising and setting, at noon, and at midnight. At noon, the thousand and one names of the sun in Hindi were repeated. The celebrant bore the frontal mark, and closing each ear with one finger, whilst he rested the closed fist on either cheek, he kept whirling round during the repetition. At midnight and at sunrise, the royal drums were beaten. In the morning, the king neither bathed nor ate until he had seen the sun; after which he repeated the names of the planet on his beadroll, and then presented himself to the people, all ranks of whom were assembled below his window, and prostrated themselves on the ground, as soon as he made his appearance.

The Brahmans now composed a new string of the thousand and one names of the sun. They pretended to consider the emperor as an Avatár, like Ráma or Krishña. They cited texts from their old books, prophesying the birth of a king in India, who should be of foreign extraction, but who should protect cows, patronize Brahmans, and govern the world with justice. They shewed these prophecies to Akbar, and he gave credit to them.

The patronage of Akbar was not confined to the Brahmans, nor even to the Hindus, as he erected two extensive edifices without the city, one appropriated to Mohammedan, and one to Hindu ascetics: these were called Kheirpur and Dharmapur. He also

---
were not a king. I would leave off eating flesh at once; and now it is my intention to quit it by degrees." Ay. Ak., I, 104.

gave a habitation to the Jogís, and associated with them on the most familiar footing, visiting the *math* by night almost unattended, and holding scientific and religious conversations with them. They initiated him into all their knowledge and practices, so that he sometimes showed gold, which he pretended was of his own making. On the Siva Rátri, a great festival of the Jogís, he eat and drank with them, expecting to prolong his life fourfold thereby. He wore his hair after their fashion, and anticipated the liberation of his soul by the fontenelle, as they teach.

His attachment to the solar worship, however, was not weakened; and by his encouragement Mullá Shiri wrote a poem in praise of that planet, in a thousand verses, which he called the Hazár Shai'a. In the year of the Hijrí 990, at the Sankránti (or passage of the sun from one sign to another), at the commencement of the year, a grand festival was held, on which occasion many adopted the new religion, receiving instead of a certificate the picture of the king [1]. This they had richly ornamented, and wore about their persons, on their turbans, or some conspicuous part of their dress. The form of address used by the followers of Akbar, on their meeting or in their notes, was Alláhu Akbar, God is great; and when two of them met, one used the same phrase, to which the reply was, Jil o Jelálahu, To him be glory.

---

[1] Abúlfazl calls this certificate the Shust. See Áy. Ak., I, 219.

About his time the Prince Selím[1], having attained his sixteenth year, was married to the daughter of Rájá Bhagaván Dás. A portion of two crore of rupees was settled on the bride. The king, with the head Kází and other law officers, went to the palace of the Rájá, where the marriage ceremony was performed in their presence, agreeably to the Hindu ritual. The king conducted the bride to the palace.

In Hij. 995 new enactments were issued. A man was restricted to one wife, unless she proved barren. Widows were permitted to marry again. Virgin widows, amongst the Hindus, were not allowed to burn with the bodies of their husbands; but this law was subsequently cancelled, and permission to burn was granted to all, provided the act was voluntary, and nothing like compulsion was used. In the first case, a whimsical compromise was sanctioned: the living widow might be transferred to a man whose wife was at the same time dead; and his dead wife was then burnt in her place, on the same pile with the husband of the widow. In all legal causes between Hindus, a Brahman was to judge; in those between Mohammedans, the Kází. The ordeal was administered to the defendant in the former case, where an oath was otherwise required. Bodies were to be buried with the feet to the east, and people were commanded to repose in the same direction. Persons in the lower orders of society were interdicted from

---

[1] Akbar's eldest son, who succeeded him under the title Jehángir.

the study of poetry, which was only calculated to foster refractory humours, and occasion public commotions.

In the thirty-sixth and thirty-ninth years of the emperor's reign some additions to these provisions were made. The flesh of cows, buffaloes, horses, camels, and sheep, was prohibited. The *Mohammedan* rite of circumcision was not to be practised on boys under the age of twelve, and after that only with their own consent. In all marriages, the age of the parties was verifiable before the Kotwál. All persons were declared free to choose their own religion; but if a Hindu female were induced, by affection for a man of the Musalman persuasion, to join that faith, she might be compelled to abandon it, and be compulsorily reattached to her original creed. Every one was permitted to erect temples, mosques, churches, or tombs, according to their own inclination.

This terminates the code of religious legislation which our author has commemorated, and these different enactments enable us to form a tolerably correct notion of the system which Akbar was anxious to introduce.

The first thing that is very apparent, is a decided hostility to the Mohammedan religion. It would not probably have been safe to have attempted its direct suppression; and it would have been also inconsistent with the universal toleration, intimated in the above rules, and, as is expressly stated, frequently enjoined by Akbar himself. The Mohammedan creed was therefore undermined, rather than assaulted, and its subversion aimed at by throwing it into contempt and disrepute. And whilst all its leading dogmas were denied, its observances contemned, and its laws counteracted by opposing regulations, many enactments apparently of an insignificant nature are not, with advertence to the general object, without importance.

Akbar was probably aware of the necessity of a popular system for the maintenance of religious impressions; and with this view, he may have endeavoured to give currency to the adoration of the planets, and especially of the sun. How far he concurred in this worship, except as symbolical, since he professed to inculcate the unity of the Deity, and called his faith, according to our author, the Tauhíd Iláhí, is doubtful. That he did incline to the moral and metaphysical notions of the Hindus, is very probable; and he may have been tempted to attach more importance to their mysticism than became an intelligent mind. At the same time, the following anecdote, related by Abd ul Káder, shews he was not so readily the dupe of credulity, as might be inferred from the interest he is said to have taken in the acquirement of the *Yoga*.

In the thirty-fifth year of Akbar's reign, it was said of Sheikh Kamál Biábání, that he was endowed with the miraculous power of transporting himself instantly to a distance, so that a person who had taken leave of him on one side of the river would, upon crossing to the other, be again saluted by his voice. Akbar went to see him, and begged him to communicate his skill, offering in exchange for it his whole kingdom. The Sheikh refused to instruct him. On this Akbar ordered him to be bound hand and foot, and threatened to have him tossed into the river, where, if he possessed the faculty to which he pretended, he would suffer no injury; and if he was an impostor, he would be punished deservedly for his fraud. This menace alarmed the Sheikh: he confessed the whole to be a trick, practised in confederacy with his son, who was covertly stationed on the opposite side of the stream, and counterfeited his father's voice.

Whatever we may think of the proposed result, we can scarcely question the judiciousness of the means; and the enactments above enumerated were well calculated to abrogate the Mohammedan creed, and erect on its ruin a modification of Hinduism less gross than the prevailing polytheism. There is one part of the plan, however, which is less entitled to approbation; and we can scarcely reconcile Akbar's assumption of a more than human character with the good sense displayed in the general prosecution of his reform. At the same time, it is not improbable that the personage was only politically enacted, in order to give greater weight to his innovations. In fact this seems to be intimated by our author, who alludes to a discussion between Akbar and Bhagaván Dás, in which he says, they concurred in the opinion, that many would be ready to acknowledge the existence of defects and errors in both the Mohammedan and Hindu creed, but that few or none would submit the correction of them to any existing authority. It was therefore to obtain the influence so necessary, and yet so difficult to be acquired, that Akbar made himself be recognised as the vicegerent of God.

We are now, then, in possession of the leading features of Akbar's religious system; and although it might have been an improvement upon any one then established, it was too little in harmony with the feelings of any class of his subjects to be generally or permanently diffused. The author of the Muntakhab mentions one insurrection occasioned by the attempt; and as we find these years of Akbar's reign continually agitated by domestic disturbances, it is probable that they were not unconnected with religious resentments. At all events, the new code enjoyed a very short existence and quickly expired under the indifference of Jehángír[1] to any mode of faith.

---

[1] At the same time, it is probable that Jehángír was rather, for some period at least, inclined to imitate his father's example; and the famous Zodiac Coins are evidently connected with the planetary worship, and the festival of the new year. The set, nearly complete, have been all met with, it is believed; and one of the most common is a gold coin bearing the figure of Jehángír on the face, and the sun on the reverse. This is dated at Ajmír 1023, or nine years after his accession. We have heard also of one of this description, which was struck apparently by Akbar, dated in Ferwardin Iláhi, or the first month of the first year of Akbar's era, leaving consequently no doubt of these coins being rather medals than coins, struck at the festival of the Nauroz, or new year. Their being only accidentally struck will explain Abúlfazl's omission of them in the various coins of Akbar's currency.

INDEX.

Abd ul kdder p. 380, 390, 398.
Abd un nabi 383.
Abd us sdmad khdn 131.
Abbayaprada 24.
Abhidharma 330.
Abjapdni 21, 24 f.
Abú abdallah shdfi 382.
Abú hanifah 382.
Abulfazl 355, 380, 386, 389, 392 ff.
Achald saptami 196.
Achamana 85.
Achdrya 18, 291.
Achyuta 163.
Adhdra 23.
Adhwaryu 254, 283, 300.
Adibuddha 12, 14, 25, 30, 361.
Adigranth 124 f., 129, 145 f.
Adipurusha 149.
Adityabandhu 2 f.
Adityardra 109.
Adwaita 97.
Agastya 207.
Agastyatirtha 22.
Aghora 215.
Aghoraghania 268.
Agni 23, 38, 248, 255 f. 298 ff.
296, 302.
Agnihotra 182.

Agnimitra 351.
Agnipur 23.
Agnyddhina 281.
Agrabdyana 181.
Aharaniya 281, 286 f.
Ahmed 317.
Ahmad shdh 152 f.
Aitareya bráhmana 249, 259 ff.
264 f.
Aihwarika 12, 21 f., 25, 28.
Aiswarya 363.
Ajdtasatru 344.
Ajigartta 253 ff.
Ajita 24.
Ajitd 39.
Ajya 269.
Akdlamrityu 24.
Akali 131 f., 145.
Akaratirtha 12 f.
Akdayogini 21.
Akbar 127, 355, 379-410.
Akshobhya 11 f., 14, 35 f.
Ali 382.
Ali babah 383.
Alobhya 313.
Aluwdid 139.
Amara 2.
Amaradds 124.

96

INDEX.

Amararati 16.
Ambarisha 247.
Amita 18 f.
Amitābha 12, 14, 85 f.
Amitaruchi 11.
Amogha 11, 14.
Amoghapāśa 23, 31.
Amoghasiddha 12, 35 f.
Amogharati 16.
Amrītsar 127, 137, 144 f. 149.
Ananda 23, 330, 333, 342.
Anamtagamja 13 ff.
Anantatīrtha 22.
Angada 124.
Āndhra 257.
Āndhrabhritya 354.
Angiras 257.
Anís 30.
Ansmarī 289.
Anupamad 5.
Anurādhapura 352, 369.
Anustaraṇī 286.
Apardjita 24.
Apardjitā 38.
Āpastamba 259.
Aparimitāyu 24.
Apsaratīrtha 22.
Argha 213, 215.
Arghamantra 215.
Arghya 163, 200.
Arhat 21, 27.
Arjuna 22, 312, 336 f.
Arjunamal 125, 127 f. 145, 148.
Arkabandhu 10.
Arthi 146.
Aruna 5.
Aryāvartta 32.

Ashāḍhā 291.
Aśhtaka 258.
Ashtakādrāddha 182.
Ashtamīvrataridhāna 4, 31 ff.
Aśoka 344, 348 f. 351.
Asura 337, 342.
Aśvalāyana 182, 264, 276, 279 ff.
    287, 291, 294, 297 ff. 307.
Aśvattha 6.
Aśvina 191, 256.
Aśvinī 336.
Atharvaveda 46, 283.
Aīlakdsa 234.
Aīlāiajā 232.
Atikakathā 331 ff.
Aukhpaśākhā 295, 302, 307, 309.
Aurangzeb 130.
Avalokita 27.
Avalokiteśvara 13 f. 334, 356.
Avatāra 65, 221, 316, 394.
Avidhard 274 ff. 293.
Avidyā 341.
Ayīnī akbarī 379, 386, 393 ff.
Ayodhyā 247.

Bābā ndnak 122 ff.
Bābkraca 257.
Balaka 344.
Baldewa 20.
Balwant sing 246.
Banda 130 f.
Banddī 131.
Bandhudatta 22.
Bandumati 5.
Banga, Bangadaśa 29.
Bauddha 2 ff. 13, 21, 25 ff. 316.
Baudhāyana 264, 283.

Bâwannabandhana 162.
Bâwannapauti 162.
Bhadani 148.
Bhadrakālī 38. 189.
Bhadrakalpa 32.
Bhagavān 149.
Bhagavān dās 396. 399.
Bhāgavatapurāṇa 69.
Bhagavatī 22.
Bhagīratha 168.
Bhāgīrathī 168.
Bhairnyekādaśī 203 f. 206. 210.
Bhairava 24. 30. 32.
Bhangī 137.
Bhadrachodja 297. 300 ff. 307.
Bharata 32.
Bhāskarasaptamī 194.
Bhardai 142.
Bhavishyottarapurāṇa 153. 163.
    203. 205. 231 f.
Bhikshu 21. 35. 241. 359.
Bhikshunī 359.
Bhilsa 250.
Bhīma 203. 205.
Bhīmachoddaśī 205.
Bhīmasena 336.
Bhīshma 201 ff.
Bhīshmapanchaka 203.
Bhīshmāshṭamī 201 ff. 210.
Bhogapandikei 173.
Bhogapongal 173.
Bhoi, Bhoṭiya 2 ff.
Bhrigu 264.
Bhūta 34.
Bijisoko 19.
Birbal 387 f.
Bodhimanda 341.

Bodhisattva 15. 19. 23. 25. 29.
    87. 313. 334. 337. 340. 342.
    356. 361. 365.
Brahma 91. 93. 95. 113.
Brahmā 15. 47. 53. 55 f. 62. 91 ff.
    102. 141. 189. 193. 211. 217.
    337 f. 385.
Brahmajālasūtra 364.
Brāhmaṇa 49 ff. 106 f. 202. 263.
    296. 302.
Brāhmaṇa (n.) 249. 259 ff. 265. 281.
Brāhmanī 21.
Brahmapurāṇa 63. 181. 183. 189.
    206. 299.
Brahmavaivarttapurāṇa 69. 94.
    193.
Buddha L 4. 19 f. 21. 24. 26. 81.
    35 ff. 310 ff.
Buddhaghosa 331 f.
Buddhamaṇḍala 34.
Buddhavachana 333.
Birvamangal 244 ff.

Chailako 21.
Chaitanya 226.
Chaitra 159.
Chait sing 246.
Chaitya 344.
Chakravarttī 348.
Chamasa 286.
Chāmuṇḍā 268.
Chaṇḍavīra 24.
Chaṇḍī 39.
Chandragiri 22.
Chandragupta 312.
Charak pūjā 78.
Charat sing 138.

Chdrugiri 17.
Chdrrdka 86 f.
Chinidmatitirika 19 f.
Childbhrashid 303.
Chobhddeo 23.
Chuid bhikshuni 21.
Chushild 39.

Dabistdn 379.
Daitya 66.
Ddkini 34.
Dakshina 281. 286. 289.
Dalai lama 358.
Damaga 20.
Danhi 28.
Dasahard 148.
Dasama pddshdh kd granth 129.
Dasaratha 55. 264.
Dattdtreya 207.
Deand 36.
Deva 341.
Devabhuti 353.
Devadattdgraja 10.
Deodli 148.
Derardta 257.
Devasuka 82.
Devi (m.) 884.
Devi 22. 38. 184 f.
Devimdhdtmya 68.
Devipurdna 185.
Dhanara 24.
Dhanadd 22.
Dhantila 19.
Dhanuhasta 39.
Dhard 190.
Dharma 329. 336. 356.
Dharmamandala 37.

Dharmardja 203.
Dharmarakshita 351.
Dharmasutra 281.
Dharmapur 394.
Darmchand 124.
Dhdtri 272.
Dhattura 217.
Dhavala 201.
Dhriti 190.
L'holdsamudra 168.
Dhydnibodhisattwa 11.
Dhydnaprochha 22.
Dhydnibuddha 12 f. 24. 26. 356.
361.
Dighanikdya 342.
Dipani 39.
Dipankara 13.
Dipawansa 331 f.
Divya avaddna 334.
Dolaydtrd 222 ff.
Dolotsara 222. 230.
Dona, Drona 343.
Drishtarupd 39.
Duskihd 233 f.
Durgd 15. 78. 142. 191. 244. 268.
Durgdkunda 244.
Durgdpujd 78. 191.
Dured 34.
Duti 39.
Dvijihagdwani 352.
Dwdparayuga 253.
Dwdrakd 71.

Ekoddishia 292.

Fa hian 318. 324. 327. 354. 369.
Fan 324 f. 327.

INDEX. 405

Farid ad din 126.
Ferishta 379.
Firiz 380, 387
Futtchpur 381.

Ganapatihridayd 12.
Gandharva 38, 337, 342.
Gandhela 18, 32.
Ganeśa 21, 28, 83, 356.
Gangādagar 163 ff.
Gārhapatya 231, 286 f.
Garita, Garuteia 12.
Gātha 248.
Gauri 184 f. 190.
Gautama 7 ff. 345, 357.
Gayd 341.
Gāyatrī 56.
Ghazi 187.
Ghanidkarna 221 f.
Ghanidkarnaprajñd 221 f.
Ghaleśwara 12, 32.
Ghazidli 386.
Ghorarūpd 39.
Ghori 39.
Girdhara 75.
Gobhila 181 f. 283.
Gokarna 16, 19.
Gokarneśwara 16, 32.
Gokula 285.
Gola 162.
Goloka 110.
Gopa 226, 282.
Gopāla 55, 66, 171.
Gorakhnāth 30.
Gorakhpur 343.
Gosdin 226.
Gotama 302.

Gotīputra 351.
Govinda 55, 163.
Govindadīcddāsi 221.
Govindasinh 131, 142.
Grahamdirikā 12.
Grihyasūtra 276 ff.
Guhyaderi 23.
Guhyeśwarī 14, 22, 32.
Guhyeśwarī ghāt 19.
Gūjar 143.
Guṇākar 23.
Gáng mahal 391.
Guru 32, 36, 54, 124 ff. 197.
    281, 291.
Gurugovind 128 ff. 142, 143.
Gurumatd 134, 141.

Hakim abūl fateh 390.
Hanifiah 382.
Hanumān 21, 28, 33, 169.
Hara 217.
Hargovind 127.
Hari 75, 145, 147, 149, 163.
Harihariharichha 23.
Harimandir 145.
Harikchandra 250 ff.
Hdriti 21, 33.
Haricanda 205.
Hdrivdsa 195.
Haviryajna 281.
Hayagriva 24.
Hazār shaia 395.
Hemachandra 8 ff. 26.
Hemanta 181.
Hevajra 24.
Hiuen tsang 324, 327, 330, 335, 354.
Holi 148, 165, 222 ff. 244.

INDEX.

Holikd 231 ff.
Homa 205, 232, 234, 389.
Hotri 254, 253.

Ikrâm daoud 382.
Ikshwâku 250 ff.
Ildhi 393.
Indra 20, 38, 50 f. 111, 206, 248 f.
    252 f. 256, 336.
Indri 39.
Îsâna 38, 178, 214.
Îsânasanhitâ 211, 219.
Îsvara 18, 214, 218 f.

Jdgarana 218.
Jaganmdid 78.
Jagannâth 55.
Jaina 10, 86 f.
Jamachho 22.
Jamadagni 254.
Jambûki 39.
Janârdana 232.
Japa 146, 216.
Jdi 142.
Jaid 24, 30.
Jaiddhara 24.
Jâtavedah 296.
Jalochha 22.
Jaya 24.
Jayâ 38, 205.
Jdyâ 264.
Jayadeva 74.
Jayantisaptami 197.
Jayasinha 153, 162.
Jayatîrtha 20.
Jehângir 395, 400.
Jina 11, 13, 17.

Jinendra 5 f.
Jivaloka 276.
Jnânatîrtha 19 f.
Jogi 395.

Kabir 125.
Kakutsa 18.
Kâlanirnaya 153.
Kâlî 73, 62, 94, 142, 268.
Kâlikâpurâna 94, 268.
Kalinga 344.
Kaliyuga 253.
Kalpa 9.
Kalpadruma 153, 162, 195, 205,
    209, 219, 222.
Kalpataru 195.
Kâma 192, 230 f. 340.
Kâmadahana 230 f.
Kamâl bidbdsi 398.
Kâmarûpa 22.
Kâmatîrtha 19 f.
Kâmbojini 89.
Kanaka 6 f. 13.
Kanakavarnanitra 335.
Kânchana 8.
Kanishka 329.
Kansa 66.
Kapâlamâlâ 89.
Kapâlini 89.
Kapila 167 ff. 346.
Kapilapur 6.
Kapilavastu 338, 346.
Kâpileya 257.
Karkota 23, 82.
Kârtik 168, 184, 202.
Kârttikeya 193.
Kâsîkhanda 195.

INDEX. 407

Kâśyapa 6 ff. 13. 27. 330. 342. 352.
Kâtyâyana 286.
Kauśika 283.
Keśa chaitya 22.
Keśavatî 22. 32.
Ketakî 217.
Ketumatî 7.
Khadgî 28.
Khadgahastâ 39.
Khaganja 16.
Khagarbha 13 ff. 19.
Khâdira 135. 140 f. 142.
Khatvâṅga 39.
Kheirpur 334.
Khir khân shirodnî 383.
Khristasaṃgîta 87.
Kîla 17.
Kîlakeśvara 17. 32.
Kiliśaravadand 12 f.
Kobad 330.
Koṭilakshdkshi 12 f.
Krakuchchhanda 6 ff. 13. 22.
Krishna 16. 55. 65 ff. 110. 163. 173. 221. 224 f. 232 ff. 264. 347. 385. 394.
Krishnaguth 71.
Krishnârudrî 38.
Kritayuga 233. 253.
Kshatriya 22 f. 47. 49. 106 f. 202. 251. 254. 263. 287. 296.
Kshemavatî 8.
Kshitigarbha 13 ff. 18.
Kudimdr 148.
Kulika 17.
Kullûkabhaṭṭa 302.
Kumâra 24. 28. 33.
Kumârilabhaṭṭa 386.

Kumbha, Kumbhî 292.
Kumbheśvara 32.
Kundachaturthî 184.
Kurukshetra 304.
Kula 343.
Kuśinagara 343.

Lakshmî 157 ff.
Lalitachaitya 22.
Lalitapur 25. 29.
Lalitavistara 323. 335. 337 ff.
Laṅkâ 204.
Laṅkâvatâra 21.
Lichhavi 344.
Liṅga 15 ff. 55. 63. 211. 214. 216 ff.
Liṅgapurâṇa 94. 219.
Liṅgâyit 71.
Lochanâ 12. 27. 35 f.
Loka 231.
Lokadhâtu 29. 32 f.
Lokaikabandhu 9.
Lokanâth 16. 18. 27.
Lokeśa 22.
Lokeśvara 17 ff. 23 ff.

Mâdhava 162. 366.
Madhuchhandas 258.
Mâdhyamika 353.
Magadha 344.
Mâgha 158 ff. 181 ff. 211. 223.
Mahâbhârata 66. 205. 264. 304. 312. 326. 330. 334.
Mahâchîn 27.
Mahâdeva 231.
Mahâkâla 21. 24. 142.
Mahâkâlî 38.
Mahâkâśyapa s. Kâśyapa.

Mahāmantrānusāriṇī 13.
Mahāmāyā 355.
Mahāmayūrī 13.
Mahāparinirvāṇasūtra or
Mahāparinibbānasuttam 342.
Mahārudri 89.
Mahāsīpā 39.
Mahāsahasrapramarddinī 13.
Mahāsaptamī 197.
Mahāsattva 342.
Mahāketarati 13.
Mahāving 136.
Mahāvīvaka 342.
Mahātattva 39.
Mahātmya 68.
Mahāvaṃso 321, 331 f.
Mahāyāna 335.
Maheśa 17.
Maheśvara 217, 222, 337, 342.
Mahī ad dīn 355.
Mahidds 387.
Maitreya 7, 8, 13 ff. 342, 362.
Makara 159, 163, 192.
Makarasankrānti 159 f. 161, 170.
Makarasaptamī 210.
Mākarīsaptamī 195 ff.
Makhdūm al mulk 383.
Mālatīmādhava 264.
Mālinī 39.
Mallikārjuna 220 f.
Māmakī or Māmukhī 12, 35 f.
Mān 385.
Maṇḍala 34, 36 f.
Manddrashashiśī 114.
Māndhātṛisūtra 335.
Mangala 15.
Manibhava 12.

Manichūḍa 16.
Manikuṇṇa 13.
Manilingeśvara 32.
Maṇimati 32.
Manipadma 356.
Manjubhadra 28.
Manjudeva 15, 17.
Manjugarita 17.
Manjughosha 28.
Manjundth 13 ff. 24, 27.
Manjupaṭṭana 27.
Manjuśri 27 f. 32, 334, 356.
Mānsadshīaka 161 ff.
Mantra 183, 213 ff. 219 ff. 242, 300, 303.
Mantramahodadhi 219.
Manu 49, 53, 61 f. 102, 182, 264, 290, 302, 313.
Māra 340.
Mārgaśīrsha 15, 191.
Markaṃya 24.
Mārichi 13, 27.
Maśk 395.
Mathurā 66, 148, 232.
Mātṛi 213.
Mātrikā 22, 33.
Mātrikānyāsa 213.
Matsyapurāṇa 189, 219.
Matsyendranāth 30.
Mātṭupongal 171 ff.
Maudgalyāyana 351, 356.
Māyā 98 f. 338, 346.
Māyādeviśuta 10.
Medhā 100.
Meld 164 f. 220 f.
Mesha 159.
Mīmāṃsaka 259, 366.

INDEX. 409

Mimânsâkâra 302.
Minâ dhîrmal 148.
Mirâbdi 74 f. 126.
Misal 134. 141.
Mitâkshard 181 f.
Mitra 51.
Moggaliputta 351 f.
Mohammed 128.
Mohammed yezdi 386. 380.
Mohîn ad dîn 390.
Moksha 113.
Mrichchhakati 360.
Mriga 159.
Mrityu 271.
Mukti 113.
Mûlamandala 37.
Mullâ shiri 395.
Munîamdlini 184.
Muntakhab at tewârikh 380. 400.
Murad 387.
Musandid 148.
Mûsica 258.

Nddir shdh 132.
Nâga 17. 19. 23. 327. 311. 314.
Nâga (tree) 7.
Nagarakot 388.
Nâgârjuna 334.
Nâgasena 334.
Nâgavdsa 14. 32.
Nâgpur 23.
Naipâliyadevatâkalyânapancha-
viméatikâ 5. 11 ff.
Nakshatra 292.
Nakula 336.
Nâmsangiti 21.
Nânak shdh 122. 135. 141. 144.

Nârada 231. 250 ff.
Narasinhapurâna 200.
Nârdyaniyupanishad 295. 307 f.
Narendra deva 25. 29 ff.
Nat 26.
Nauroz jeldli 388. 400.
Nausdri 389.
Newdr 1.
Newdri 5.
Nezhet al ma'drij 395.
Nila 23.
Nirmala 124. 142. 145 f.
Nirmalatîrtha 19 f.
Nirńayâmrita 183.
Nirodha 329. 317. 362 ff.
Nirydtana 36.
Nitya 131.
Nrisinha 221.
Nrisinhadeviddsi 221.
Nyagrodha 6.
Nyâyika 85. 90. 97. 100.

Pachiliraivi 19.
Pada 147.
Padmapâni 14. 18. 27. 29. 31. 334.
Padmapurâna 162. 219.
Pdhul 148.
Paijacana 264.
Panchaidkini 39.
Panchâla 32.
Pancharakshâ 12 f.
Pancharatna 168.
Panchavinsati 5. 29. 31 f.
Pândava 336.
Pânini 326.
Pânduva 19. 86.
Parameśvara 142. 149.

27

INDEX.

Pdraskara 281.
Parainhastd 79.
Parrata 250.
Púrcati 20. 21. 30. 77 f. 215. 231.
Pdrratiya 1.
Pdispata 30 f.
Painpati 28. 217.
Pdiald 5.
Pdidia 17.
Pdjalipstra 354.
Pdtanjala 85. 90.
Patan 19.
Pausha 158. 161.
Paushya 170.
Parana 292.
Perum pongal 172 f.
Phalgu 224.
Phdlguna 181. 208 ff.
Phalguni 211.
Phanikehoara 32.
Phanindresirara 16.
Phulchok 22.
Phullochka 22.
Phúsinkkel 19.
Pishiaka 161.
Pishiakasankrdnti 161.
Pitri 61 ff. 161. 178. 201. 208. 210. 271. 292.
Piyadasi 348.
Pogipanikkei 173.
Pongal 170 ff. 178.
Potala 24.
Prabhd 190.
Prabhdrati 32.
Prachanda deva 23.
Prajdpati 255.

Prdjdpatya 303.
Prajnd 12. 14. 27. 32.
Prajnapti 26.
Prakriti 96.
Pramodatirtha 20.
Pratingird 13.
Pratisard 13.
Prithwigarbha 18.
Priyarrata 183.
Proshihapadd 291.
Puchhdgra 23.
Pulastya 205.
Pulinda 258.
Pundarika 5.
Pándra 258.
Puniyatirtha 19.
Purdna 67 ff. 86 ff. 93. 101. 141. 153. 219. 231. 269. 298. 351.
Púrnimd 230.
Purushamedha 268.
Purushottama 201. 304.
Púrvamindmed 85. 91.
Pushkara 63.
Pushpanydsa 35.
Pushti 190.
Pútand 232.

Ruidhd 66. 70 ff. 94. 110.
Rádhdkduta deva 294 ff.
Raghu 233.
Raghunandana 61. 157. 181 ff. 196. 201. 288. 300. 307.
Rajasúya 254.
Rdjatarangini 33.
Rdjatirtha 19 f.
Rdkkibandhana 389.
Rdkshasi 231 ff.

INDEX. 411

Rāma 21, 55, 65 f. 75, 110, 142,
149, 169, 202, 264, 366, 394.
Rāmānanda 72, 126.
Rāmānandi 168.
Rāmānuja 71 f.
Rāmāyaṇa 65, 247 ff. 264, 380.
Rāmādds 127.
Rāmmohan rāy 44, 52, 89, 91.
Rāmrdyi 148.
Raṇachhor 74.
Ranjit siṅg 135 ff.
Raśantichaturtkadi 183 f.
Ratnasaptami 196.
Rati 192.
Ratnacheḍa 16.
Ratnagarbha 13.
Ratnaliṅgeśvara 15.
Ratnasambhava 12, 14, 35.
Ratnodbhara 34.
Rāvaṇa 21.
Ravirāva 129.
Rdzi 386 f.
Rekhta 147.
Reṇu 257.
Ribhu 48.
Ṛichika 247.
Ṛigveda 15 ff. 219, 243 f. 254,
259, 270 ff. 274, 282, 286, 290 ff.
298, 302, 305 ff.
Ṛishabha 257.
Ṛishi 17, 247, 365.
Rohiṇi 198.
Rohita 251 ff.
Rudra 20, 216 f.
Rudrākska 217.
Rudrayāmala 219.

Śabara 258.
Śabdakalpadruma 294.
Śaiva 15, 26, 30, 67, 71 ff. 142,
165, 182, 211, 229.
Śākdshiami 208 ff.
Śakra 237.
Śākta 26, 28, 78, 182, 184.
Śakti 12, 14, 34, 78, 94, 97, 214.
Śākya 6 ff. 10, 13, 21, 23, 27, 32,
36, 323, 333, 336 f. 339, 341 ff.
Śaṅkara 215 ff.
Śaṅkarāchārya 71, 79, 366.
Śaṅkaratīrtha 19 f.
Śaṅkuśuka 271.
Śāntanu 202.
Śāntapur 23.
Śāntairi 23.
Śāntatīrtha 19 f.
Śāradātilaka 189.
Śārdūlardhana 28.
Śāriputra 352, 356.
Śatapathabrāhmaṇa 268.
Śikhādhara 28.
Śikhi 5, 8, 13.
Śikhs 121 ff. 150.
Śiloṣṇid 232.
Śirīsha 6.
Śiruka 24, 27.
Śishya 124.
Śiśira 181.
Śitaḷa 21.
Śitaḷāpūjā 191.
Śitaḷāshashṭhī 192 ff.
Śiva 1, 15, 21, 24, 28, 30, 34,
53, 55 f. 63 f. 71 ff. 91 ff.
141 f. 184 ff. 188, 211, 213,
217, 222, 229, 231, 268.

412   INDEX.

Śivd 38.
Śivalinga 217.
Śiramārgi 30.
Śivapura 22.
Śivapurāña 218 f. 222.
Śivarahasya 219.
Śivarātri 210 ff. 395.
Smaddna 300.
Śobhanavati 6.
Śrāddha 61 ff. 87. 167. 181 ff.
Śramaña 312. 314. 345.
Śrautasūtra 280 ff. 290 ff.
Śrāvaka 21.
Śrī 187.
Śrīdhara 163.
Śrīgiri 17.
Śrīmanju 23.
Śrīpanchami 187 ff.
Śrīparvata 221.
Śrīśānta 23.
Śrīvatsa 15 f.
Śrotriya 291.
Śuddha 211.
Śuddhakāvāsakāyika 342.
Śuddhitattwa 298.
Śuddhodana 9 f. 338. 346.
Śūdra 49. 106 f. 163. 202. 263. 288.
Śūlapāni 217.
Śunahpuchchha 254.
Śunaḥśepha 217 ff.
Śunolāngūla 254.
Śyāmā 78. 184.

Sadikunwar 137.
Saddharmalaṅkāratāra 363.
Saddharmapuṇḍarīka 328. 366.

Sādhavd 300 f.
Sādhvī 71.
Sadyojāta 215.
Sagara 157 ff.
Sahā 32.
Sahadeva 336.
Sahagamana 295.
Sahalokadhātu 33.
Sahamaraña 295 ff.
Sahamarañavidhi 298. 301. 307.
Sahyādri 353.
Saldtara 326.
Sāmaveda 46. 254. 282. 306.
Samantabhadra 14 f. 17.
Sdmayāchdrikasūtra 281.
Sambhu 14. 23. 28.
Sambhunāth 14. 21.
Sambhupurāña 14. 19. 23. 27.
Sampatpradā 12 f. 27.
Samvara 24. 32.
Samratsarapradīpa 187.
Sānchi 350. 352.
Sandhyā 145.
Sangat 124.
Sangha 356.
Sanghamandala 37.
Sanhitā 55. 260 ff.
Sankalpa 168. 213.
Sānkhya 85. 90. 96 f. 100 f. 113.
Sāṅkhyakārikā 96. 101 f.
Sankochha 22.
Sāṅkhāyana 283.
Sankrānti 159. 395.
Sankriti 202.
Sansār chand 137.
Samskāra 280. 283.
Sapatnī 292.

INDEX. 413

Saptabuddhastotra 5 ff.
Saraswati 197 ff.
Sdrndth 354.
Sarvanivaranavishkambhi 13 f. 18.
Sarvapdda 17.
Sarvârthasiddha 10.
Sarvéśvara 17.
Sati 60. 274 ff. 293 ff.
Satlakshaṇatîrtha 20.
Satndin 149.
Saukharati 24. 29.
Sautrāntika 363.
Savitri 255.
Suyana 259. 267. 275 ff. 294 ff.
308 f.
Selim 396.
Selim chishti 381.
Shâfi'ah 382.
Shâh zemân 137.
Sheildapur 391.
Shashthi 193.
Shaitiladdna 206 ff. 210.
Shi'áh 382.
Shipphuchchho 22.
Siddhārtha 339. 346.
Sikri 881.
Sindùra 300.
Sing, Sinh 128.
Sinhakeli 25.
Sinhini 22. 32.
Sitd 65. 110.
Sitâkund 169.
Skanda 22.
Skandapurâna 202.
Smriti 208.
Soma 50. 281.
Somayajna 281.

Somnâth 64.
Sthalakâli 38.
Sthâpa 344. 349. 352 ff.
Subahu 351.
Sudhana 24.
Sudhanvan 366.
Sûfi 73. 122. 385 f.
Sugata 6. 37.
Sunni 382.
Suraj ad daula 212.
Sûryapongal 173.
Sûtra 320. 332. 342. 365.
Sûtrakâra 302. 307.
Susrata 193.
Suyarasa 253. 257.
Svabhâdrika 12 f. 21 f. 24 ff. 363.
Svayambhû 11. 15. 27.
Svayambhûchaitya 32.
Svayambhûndtha 34.
Svayambhûpurâṇa 23.

Tadakong 23.
Taishya 170.
Taittirîya 283. 295. 302. 307 f.
Taittirîya âraṇyaka 308.
Tâj ad din 395 f.
Tâj al 'arafîn 385.
Tantra 2. 29. 33. 77. 79. 81. 150.
184. 219. 330.
Tântrika 4. 21. 30 ff. 39.
Tapas 10.
Tdrd 19. 27. 35 f.
Tdrdtîrtha 22.
Tarkshya 20.
Tathâgatha 31. 39.
Tatkartâ 149.
Tauhid ildhi 398.

Tegh bahādur 128, 148.
Tīkā 389.
Tila 206.
Tilūd 161.
Tilūdsankrānti 161.
Tīrtha 19, 22.
Tīrthaka 365.
Tithi 211.
Tithikṛitya 157.
Tithitattva 151, 157, 187, 201, 219.
Trayastriṅśat 314.
Tretāyuga 253.
Tridaṇḍvari 39.
Trikāṇḍadeśa 27 f.
Trilokarāśaṅkara 23.
Trilokarīra 24.
Tripiṭaka 329, 331 ff.
Tsong kaba 375 f.
Tushita 336 f.
Tushitapur 7.
Tushti 100.
Tüyü khed 23.
Turashīrī 272.

Udakakarma 290.
Uddal 124, 145.
Udgātṛi 254, 287.
Udiya, Udiyāna 13.
Udumbara 5.
Umā 38, 78, 181 ff. 211, 215.
Upachhandaka 32.
Upāli 330.
Upanishad 65, 83 ff.
Ushas 256.
Ushnīshakarpaṇḍ 12.
Uttaramīmāṅsā 85, 90.
Uttarāyaṇa 138 ff. 196.

Vāḍiraj 29.
Vāgrīndra 22.
Vāgmati 16, 18, 22, 32.
Vaibhāshika 363.
Vaidyanāth 220 f.
Vaipulyasūtra 333 f.
Vairochana 12, 14, 35 f.
Vaiśeshika 85, 90.
Vaishṇava 67, 71 ff. 126, 142, 163.
Vaidya 19, 106 f. 202, 263, 296.
Vaitānika 281.
Vairasvata 32.
Vajaneyīsanhitā 306.
Vajra 35.
Vajrāchārya 17, 20, 21.
Vajradhātrī 12.
Vajradhvrid 35.
Vajrahastā 39.
Vajrapāṇī 13 ff. 17.
Vajrapushpa 35.
Vajrasattva 12, 37, 39.
Vajrasattvātmika 12.
Vajravīdrādriṇī 12.
Vajravīra 21.
Vajrayoginī 21.
Vajreśvari 39.
Vallabha 72.
Vāmadeva 215.
Vānaprastha 313.
Varada 24.
Varaddehaturthi 184 ff.
Vartika 207.
Vardhadueddaśi 207.
Varuṇa 51, 195, 251 ff. 254 ff.
Vasanta 231.
Vasantapanchami 191 f. 209, 223, 227, 229.

INDEX. 415

Vasentotsara 209. 223.
Vaṃśika 251.
Vastudera 161.
Vasudera 55. 163.
Vāsudera 209.
Vasundhará 3. 7. 13. 22.
Vasujur 23.
Vattagdmini 331.
Vidya 23. 50 f. 336.
Vidyapur 23.
Vidyapurdna 219.
Veda 44 ff. 86 ff. 101. 107. 259.
  265. 269. 291. 295 ff. 327.
  348.
Vedánta 62. 73. 85. 88. 90. 97 ff.
  113. 122.
Venga 25. s. Banga.
Veshas 250.
Vichitrandiak 121.
Vidhānaaaplawi 200.
Vidhātri 32.
Vidyādāri 26.
Vidyādhari 26.
Vighnardja 23.
Vikdra 349. 357. 365.
Vijamantra 21.
Vijaya 24.
Vijayā 34.
Vijayaikadaśi 219 f.
Vikramēśa 19.
Vikramēśvara 32.
Vilva 217 f.
Viná 192.
Vinaya 330 ff. 360.
Vindhyadeśini 78.
Vipakyi 5. 8. 13 f. 22.
Viripa 20.

Vishnu 2. 15. 28. 32. 53. 55 f.
  63 ff. 71 ff. 91 ff. 111. 149.
  162. 167. 187. 203. 205. 208.
  211. 217. 221. 275. 336. 382.
Vishnudvīpa 344.
Vishṇupurāṇa 48. 70. 91. 102.
  104. 181. 208. 232.
Viśvabhū 5. 8. 13.
Viśvadera 161 203. 251.
Viśvāmitra 248. 254. 257 ff.
Vishkambhi 18.
Vitardga 15. 17 f. 27. 32.
Viśaucat 186.
Vupadera 64.
Vraj 110.
Vrata 205.
Vratapati 215.
Vratárka 153.
Vṛndāraṇ 66. 235 f.
Vyāghrapāda 302.
Vyāghrini 22. 33.
Vyāsa 17 f. 67. 91. 97. 202.
  317.

Yajamāna 281.
Yajnavalkya 290.
Yājñiki upaniṣhad 308.
Yajurveda 46. 254. 268. 282. 301.
Yaksha 38. 337.
Yakshamalla 23.
Yakshini 21.
Yama 24. 58. 71. 183 f. 205 f.
  218. 271. 273. 286. 289.
Yamahārdikā 32.
Yāʼkūb 386.
Yantra 82.
Yoga 80. 398.

416   INDEX.

Yogdehdra 363. | *Yuga* 208.
Yogdmbara 24. | *Yugdityd* 207 f. 210.
Yogi 30. |
Yogini 21. 33 f. 39. | Zechariah 351.
Yudhishihira 232 f. 336. | *Zeik khdn khota* 389.

CORRECTIONS AND ADDITIONS.

Page 21 L. 15 read: *Sitald*.
- 23 - 17 - Guṇākar.
- 81 - 10 - *Yoga*.
- 129 - 11 - Náiak.
- 163 - 16 - Vasudeva.
- 178 - 5 - something else.
- 186 add to Note ***: M. Richard, Traditions populaires de l'ancienne Lorraine. Remiremont: 1848, p. 61 ff.
- 187 L. 13 read: *Mdgha*.
- 193 - 28 - Forbes.
- 203 - 14 - Dharmarája.
- 217 add to Note *: Cf. also Vratárka, Calcutta edition, fol. 136.
- 244 L. 25 add: N. Hocker, die Stammsagen der Hohenzollern und Welfen. Düsseldorf: 1857, p. 139.

www.ingramcontent.com/pod-product-compliance
Lightning Source LLC
Chambersburg PA
CBHW032143010526
44111CB00035B/1041